BLINDED BY SIGHT

*Seeing Race Through
the Eyes of the Blind*

Osagie K. Obasogie

Stanford Law Books
An Imprint of Stanford University Press
Stanford, California

Stanford University Press
Stanford, California

This book has been partially underwritten by the Stanford Authors Fund. We are grateful to the Fund for its support of scholarship by first-time authors. For more information, please see www.sup.org/authorsfund

Printed in the United States of America on acid-free, archival-quality paper

Library of Congress Cataloging-in-Publication Data

Obasogie, Osagie K., author.
    Blinded by sight : seeing race through the eyes of the blind / Osagie K. Obasogie.
        pages cm
    Includes bibliographical references and index.
    ISBN 978-0-8047-7278-5 (cloth : alk. paper)
    ISBN 978-0-8047-7279-2 (pbk. : alk. paper)
    1. Race awareness—United States. 2. Blind—United States—Attitudes. 3. Race—Social aspects—United States. 4. Race discrimination—Law and legislation—United States. 5. Post-racialism—United States. 6. United States—Race relations. I. Title.
E184.A1O19 2013
305.800973—dc23
                                                                            2013013770

ISBN 978-0-8047-8927-1 (electronic)

BLINDED BY SIGHT

That Justice is a blind goddess
Is a thing to which we black are wise
Her bandage hides two festering sores
That once perhaps were eyes.

Langston Hughes, 1923

Contents

Acknowledgments

There is simply nothing more important in life than being surrounded by a loving family, supportive friends, and thoughtful colleagues. And, in this regard, I am the luckiest man on earth.

All that I have achieved in life is the result of the loving home and upbringing provided my parents, Dr. A. O. Obasogie and Mrs. Faithe Obasogie, and my sister, Imuetinyan. They have been unbelievably supportive in allowing me to pursue my interests and passions. But they are also most responsible for shaping my sociological imagination and legal sensibilities. I am eternally thankful for their efforts, wisdom, love, and sacrifice in cultivating my curiosities and developing my sense of justice.

This project started around 2005 after I viewed the film *Ray*, which portrays the life story of the talented musician Ray Charles, who was Black and blind. I was immediately struck by the fact that although Mr. Charles became blind as a young child, he had a remarkably strong sense of race throughout his life—a sense that, in many ways, belied the emphasis on vision that orients sighted people's understanding of race. I was intrigued by this notion that a blind person could share the same racial sensibility as sighted individuals. At the time, I assumed that this was an active area of scholarly research. I wanted to learn more, so I examined the literature. I was surprised to find that no one had studied blind people's understanding of race, which speaks to the strength of the assumption that race is self-evidently known and defined by visual cues. After stumbling across this remarkable gap in the literature, I began this research project.

It has been quite a journey. I am first and foremost indebted to the more than one hundred respondents who graciously shared their thoughts and experiences with me. I am always impressed by the courage and kindness that it takes for respondents to tell a complete stranger the most intimate details of their lives. I am also thankful to the advisers and colleagues who have shaped this book into its current form. Lauren Edelman has been amazing; I am deeply appreciative of her patience, guidance, and encouragement throughout this process. Kathryn Abrams, Catherine Albiston, Neil Fligstein, Ian Haney López, Angela Harris, Kristin Luker, Melissa Murray, and Sarah Song also offered remarkable insights that were instrumental in the early development of this project. Several others have also played key roles in helping this project evolve: Ashutosh Bhagwat, Khiara Bridges, Devon Carbado, Benjamin Depoorter, Kimani Paul-Emile, Katherine Franke, Laura Gómez, Cheryl Harris, Jerry Kang, Sonia Katyal, Ethan Leib, Laura Beth Nielson, Dorothy Roberts, Aliya Saperstein, Carroll Seron, Kendall Thomas, and Joan Williams. Katy Chase, Catherine Davidson, and Nancy Zhang provided excellent research assistance. And a special thank-you to Kate Wahl, Michelle Lipinski, Frances Malcolm, Mary Ray Worley, and Tim Roberts at Stanford University Press for their wonderful editorial assistance.

Portions of this book previously appeared in my doctoral dissertation and in these published articles: Osagie K. Obasogie, *Do Blind People See Race? Social, Legal, and Theoretical Considerations*, 44 LAW & SOC'Y REV. 585 (2010); Osagie K. Obasogie, *The Return of Biological Race? Regulating Race and Genetics Through Administrative Agency Race Impact Assessments*, 21 S. CAL. INTERDISC. L. J. 1 (2012); and Osagie K. Obasogie, *Can the Blind Lead the Blind? Rethinking Equal Protection Jurisprudence Through An Empirical Examination of Blind People's Understanding of Race*, 15 U. PA. J. CONST. L. 705 (2012). Many thanks to these journals' editors for their tireless work.

I have been quite fortunate to have the opportunity to develop this project as a faculty member at the University of California, Hastings College of the Law, and the University of California, San Francisco (UCSF) Department of Social and Behavioral Sciences (SBS). The faculty, staff, and administration at these institutions have created a wonderful environment for research and writing, and I am forever indebted to them for their support. A special thank you to former UC Hastings Chancellor and Dean Nell Newton, current

UC Hastings Chancellor and Dean Frank Wu, UC Hastings Academic Dean Shauna Marshall, former UCSF SBS Department Chair Howard Pinderhughes, and current UCSF SBS Department Chair Ruth Malone for their support throughout this process.

From 2008 through 2010, I was a Visiting Scholar at UCSF Center for Health and Community (CHC). CHC Director Nancy Adler has been an amazing presence in my professional development, and I owe her and many other CHC affiliates—especially Paula Braveman, Ray Catalano, Robert Hiatt, William Satariano, and S. Leonard Syme—a tremendous debt of gratitude for allowing me to partake in their remarkably enriching community of scholars. I am also thankful for the opportunity to work with the Center for Genetics and Society, which has in many ways become my second family over the years. Richard Hayes and Marcy Darnovsky are simply two of the best people that I have ever met; their passion for and commitment to social justice has left a lasting imprint on me. Francine Coeytaux, Jessica Cussins, Alexander Gaguine, Charles Garzón, Douglas Pet, Jesse Reynolds, Pete Shanks, Emily Smith Beitiks, and Diane Tober have been wonderful colleagues, and I look forward to our continued work together.

And last but not least, a special thank you to the lovely Ms. Ellis, who has been a devoted partner since the very beginning of this book project.

Preface

I was born and raised in Southwestern Ohio, right along what many consider to be the northernmost edge of the Bible Belt. Like most people in the area, I was raised in a fairly religious household; my parents are devout Christians. Southern Baptists, to be exact. Church attendance every Sunday, if not a time or two during the week, was a foregone conclusion. Our family was active in church life; my father occasionally served on various committees, and I cannot remember a time when my mother did not teach Sunday School.

Looking back on this part of my childhood, several of my fondest memories are tied to faith and religion. I remember being a small boy, kicking off the uncomfortable loafers my parents made me wear to service, crawling up in the pew next to my mother, and dozing to sleep with my head on her lap. I also remember watching my father's head nod up and down during exceptionally long sermons and my mother lovingly pinching him to stay awake. On the car ride home, he would always defend himself, saying "I wasn't sleeping. I was resting my eyes." Or, my personal favorite: "My eyes were closed because I was praying to the Lord."

Other childhood memories include scrambling Sunday mornings to memorize the weekly Bible verse so as to not disappoint my Sunday School teacher, who, at times, was my own mother; gazing at my watch as it struck 12:30, praying to God that the pastor would let us out in time to catch the kickoff of the Sunday afternoon football game; and standing next to my father as he belted hymns that ricocheted throughout the church in a baritone that still echoes in my mind.

But of all of these moments tied to faith that shaped my childhood, probably the most impressionable happened while at home. Although my family has been a member of our town's First Baptist Church since I was an infant, my father also followed the ministry of Fredrick K. C. Price, a now semi-retired Los Angeles–based televangelist whose weekly sermons reached an estimated 15 million homes each week.[1] Price's sermons were in many ways the soundtrack of my adolescence. Much of his ministry focused on achieving economic stability and prosperity through a faith-based lifestyle. This theme has a particular resonance with my father, whose personal life is heavily influenced by Christ's teachings and whose professional life involved teaching business and economics to college students.

Price is impressive in many ways.[2] His energy and passion radiate through the screen. and his commitment to social justice and improving the condition of urban America is unwavering. He has a way of preaching that is at once plainspoken yet pregnant with meaning and layers. Price is able to make the Bible's age-old teachings and stories directly relevant to the day-to-day experiences of contemporary Americans in a manner that does not simply ask "What would Jesus do?" but engages the nuances of modern life through a theological lens that many find inspiring. This explains, in part, why his ministry has become so influential both in the United States and abroad.

Initially, I didn't pay that much attention to Price's sermons. They were certainly entertaining. But they mostly existed as white noise in the background while eating dinner or doing chores around the house. Over time, however, Price's catchphrase—from 2 Corinthians 5:7, which he repeated verbatim at the end of every telecast—increasingly intrigued me over the years: *"For we walk by faith, not by sight."*

Walking by faith rather than sight? This idea puzzled my adolescent mind. Price offers an interesting description of the passage: "It is not like seeing with your eyes. This scripture is talking about the difference between walking by the things of the Spirit of God, which operates by faith, and walking by what your five physical senses tell you. I like to paraphrase this verse like this: *We walk by the Word and not by our senses.*"[3] Price's take is a fairly common interpretation that draws attention to the rather delicate relationship between faith and knowledge—what we believe and what we know—which is part of a much broader philosophical discussion beyond this book's scope. But what is worth pointing out in this passage, from a theological perspective, is the superficiality of our sensory experiences—especially sight, which is often privileged as an impartial barometer of reality. What we see is often understood and experienced as a self-evident, obvious, and unmediated way to engage the world around us. Sight is privileged because of its seeming objectivity; colloquialisms such as "what you see is what you get" and "seeing is believing" highlight the commonsense that visual perception is an objective engagement with the world that is "real" and "tangible" outside of any subjective influences. Thus, our eyes are thought to merely witness what objectively exists; other cognitive processes then interpret these observations.

The sociological distinction between theory and data mirrors, in some ways, lay distinctions between faith and knowledge in that there are things that we believe to be true yet have no supporting evidence and things that we know to be true through observation. But, 2 Corinthians 5:7, as well as certain aspects of Christian theology, encourage a different approach to thinking about this relationship between faith and knowledge—one that does not juxtapose these concepts. David Lipe writes:

> The Bible clearly teaches in different ways that faith and knowledge are not to be set in contradistinction. Faith and knowledge never are contrasted in the New Testament. Faith is contrasted with sight—not knowledge or reason. In Hebrews 11:1 we read: "Now faith is the substance of things hoped for, the evidence of things not seen." Further, Paul wrote in 2 Corinthians 5:7: "For we walk by faith, not by sight." These verses make it clear that faith is set in contrast to "walking by sight." Sight is a type of sense perception, and therefore a means of attaining knowledge. Thus, faith, instead of being contrasted with knowledge, is contrasted with a means of attaining knowledge. This does not mean faith and sight cannot function together. Jesus said: "Thomas, because thou hast seen me, thou hast believed" (John 20:29). Thomas' faith was based on the evidence of his senses—namely, his sense of sight. Again, Jesus said to Thomas: "Blessed are they that have not seen, and yet have believed" (John 20:29). *This shows that there can be faith where there is no sight, but note that the verse does not say there can be faith where there is no knowledge.*[4] [emphasis added]

Thinking about faith in contrast with sight rather than knowledge gives it substance while, at the same time, deprioritizes vision as a self-evident or objective way to understand reality. Another way to think about the verse from 2 Corinthians is that we "walk" or navigate the world through the sub-stance of our beliefs, not by ephemeral sensory perception. While there is cer-tainly a relationship between what our senses perceive and our substantive thoughts, 2 Corinthians 5:7 suggests that our tendency to treat vision as a self-evident means of understanding the world might lead us to miss impor-tant yet unseen mechanisms that shape our core beliefs and orient our lives outside of immediate sensory perceptions. Indeed, this is the take-home mes-sage from Reverend Price's weekly refrain of this verse: faith shapes our per-ception of the world—a socially driven orientation gained through fellowship with other believers that generates a shared lens through which to "see." That is what makes the idea of walking by faith counterintuitive: that visual per-ception is not merely an individual sensory experience of "seeing" freestand-ing objective "things." Rather, our seemingly objective engagements with the world around us are subordinate to a faith that orients our visual experience and, moreover, produces our ability to see certain things. *Seeing is not believ-ing*. Rather, to believe, in a sense, is to see.

BLINDED BY SIGHT

Introduction

THIS BOOK STARTS WITH A FAIRLY STRAIGHTFORWARD QUESTION: how do blind people understand race? Given the vast and sprawling writings on race over the past several decades, it is surprising that scholars have not explored this question in any real depth. Race has played a profound and central role to human relationships. Yet how is it possible that this basic question has escaped deeper contemplation?

This gap in the scholarly literature and public discourse points to a fundamental assumption that we almost all make about race, its significance, and its salience.[1] Race has been central to human relationships. Yet, there seems to be at least one thing that most people can agree upon: that race is, to a large extent, simply what is seen. There are surely many variables that inform individuals' racial consciousness, such as religion, language, food, and culture. But race is primarily thought to be self-evidently known, in terms of reflecting the wide variation in humans' outward appearance tied to ancestry and geographic origin such as skin color, hair texture, facial shapes, and other observable physical features. Thus, race is thought to be visually obvious; it is what you see, in terms of slotting visual engagements with human bodies into predefined categories of human difference, such as Black, White, and Asian. Given the dominant role these visual cues play in giving coherence to social categories of race, it is widely thought that race can be no more salient or significant to someone who has never been able to see than the musical genius of Mozart or Jay-Z can be salient to someone who has never been able to hear.

Therefore, one plausible explanation for why questions concerning blind people's understanding of race have not been explored is that, from a sighted person's perspective, the answer seems painfully obvious: blind people simply cannot appreciate racial distinctions and therefore do not have any real racial consciousness.

This pervasive yet rarely articulated idea that race is visually obvious—a notion that I call *"race" ipsa loquitur*,[2] or that race "speaks for itself"—has at least three components: (1) race is largely known by physical cues that inhere in bodies such as skin color or facial features,[3] (2) these cues are thought to be self-evident, meaning that their perceptibility and salience exist apart from any mediating social or political influence, and (3) individuals without the ability to see are thought, at a fundamental level, to be unable to participate in or fully understand what is assumed to be a quintessentially ocular experience. Through this *"race" ipsa loquitur* trope, talking about race outside of visual references to bodily differences seems absurd, lest we all become "colorblind" in the most literal sense. Indeed, as I discuss in Chapter 4, much of the ideological value in the emerging colorblindness discourse works from the idea that race and racism are problems of visual recognition, not social or political practices.[4]

But, how much does the salience of race—in terms of it being experienced as a prominent and striking human characteristic that affects a remarkable range of human outcomes—depend upon what is visually perceived? To play upon the biblical reference to 2 Corinthians 5:7 discussed in the Preface, do we simply "walk by sight" in that the racial differences are self-evident boundaries that are impressionable on their own terms? Or, is there a secular "faith" about race that produces the ability to "see" the very racial distinctions experienced as visually obvious? And if we take this idea seriously, that the visual salience of race is produced rather than merely observed, precisely what is at stake—socially, politically, and legally—when we misunderstand the process of "seeing race" as a distinctly visual rather than sociological phenomenon?

I push the boundaries of the *"race" ipsa loquitur* trope by investigating the significance of race outside of vision. I critique the notion that race is visually obvious and suggest that the salience of race, in terms of its visually striking nature and attendant social significance, functions more by social rather than ocular mechanisms. Though perhaps counterintuitive, I begin with the hypothesis that our ability to perceive race and subsequently attach social meanings to different types of human bodies depends little on what we see; taking vision as a medium of racial truth may very well obscure a deeper understanding of precisely how race is both apprehended and comprehended, and thus how it informs our collective imaginations and personal behaviors as well as how it plays out in everyday life.

I explore this issue through a series of interviews with people who have been totally blind since birth. Since race is strongly connected to visual cues, it is largely assumed that race must be of diminished significance to blind people's daily lives. But this may not necessarily be the case. All things being equal, race may very well be as significant—even *visually* significant—to the blind community as it is to sighted persons. Moreover, it is likely that the social, cognitive, and other nonvisual interactions shaping blind people's racial experiences are not unique to them. A comparative approach that analyzes the racial experiences of blind and sighted people can offer important insights into the ways in which fixing race as a visual experience may limit a deeper understanding of the extent to which race shapes everyday life, and everyday life shapes our ability to see race. Therefore, exploring blind people's racial experiences and understandings may provide a rich grounding from which to appreciate how race is not simply what we see. Rather, there may be social practices that produce our very ability to see race.

The findings from this research are quite surprising. After conducting over a hundred interviews with blind individuals—people who have never seen anything, let alone the physical traits that typically serve as visual markers for racial difference—one consistent theme resonates throughout the data. Blind people understand and experience race like everyone else: visually. That is, when asked what race is, blind respondents largely define race by visually salient physical cues such as skin color, facial features, and other visual characteristics. But what stands out in particular is not only blind people's visual understanding of race, but that this visual understanding shapes how they live their lives; daily choices, experiences, and interactions such as where to live and whom to date are meditated by visual understandings of race in the blind community as much as they are among those who are sighted. Despite their physical inability to engage with race on the very visual terms that are thought to define its salience and social significance, blind people's understanding and experience with race is not unlike that of sighted individuals.

These data present a tremendous challenge for existing lay and scholarly conceptions of race. How can it be that individuals who cannot see have a *visual* understanding of race? And how is it possible that this visual understanding is so significant that it fundamentally shapes their everyday lives just as it does for anyone else? How can someone not have vision, but be able to, for all intents and purposes, "see" race? *Blinded by Sight* unravels this mystery so as to understand this phenomenon as an empirical matter. Through qualitative research methods, I capture these experiences and unearth the broader sociological patterns that give rise to blind people's ability to "see" race. These empirical findings can have wide-ranging implications for rethinking the relationship between race, legal doctrine, public policy, and social relations. This research ventures into an area that many assumed did not exist in any meaningful sense—the racial lives of blind people and, moreover, the visual acuity with which they experience race—and uses the empirical data to discuss this discovery's implications for reconceptualizing the ways that race plays out in law and society.

I leverage these empirical findings to intervene in at least three separate scholarly conversations relevant to race, law, and society. At the broadest level, this book offers a fresh intervention into a concept that is so prominent and unthinkingly accepted across almost all areas of race scholarship that it is rarely subject to any meaningful critique: the social construction of race. The idea that race is a social construction is often meant to convey that the meanings placed upon particular racialized bodies are not caused by nature or driven by inherent biological differences. Rather, these meanings and their attachment to specific groups are a product of social, economic, and political forces. Social constructionists have paid painstaking attention to this meaning-making process and how specific concepts come to attach to certain groups, whether it is eastern European immigrants "becoming" White or the racialization of Mexican Americans.[5] However, this emphasis on meanings attaching to bodies has obscured a more fundamental question: how does race itself become visually salient? More so than meanings adhering to bodies, there seems to be an underlying social process that produces the visibility of group difference. It is largely assumed that racial differences become salient merely because they are self-evident and visually obvious, but this book challenges this idea and contributes to broader constructionist debates by developing a *constitutive* theory of race that highlights the way in which social practices produce the ability to see and experience race in particular ways.

Secondly, I use the data collected on blind people's visual understanding of race to offer critical new insights and interventions into law—specifically Equal Protection jurisprudence. Fourteenth Amendment Equal Protection jurisprudence has offered the most robust legal mechanism from which to advocate racial equality for disadvantaged minorities. Equal protection has been at the heart of the United States' most heated and divisive debates on race, from school desegregation to affirmative action. However, what is uncovered in Part 2 is that despite shifting understandings and applications of the Equal Protection Clause, a basic assumption about race has been enmeshed throughout the jurisprudence: that it is visually obvious and its salience stems from self-evident visual cues. This understanding of race drives the legal and moral basis for the Court's ability to review and strike down laws that impermissibly categorize individuals by race. I will argue that this limited understanding of how and why race becomes salient warps Equal Protection jurisprudence by treating race as a visually obvious and self-evidently knowable trait, which fails to take account of the sociological factors that produce our very ability to see racial differences. Thus, by engaging the qualitative data discussed in this book, we gain an empirical basis from which to rethink Equal Protection's normative contours with respect to the scrutiny inquiry, the intent doctrine, and theories of colorblindness that have come to orient this body of law.

As a third intervention, this book attempts to draw attention to the scholarly opportunities that await when Critical Race Theory and empirical methods are brought into conversation with one another. Historically, these two fields have not had a comfortable relationship. Critical Race Theory—a field that has been skeptical of the idea that the complexity of human relationships and group interactions can be fully captured through observation and measurement—has not always embraced social science methods. Instead, critical race theorists have used other approaches—textual and doctrinal critiques, personal narratives, among others—to unearth the various forms of oppression embedded in seemingly neutral social norms and legal rules. Social scientists, on the other hand, appreciate and engage theory yet nonetheless privilege what they consider to be the objective assessment of scientifically collected data. These tensions have led to a fragmented race scholarship. For example, the claims made by critical race theorists may not be as strong as they otherwise could be since their hesitancy to engage empirical methods and datasets makes it difficult to verify these perspectives as bona fide social phenomenon. At the same time, the social sciences' emphasis on observable and measurable data does not fully attend to the often transparent manner in which racial hierarchy and White racial privilege shape law and social relations—a process that can only be fully revealed through humanistic endeavors and often escapes capture by empirical measures. I attempt to mitigate this tension by giving further voice to a nascent but blooming project that is at once conceptually oriented by Critical Race Theory while also based upon traditional qualitative research methods.[6] The hope of this intervention is to further establish a new approach to race that blends these two fields to produce race scholarship that is both theoretically sophisticated and methodologically rigorous—an *empirical Critical Race Theory* that at once uses critical race perspectives to deepen the interrogation and analysis of empirical findings while also further substantiating Critical Race Theory's critique and normative aspirations through engaging empirical methods.

Blinded by Sight is somewhat unconventional in its scope and method. Not only do I ask the novel question about blind people's understanding of race and approach it in a unique way, but I pursue this work through a mixture of personal stories, pop culture references, empirical research, doctrinal critiques, sociological references, and other narratives. This may seem odd to some readers but nonetheless reflects my training as a legal scholar and social scientist working at the intersection of several fields to offer new insights that can hopefully make a contribution to both public and scholarly conversations on race. Race scholarship is in a moment of crisis and it will take unconventional tactics to reboot the race conversation in pursuit of racial justice. It is my ultimate goal for this book to not only offer a thoughtful scholarly discussion about a sociological phenomenon with important legal and policy implications, but to also provide a broader intervention into lay understandings of race that is readable and serviceable to a wide audience.

Each chapter begins with a short story or essay that introduces the ideas and concepts discussed in that section. In Chapter 1, I provide an overview of the context from which most race scholarship moves forward—the social construction of race—to situate the gap that can be filled and contributions that can be made by inquiring into blind people's understandings of race. Chapter 2 offers an in-depth discussion of the theoretical contexts and methodological approaches behind this research question in order to provide insight on how I approach empirical research and the theories of race I develop. Here, I propose a *constitutive theory of race* that draws upon yet goes beyond the constructionist focus on how social meanings attach to bodies to offer an understanding of how racial bodies become visually salient in the first place. This chapter also discusses initial findings from the empirical data showing that blind people have a visual understanding of race. Chapter 3 continues this discussion of the empirical data to sketch out the ways in which blind people not only have visual understandings of race, but that these understandings orient their daily experiences as much as they do for sighted individuals. This suggests that shared social practices rather than any sense of obviousness produces the visual salience of race—a finding that runs counter to lay and scholarly understandings of racial difference. Where Part 1 discusses the data that I collected and research findings, Part 2 discusses their broader social and legal ramifications. Chapter 4 explores their implications for colorblindness—a normative theory of law and public policy that advocates racial nonrecognition in all government decision making that is based, at least in part, on a metaphor premised upon the idea that blindness to color difference leads to equitable outcomes. I use the data from my research to empirically destabilize colorblindness as a metaphor and the problematic reasoning it promotes. Chapter 5 then discusses these findings' implications for legal doctrine—specifically Equal Protection law, whereby its theory of race and remedial approaches revolve around the idea that the salience of race emanates from its visual obviousness. In Chapter 6, I conclude with a broader discussion of this research's significance for lay and scholarly understandings of race, particularly in relation to emerging claims that we have now entered a post-racial era.

PART I
   "FOR WE WALK BY FAITH,
   NOT BY SIGHT"

1   Critiquing the Critique

Beyond Social Constructionism

I N THE MIDST OF THE GREAT DEPRESSION AND WORLD WAR I'S
aftermath, 1930s American foreign policy could best be described as
isolationist; neither politicians nor the American public had much of a stom-
ach for getting involved in then-emerging global conflicts across Europe and
the Pacific. While the United States offered various forms of aid to countries
like England to assist in fending off German aggressions, America remained
formally neutral as the world entered the Second World War. That is, until
December 7, 1941, when Japan's bombing of Pearl Harbor led to over two thousand casualties. Isolationism, as a foreign policy, was no longer a viable or
desirable option.

While the attack on Pearl Harbor changed the United States' approach
to international politics, it also had a distinct impact on the country's racial
politics. Surely anti-Asian and specifically anti-Japanese sentiments existed
prior to 1941, but Pearl Harbor changed and intensified the underlying social
meaning of what it meant to be Japanese. Susan Moeller notes,

> The whole cartoon aspect of the Jap changed overnight. Before that sudden
> Sunday the Jap was an oily little man, amiable but untrustworthy, more funny
> than dangerous. After December 7, the Japanese were depicted by stereotype.
> The Japanese, noted eminent columnist Ernie Pyle, "were looked upon as
> something subhuman and repulsive; the way some people felt about cock-
> roaches or mice." The Japanese were routinely referred to and pictured as

literal or figurative animals, something less than human—at best credited with "child minds." The Japanese were compared to rats and ants, and, most consistently, considered ape-like, "almost simian." Liberty Bond Drive posters depicted the Japanese as leering monkeys raping and pillaging Western women and civilization.[1] [Internal citations omitted]

In many ways, Pearl Harbor demonstrates the instability of racial meanings and how they are always in flux in relation to broader social and political dynamics. This singular act radically deepened Americans' pejorative sentiments toward Japanese people, leading to them being perceived as a distinct group with intrinsic tendencies toward treachery and duplicity. Vestiges of Pearl Harbor as an example of the social construction of race and ethnicity persist to this very day. For example, in 2004, Bill Parcels—then head coach of the Dallas Cowboys—characterized the secret plays developed by his competing offensive and defensive coordinators during practice as "Jap plays . . . surprise things."[2] But while the attack on Pearl Harbor shifted and intensified the social meaning of being Japanese among Americans, there remained one broader issue: if Japanese people ostensibly constitute an inherently duplicitous subgroup, how does one distinguish them from other Asian populations?

Much like reported incidents of post-9/11 attacks on Sikhs who were mistaken for Muslims, the bombing of Pearl Harbor also led many Americans to engage in acts of vigilantism against persons thought to *look* Japanese. The December 22, 1941, edition of *Life* magazine that shortly followed the Pearl Harbor attacks took this to be a serious problem; the editors saw it as their patriotic duty to help the American public direct its hostilities to the right ethnic group.[3] In an article titled "How to Tell Japs from the Chinese," *Life* lent its photojournalistic credibility and reach into millions of American homes to teach the public how to visually differentiate Japanese from Chinese, the latter being our ally during the war. The *Life* article is fascinating in many regards. But what perhaps stands out the most is how it acknowledged the problematic myths surrounding various notions of racial purity and inferiority that drove Nazism and eugenics, yet ultimately saw its journalistic project of "seeing racial difference" as distinct from and innocent of this form of racism. This move—stigmatizing Japanese people as a group while self-consciously distinguishing such racial and ethnic stigmatization from that which was used by Nazis—was not uncommon during this period. A prime example occurred in *Korematsu v. United States*, the 1944 Supreme Court decision upholding the

Executive Order excluding Japanese Americans from parts of the West Coast and permitting their internment during the war. In the decision, Justice Black took great pains to distinguish the United States' internment camps from German concentration camps.[4] Similarly, the *Life* article noted, "To physical anthropologists, *devoted debunkers of race myths*, the difference between Chinese and Japs is measurable in millimeters. . . . Physical anthropology, in consequence, finds Japs and Chinese as closely related as Germans and English. It can, however, set apart the *special types* of each national group" (emphasis added).

From this perspective, race myths are a presumably illegitimate product of *subjective* racial prejudice, which is wholly distinct from the ability to use visual cues to *objectively* appreciate scientific and measurable differences between Japanese and other Asian groups. What remains resilient in this formulation is the notion of *racial typologies*—that humans can be divided into basic racial groups that are biologically distinct—which itself promotes racial hierarchy by substantiating the idea that social categories of race reflect natural "types" of human groups with inherent abilities and disabilities. The *Life* article constructs racial and ethnic differences as being quantifiable down to the smallest units of measurement, suggesting not only that racial and ethnic difference are an objective reality but also that the lay eye can detect such visually obvious differences—that is, if it knows what to look for. *Life* happily assumed the responsibility of training Americans' visual sensibilities through a series of images that attempted to mark out the obvious visual distinctions one should look for to properly differentiate friend from foe. *Life* described "the typical Northern Chinese . . . [as being] relatively tall and slender built"; "his complexion is parchment yellow, his face long and delicately boned, his nose more finely bridged."[5] The first set of images focused primarily on facial distinctions, where in contrast to Chinese traits, *Life* described Japanese people as having "a broader, more massively boned head and face, flat, often pug, nose, yellow-ocher skin and heavier beard."[6] But, as shown in Figures 1 and 2, these physiological descriptors were not enough; the images themselves were marked by *Life* editors to specifically point out the visual cues that distinguish each group, whether a "more frequent epicanthic fold" or a "broader, shorter face."

A second set of images focused on physical differences in Chinese and Japanese bodies. The text of the *Life* article noted that the Chinese brothers pictured in Figure 3 represent a typical "lanky, lithe build," while Japanese people, as shown in Figure 4, "exhibit squat, solid, long torso and short stocky legs."[7]

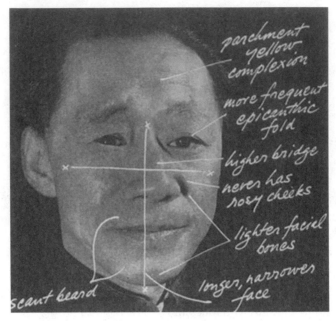

FIGURE 1. "Typical" Chinese facial characteristics as depicted in *Life* magazine, December 1941. Photo by Carl Mydans/Time & Life Pictures/Getty Images.

The *Life* article even went so far as to claim that when Chinese become "middle aged and fat, they look more like Japs."[8] But *Life* cautioned its readers to pay attention not only to visual cues of a physiological nature, but also to those that manifest themselves through cultural differences: "an often sounder clue [to distinguishing between Chinese and Japanese] is facial expression, shaped by cultural, not anthropological, factors. Chinese wear rational calm of tolerant realists. Japs . . . show humorless intensity of ruthless mystics."[9]

These images and descriptions link the politically driven stereotype of treachery and duplicity to a visually distinguishable body that ultimately produced an understanding of the Japanese as a subhuman group.[10] The visuality of group difference emphasized by the *Life* images played an important role in the construction of racial difference by reasserting the centrality of racial typologies or the idea that distinct, biologically different racial groups exist. Part of emphasizing Japanese difference from both ourselves as Americans and Chinese as Allies is to suggest that their inherently duplicitous nature manifested itself in or correlated with physical differences that are visually

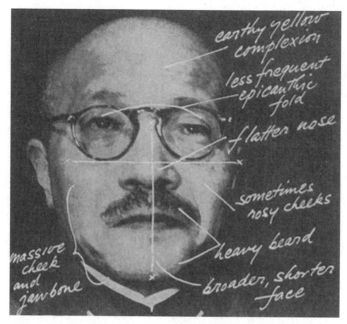

FIGURE 2. "Typical" Japanese facial characteristics as depicted in *Life* magazine, December 1941. Black Star.

obvious if you know what you're looking for. That was the point of the *Life* magazine photo spread: to teach Americans how to visually distinguish human bodies to ascertain these typologies and tendencies.

Such efforts impacted Americans' view of the Japanese and Japanese Americans. In many ways, Americans despised the Japanese more than other nationalities we were at war with; the idea of racial difference played a distinctive role both in how the Japanese were understood on their own terms and, in a comparative sense, in relation to Germans and Italians. Not only were Japanese dehumanized by cartoonists, journalists, and others as being apes, monkeys, and rodents—whereby their seeming physical distinctions blurred seamlessly with the bestial form to which they were being compared—but the comparative political rhetoric surrounding discursive references to America's enemies during World War II treated the Japanese as a separate and monolithic group. Germans and Italians, on the other hand, continued to enjoy the perception of being diverse in temperament. This shaped policy choices during the war, such as the widespread exclusion and interment of Japanese Americans without any similar treatment to German or Italian Americans.[11]

FIGURE 3. "Typical" Chinese body as depicted in *Life* magazine, December 1941. Photo by Carl Mydans/Time & Life Pictures/Getty Images.

This slice of World War II history introduces a key concept at the heart of almost all modern race scholarship: the social construction of race. The rapidly shifting meanings and ideas surrounding race and ethnicity in the wake of the bombing of Pearl Harbor shows how racial meanings are neither static nor timeless. Rather, they are constructed by social, economic, and political developments that can rapidly attach new meanings to racialized bodies with a power and force that can make these newly constructed meanings seem like an essential aspect of group membership. This, in short, is the social constructionist thesis: social forces—not nature or anything intrinsic to racial groups—produce the meanings that come to be associated with racial difference. The constructionist project largely involves fleshing out

FIGURE 4. "Typical" Japanese body as depicted in *Life* magazine, December 1941. © Bettmann/CORBIS.

the social processes—such as the politics of war—leading to the creation of social meanings, their attachment to bodies deemed racially different, and the subtle dynamics leading these meanings and attachments to be rearticulated as a natural, inherent, and timeless group traits.

But the *Life* magazine images bring another dimension of racialization to the forefront: the extent to which constructed meanings are assumed to be both essential to racial difference and visually obvious *at the very same time* that these ostensibly self-evident traits require meticulous policing, training, and visual instruction in order for differences to become publicly visible in a presumptively consistent and coherent manner. Thus, not only are racial meanings such as Japanese duplicity constructed, but social forces (such as photojournalism) also produce the very ability for individuals to clearly see racial differences in a manner that is experienced as being self-evident.

This other dimension regarding the productive forces behind racial difference *becoming visible* (rather than simply being visually obvious on its own terms) has not been a significant part of the social constructionist project. These productive forces leading up to race becoming visible yet experienced as self-evident is what I identify as the *constitutive theory of race*. An important though usually ignored tension within the social constructionist perspective is that it assumes that the visual salience of race is largely obvious; race is thought to speak for itself. The visibility of racial difference—hair color, facial features, and other visual cues thought to definitively mark group membership—is largely conceptualized as existing anterior to any social process; both lay persons and race scholars tend to treat race as something that is coherent and "known" through mere observation. The social constructionist literature has paid exhaustive attention to situations such as how the politics of war lead pejorative social meanings to attach to Japanese physiological distinctions such as the flat nose and broad face marked out by the photos in *Life*. But less attention has been paid to how social forces such as the *Life* magazine photo spread produce the very ability to see race in particular ways that come to be experienced as visually obvious yet require remarkable amounts of work to create salient and coherent boundaries of visual (and visible) difference.

By drawing attention to the constitutive social practices that give rise to individuals' ability to see race in certain ways, this book intervenes into the existing theoretical and conceptual gaps in race scholarship that largely frame racial difference as being self-evident and visually coherent on their own terms. In addition to exploring the contributions and limitations of the social constructionist literature, this chapter puts the existing literature in conversation with other perspectives not typically part of the race canon that are more sensitive to the ways in which social practices produce the ability to see human difference. This provides the theoretical orientation for the empirical project—teasing out blind people's understanding of race—that is at the core of this book that, in itself, generates a new standpoint from which to both critique and expand social constructionism in order to understand the social practices behind visual experiences.

The theoretical project of destabilizing the presumption that race is visually obvious and the empirical project of assessing blind people's understanding of race are tightly connected. Qualitative research on blind people's understanding of and experiences with race permits an empirical basis from which to rethink the obviousness that envelops the process of "seeing race" so as to better understand the social forces that influence our visual engagements. An empirical assessment of blind people's visual understanding of race can challenge the intuition that the visual salience of race—why it is conspicuous, why it seems to visually stand out as a coherent marker of human difference—stems not from it being visually obvious but rather from constitutive social practices that produce our ability to see the world in racial terms. This works from and extends existing claims regarding the social construction of race to the extent that "seeing race" is not merely a neutral observation concerning the way social meanings attach to racialized bodies. Rather, this book highlights the extent to which our eyes are trained to see race in particular ways—so much so, that even blind people see race. This has important social and legal implications; the empirical data belie the assumption that race is visually obvious—an assumption that ultimately frames important legal and policy choices in a manner that inhibits racial justice. But before moving to this empirical work and its ramifications, it is useful to situate the empirical project in the existing literature on the social construction of race that anchors almost all race scholarship while also putting this dominant approach in conversation with literatures on the social processes behind seeing difference. This allows for a better conceptual basis from which to understand this book's empirical component and broader implications.

Rarely do we dissect with any precision what social constructionism means, from what previous concepts of race the constructionist thesis emerged, and the "work" that the constructionist thesis does in modern times. In order to fully articulate the claims being made in this book, this chapter discusses the significance of the social constructionist thesis in terms of the social, political, and ideological contexts giving rise to its prominence in postwar race scholarship and public policy. Once this backdrop is established, the core contribution of the constructionist approach is brought to the forefront: to expose how social meanings attach to various bodies. I then discuss how the constructionist thesis is operationalized in current race scholarship in law and the social sciences to highlight a glaring tension: the extent to which race, as both a theoretical and an empirical matter, is assumed to be a visually stable, self-evident, and obvious variable that freely exists in the social world with a visual salience that is separate from any social process.

In other words, the constructionist approach provides a theoretically rich account of how meaning attaches to bodies and offers robust mechanisms to decouple these assumed connections to rethink the possibilities for human interaction and the social order. Yet it has not offered an empirically nuanced account of how bodies become visually salient in the first place. The gap in the literature exposed in this chapter gives rise to the constitutive theory of race proposed by this book. But first, let us spend a few moments exploring social constructionism.

The Social Construction of Race

As previously noted, the social constructionist thesis has come to stand for the idea that race does not reflect any natural differences or inherent meanings between groups. Rather, racial groupings and their attendant meanings reflect social choices and power relationships that legitimize hierarchies and social orderings that privilege one group over another. This has largely become the boilerplate starting point for how scholars think about and discuss race.[12]

But the significance of the social constructionist approach to race can only be fully appreciated in contrast to the prevailing ideas of race from which it emerged in the twentieth century: that social categories of race, based largely on phenotype, reflect inherent differences that explain groups' disparate social outcomes and justify racial subordination. While early race conversations on group inferiority and superiority often emphasized various social myths and religious explanations, scientific accounts of racial hierarchy in the West became increasingly prominent in the late eighteenth and nineteenth centuries. Thus, it is useful—both to grasp a deeper understanding of the constructionist thesis and to situate the *constitutive* theory of race developed in this book—to briefly sketch this backdrop so as to have a finer appreciation of what is meant by the now ubiquitous claim that race is a social construction.

Scientific Racism

Science has a long history of trying to use quantitative methods to show that there are measurable physical differences between racial groups that explain differences and disparities in social and health outcomes. Rather than viewing those outcomes as a product of social, economic, and political inequalities, the scientific method was used to frame differential group outcomes as a product of nature. Scholars have documented this practice across many disciplines for decades. But, Stephen Jay Gould's *Mismeasure of Man* is remarkable in detailing the ways in which biological notions of race were used in the nineteenth century to both reflect and produce notions of racial inferiority and White racial supremacy. Gould draws attention to respected researchers such as Samuel Morton, a Philadelphia physician who significantly influenced early American anthropology by offering extensive quantitative data to support a biological theory of racial difference known as craniometry. This practice linked skull size and shape with cognitive ability and moral virtue to establish a ranking system that ostensibly provided objective data to support White racial dominance.[13] Morton's research was central to nineteenth-century American polygenesis—the then-popular theory that each race had separate origins—in that it legitimated the social order through science. It is difficult to overstate his impact on public and scholarly understandings of race at the time. The *New York Tribune* wrote at his death that "probably no scientific man in America enjoyed a higher reputation among scholars throughout the world than Dr. Morton."[14]

Morton's work is a prime example of how the scientific method came to play a prominent role in shaping scholarly and lay understandings of racial hierarchy. Science assumed an even stronger role in conceptualizing race differences after the 1859 publication of Charles Darwin's *On the Origin of Species*. Darwin's theory is quite simple: organisms' traits are hereditary, adapting to environmental pressures and changing over time to confer survival advantages (evolution) through natural selection or sexual reproduction. Darwin was not the first to propose an evolutionary model for organisms' development. His contribution was to theorize how evolution happened through natural selection: mating between the strongest and most attractive individuals gives survival advantages to subsequent generations, improving organisms' overall strength and vitality.[15]

Darwinism helped resolve a virulent debate among race commentators at the time: whether all humans had one single origin (monogenism) or whether each race had different and unrelated biological origins (polygenism). Darwinism presented the great compromise that superseded this theoretical impasse. Evolution by natural selection allowed monogenists to "win" part of the argument—that humanity has one origin from which racial hierarchies with superior and inferior races evolved—while polygenists "won" in that the heritability of differences in ability appeared to be supported by the idea that great evolutionary distances separated the races.[16] Put bluntly, the racist tendencies underlying each theory led to their consensus around evolution to the extent that "it provided an even better rationale for their shared racism."[17]

The close connection Darwin drew between human evolution and the ability to empirically document its different stages fueled a flame that had already been burning since the early nineteenth century: measuring racial differences. Scientists like Morton and his successors thought that if the races represented human evolution's stages, measuring these differences would be absolutely crucial in giving these social observations scientific backing. Thus, as Thomas Gossett notes in *Race: The History of an Idea in America*, the "nineteenth century [became] a period of exhaustive and—as it turned out—futile search for criteria to define and describe race differences."[18]

The ascension of measurement to defining proper scientific thought reified the notion that observing the status quo leads to racial truth concerning groups' inherent abilities, intensifying the scrutiny given to racial bodies as a predicate for postwar race relations. Racial bodies and their performances became subject to exacting visual scrutiny in efforts to explain racial minorities' natural state as degraded and inferior. In postwar America, this type of policing became a new type of social control. The Civil War, the Emancipation Proclamation, and the Reconstruction Amendments may have formally liberated Blacks, but science became the new basis for their social and legal restraint. Blacks' limited progress was explained as natural, normal, and predictable by scientific observations; even laypeople were thought to be able to appreciate these differences by simply looking out into the world. Indeed, legal historian Ariela Gross notes that a common theme among today's historians of the nineteenth-century South is that in the postbellum world "the color line replaced the boundary between free and slave, race replaced slave status, and a regime a whiteness replaced the regime of slavery as the weapon of oppression."[19] Gross notes that science played a key role in these transformations in that "it was [during] the post–Civil War period that racial science triumphed and became the single argument for explaining 'race.' "[20] This is a subtle but important point that deserves amplification. While the Civil War and Reconstruction Amendments provided powerful mechanisms to make Blacks full citizens, there were equally powerful opposing forces determined to maintain racial subordination through different means. The increasingly sophisticated notion of race-as-biology played this key role: providing a rational, and objectively verifiable, measurement system that demonstrated racial minorities' inferiority as natural, inherent, and heritable. Within the Darwinian framework, this not only justified the status quo, but gave moral impetus to the belief that to try to change these status relationships would be contrary to evolutionary progress and thus society itself.

Social Darwinism and Eugenics

The social sciences became particularly useful in justifying inequalities "in terms of a natural hierarchy of class and race caused by a struggle for existence wherein the fittest individuals or races advanced while the inferior became eclipsed."[21] These popular terms—"the struggle for existence" or more often "the survival of the fittest"—are often attributed to Charles Darwin but actually belong to Herbert Spencer. Spencer, an Englishman, had a profound impact on American social sciences. Darwin often balked at directly applying his evolutionary thought to social relations. But, even before Darwin published *On the Origin of Species*, Spencer was developing his own pseudoevolutionary theories that treated social organisms the same way Darwin approached biological ones.[22]

Thus, Spencer advocated what came to be known as Social Darwinism: "the idea of natural selection was translated to a struggle between individual members of society[;] . . . nature's indispensable method for producing superior men, superior nations, and superior races."[23] In the context of Darwin's rock star status in the United States and the postwar need for rational explanations of human difference, Spencer's "biological analogy" was, to put it mildly, the right theory at the right time. The parallels Spencer made between the natural and social sciences were simply too elegant and seductive for Americans to resist.

Race became a key framing for Social Darwinism; Spencer analogized the evolutionary gap between savage and civilized minds as being akin to the gulf in cognitive abilities between juveniles and adults.[24] Here, as throughout this period, anthropological measurements such as craniometry merge with Social Darwinist theory to reveal the evolutionary and biological hierarchies embedded in these race discourses through quantified comparisons of geographically separated and visually distinguishable groups.

With the intellectual and "scientific" basis for conceptualizing and measuring racial hierarchy establishing itself throughout the nineteenth century, the question at the turn of the twentieth century became quite pragmatic: what should be done about it? This context gave rise to the eugenics movement, which was an international effort to use science and medicine to justify limiting the reproduction—and existence—of individuals deemed to be of an inferior racial stock while promoting the reproduction of those thought to be racially superior.[25] Known as racial hygiene, eugenics came to dominate social, political, and legal thought in the early twentieth century across America and Europe, leading to devastating public policies that facilitated an estimated sixty thousand forced sterilizations in the United States and the genocide of Jewish people and other marginalized groups during the Holocaust.[26]

Race, Reconciliation, and the Growing Acceptance of Social Constructionism

Though eugenic practices continued in parts of the United States until the 1970s, eugenics as a broad social policy for racial betterment was largely discredited by the 1950s;[27] the horrors of World War II exposed the movement's logical folly and dire consequences for humanity. The ideas of scholars who challenged scientific racism before and during the war—notable figures such as Franz Boas, Ashley Montagu, and others—became mainstream afterward. Academics gravitated toward what appeared to be a consensus view that race is not a biological concept and that group differences are attributable to social, cultural, political, and economic forces rather than heritable differences. With the radical shift in global political sentiments in the postwar period, the anti-racist scholarship that challenged eugenic worldviews during the first half of the twentieth century came to be the dominant perspective. For example, Montagu played a key role in drafting UNESCO's Statement on Race in 1950, which stated:"The biological fact of race and the myth of 'race' should be distinguished. For all practical social purposes 'race' is not so much a biological phenomenon as a social myth. . . . The biological differences between ethnic groups should be disregarded from the standpoint of social acceptance and social action. The unity of mankind from both the biological and social viewpoints is the main thing."[28] Such scientific declarations also trickled into lay discourses on race, with a *New York Times* headlines declaring "No Scientific Basis for Race Bias Found by World Panel of Experts."[29]

With this attempt to shift the political and lay conversations away from biological understandings of race came more sustained efforts in the social sciences and other related disciplines to highlight the social, political, and economic forces that produce the racial meanings that were once thought to stem from heritable genetic differences. Following the 1967 publication of Berger and Luckman's *The Social Construction of Reality*, this practice of deconstructing the presumed natural links between human characteristics and meanings to reveal their irreducibly social origins became known as constructionism. Berger and Luckman explain:

> Everyday life presents itself as a reality interpreted by men and subjectively meaningful to them as a coherent world. As sociologists we take this reality as the object of our analyses. Within the frame of reference of sociology as an empirical science it is possible to take this reality as given, to take as data particular phenomena arising within it, without further inquiring about the foundations of this reality, which is a philosophical task. . . . [However] we cannot completely bypass the philosophical problem. The world of everyday life is not only taken for granted as reality by the ordinary members of society in the subjectively meaningful conduct of their lives. It is a world that originates in their thoughts and actions, and is maintained as real by these. . . . We must therefore attempt to clarify the foundations of knowledge in everyday life, to wit, the objectivations of subjective processes (and meanings) by which the intersubjective commonsense world is constructed.[30]

By questioning the origins of the meanings that we often experience as an inherent or essential part of the natural world, the social constructionist approach has come to represent the process of disaggregating subjective social meanings (i.e., that which is constructed by social forces and human choices) from the objects and bodies that they attach to. While these meanings' adhesion to things is often seen as an inseparable part of the thing itself, social constructionists separate the two—often to highlight how society's uncritical acceptance of the natural link between meanings and things can be part of a power dynamic (such as racial hierarchy) to privilege one group over another. Thus, this emphasis on disaggregation is often in furtherance of broader notions of social justice by demonstrating that status quo inequities do not reflect any natural order. Rather, these inequities represent one particular outcome that often can be more equitably reoriented with the appropriate commitments in place.

This has become an influential if not dominant approach for scholars in law, social sciences, and humanities to understand social life, from the social construction of gender (which disaggregates normative perspectives on how men and women ought to interact from the sexed bodies that these normative relations are thought to emanate)[31] to the social construction of deviance in homeless and runaway youth (which examines how the stereotypical "meanings" of pervasive criminality among runaway and homeless youth are produced by the selective enforcement of arbitrary and ambiguous local policies rather than anything intrinsic to this group).[32] But social constructionism has probably become the most influential in understanding race.

Against the backdrop of a long history of scientific racism and biological understandings of racial difference used to justify genocide, postwar research on the social construction of race has largely come to stand for three related claims. First, social categories of race do not have any biological meaning. While there may be genetic variations linked to a similar outward appearance among various populations that can signal propensities in social and health outcomes, social categories of race do not capture these in any meaningful sense. Social categories of race and human population differences are largely discordant and do not meaningfully map onto each other.[33] Moreover, the disparate outcomes that we see between racial groups are more likely linked to social and environmental determinants rather than inherent differences between groups.[34] Second, social forces create racial boundaries and meanings. The meanings that we associate with racial groups, as well as which people are "in" and "out" of various groupings, is a sociological phenomenon linked to legal decisions, political motivations, economic dynamics, and historical contexts. Lastly, these racial meanings and boundaries themselves are unstable, varying across time and space. The racial boundaries of Whiteness were not the same in 1930 as they are today, and being Black in the United States may not be the same as being Black in parts of South America. Racial categories mutate in addition to being created and destroyed; they have little temporal or geographical stability. Therefore, the instability of racial categories and meanings as well as the frequency with which they change belie claims to their immutability.

Despite its appeal and popularity, the perspective that race is socially constructed has itself been critiqued along at least three different lines in the postwar era. After the critique of biological race "went public" through the first UNESCO Statement on Race in 1950 but before the language of social constructionism became a popular way to capture these sentiments, there were concerns that the constructionist approach might be overly political in making anti-racist claims not supported by scientific data. Of particular concern was the first UNESCO statement's condemnation of the idea that certain mental and emotional traits are distributed along racial lines[35] and the statement's concluding claim that "biological studies lend support to the ethic of universal brotherhood; for man is born with drives toward co-operation, and unless these drives are satisfied, men and nations alike fall ill."[36] Physical anthropologists and geneticists took exception to these and other conclusions, which led to the Second UNESCO Statement on the Nature of Race and Race Differences in 1951, which re-opened the possibility that emotional and mental responses may vary along racial lines and that an affirmative commitment to equality in law does not mean that racial groups are themselves biologically equal. While few researchers today would argue that race is relevant to emotional and mental abilities, biological understandings of racial difference remain common in medicine and biomedical research.[37] Therefore, there is a concern that political commitments to racial equality might unduly restrict efforts to understand human genetic variation that may very well hold significance along racial lines.

This first critique concerning the overly political nature of social constructionism leads to a second, related critique: that the constructionist approach to race does not take into account the growing body of evidence that social categories of race map on to biological differences that are observable at the molecular level and also explain various racial disparities in social or health outcomes. Burchard et al. note that three different sets of studies in population genetics "have revealed great genetic variation within racial or ethnic subpopulations, but also substantial variation among the five major racial groups."[38] Although the Human Genome Project concluded that all persons are over 99 percent similar at the molecular level, researchers continue to mine this less than 1 percent of genetic dissimilarity—noting that it represents millions of points of genetic variation—to demonstrate the heritability of racial disparities from asthma to kidney disease.[39]

The third critique is a broader philosophical assessment of social constructionism as having become an undisciplined catchall phrase that, on its face, signifies a rejection of the status quo or essentialism but, as a substantive matter, often contributes little to our understanding of the social world. As Ian Hacking argues in his book The Social Construction of What? "the use of the word declares what side one is on" as opposed to being an independently useful analytical tool.[40] While Hacking engages in a rather elaborate deconstruction of the constructionist trope, his most basic and penetrating point is that social constructionism is old wine in a new bottle; the notion that ideas and perceptions of the world are historically contingent and that things are not really what they seem has been around for centuries.[41] Yet the radicalism with which the constructionist agenda puts forth its critique often fails to acknowledge this, thus overstating what Hacking and other philosophers see as a diluted if not entirely obvious contribution to understanding social reality. With this, Hacking sees a redundancy in the term "social construction" itself. Using the example of gender (which can be conceptually extended to race), Hacking rhetorically asks, "if gender is by definition something essentially social, and if it is constructed, how could its construction be other than social?"[42] Without dismissing it in its entirety, this philosophical critique offered by Hacking asks what is being presented by constructionist approaches beyond a history of an idea's contingency, which is a form of critique that has been around for quite some time and applies to most things in the social world.[43]

Social Construction, Race Scholarship, and the Question of Vision

Virtually every question regarding the sociology of race starts from the premise that race is a social construction, which, as described above, means that racial categories and their attendant meanings do not reflect any natural or biological characteristics but rather are conventions tied to other social, economic, and political processes. Michael Omi and Howard Winant's *Racial Formation in the United States* stands out in this regard; its discussion of racial formation as the socio-historical process by which racial categories are created and destroyed is the benchmark from which almost all sociologists think about race. Omi and Winant's definition of race has been equally influential: "Race is a concept which signifies and symbolizes social conflicts and interests by referring to different types of human bodies. Although the concept of race invokes biologically based human characteristics (so-called 'phenotypes'), selection of these particular human features for purposes of racial signification is always and necessarily a social and historical process."[44] Omi and Winant's emphasis on phenotypes—defined as "the set of *observable* characteristics of an individual resulting from the interaction of its genotype with the environment"[45] (emphasis added)—highlights the extent to which racial conversations within sociology already implicate visibility as an epistemological starting point. From this perspective, race is constructed around these observable characteristics. It is the selection and attribution of meaning that necessarily constitute a social and historical process; the method through which these phenotypes or observable characteristics are invoked—vision or visual references—is outside of Omi and Winant's substantive constructionist argument and goes without meaningful critique. This approach is repeated throughout the social constructionist literature on race.

Most of what I term the existing first generation social constructionist writing on race has largely used historical evidence to develop this theory of race. Theodore Allen wrote his two-volume treatise *The Invention of the White Race* in this constructionist tradition, analyzing the transhistorical and transcontinental moments—forced labor, need for social control in modern society, and so on—that solidified racial oppression in the West to give rise to a uniquely identifiable White race where none existed before.[46] Historical approaches to understanding how previously marginalized White ethnics became part of the White mainstream are also highly regarded examples of constructionist scholarship. This includes Matthew Frye Jacobsen's examination of this "de-ethnitizing" process among European immigrants, Noel Ignatiev's specific examination of this process among the Irish, and Brodkin's related arguments concerning Jewish communities.[47] Similarly, David R. Roediger's *Working Toward Whiteness* provides insightful commentary into how White ethnics transitioned from minority status into the mainstream, complicating the previous analyses by asking "what happens when we think of assimilation as whitening as well as Americanizing?"[48] Roediger adds another layer to historical conversations on Whiteness by looking at it as a function of citizenship, while also examining how White ethnic groups' movement from society's fringes to the mainstream had the dual effect of marginalizing other minorities on both racial and citizenship grounds in terms of which groups were "real" Americans.[49] As a whole, these authors shed light on the historical instability of racial categories in a manner that draws attention to (and develops a theory of) their socially constructed nature.[50]

While the constructionist theory of race has been widely accepted among sociologists, it has been in tension with sociology's *empirical* work on race. For example, John Levi Martin and King-To Yeung conclude that the "social sciences' claim to understand race as a social construct is belied by practitioners repeated use of race as if it were a nonproblematic set of categorical divisions."[51] Martin and Yeung's research highlights a strange irony: while sociologists have come to a theoretical consensus that race is a social construction, few have taken this premise seriously as an empirical matter. Jack Niemonen similarly concludes that contrary to the critical reflection on race one might expect from sociology, race has largely been used as reified common sense, that is, that race is as we see it.[52] Where the field's empirical and constructionist leanings have coexisted rather harmoniously—such as in Ruth Frankenberg's *White Women, Race Matters* and Mary Waters's *Ethnic Options*[53]—the studies have been somewhat limited in that their empiricism is descriptive rather than explanatory; they largely get at the fluidity with which people understand and construct their own identity rather than the social practices that produce dynamic understandings of race.

Since this research regarding blind people's understanding of race looks at the interaction between the cognitive and social processes underlying blind individuals' racial perceptions, it is useful to note that the limited perspectives present in the sociology of race are also pervasive among social psychologists studying race.[54] Matthew Hunt et al. conclude that "social psychologists, as well as sociologists in other subfields, have given race and ethnicity less attention than it warrants."[55] Indeed, Hunt and his colleagues go so far as to say that "the failure to test for racial variation both reflects and reinforces the assumption that social psychological processes are universally applicable and thus generalize to different groups in stratified societies."[56] From this perspective, social psychologists are like the empirical side of their sociology of race counterparts: they assume the inherent stability of racial categories in their research without probing deeper into their actual construction.

Sociology's conversations on race are connected to research on social stratification in that questions regarding how individuals know and experience race inevitably come up against work on other forms of hierarchies in American society.[57] As a subfield of sociology, social stratification attempts to empirically demonstrate social inequalities in addition to examining their possible causes and consequences. For some, inequalities are mostly benign, inevitable, or even positive for society.[58] For others, the fact that certain physical markers become a proxy if not cause for groups' "repeat losing" signals at best an inefficiency in resource allocation and, at worst, an immoral outcome in that stereotypes and bigotry trump individual merit in determining social position.[59] Social stratification is not simply limited to conversations around structured inequality relative to class, skill set, or labor market position. Rather, such inequalities often correlate with the stereotypes and disdain associated with disreputable social groups. For example, research shows that particularly with regard to women, physical attractiveness can influence life chances and opportunities in terms of the labor market and everyday life exchanges.[60] Race also plays a central role in how society distributes resources and opportunities, though there is much debate as to when the race problem becomes a class problem.[61] Nevertheless, racial stratification is not simply about hierarchies among races but also between them. The veracity with which certain meanings attach to individuals within disreputable racial groups often depends upon their complexion: minorities with fairer skin tend to have better social and economic outcomes while individuals with darker skin are viewed less favorably by Whites and others within their own racial group.[62] What is remarkable is that this literature largely assumes that inequality and stratification are based upon visual processes; groups with disadvantaged relations to the market are visually targeted, discriminated against, and denied upward mobility.[63] The assumption is that what is visually perceptible (gender, race, body type, etc.) becomes the sociological "trigger" producing a discriminatory response, and that *but for* these visual distinctions, such stratification would not be possible. But, is what we see, in and of itself, that crucial to how groups define an "us" and "them" to apportion resources and opportunities? There are likely to be other constitutive orderings at play that make such divisions and distinctions thinkable, and talking to blind people about their racial experience can offer insight into how this works outside of direct visual perceptions.

The sociology of law is a natural disciplinary location from which to situate this project as this field has largely developed around the idea that law should be placed in a broader social context not only to understand the development of rules and rule making, but also to appreciate the effects of law on society.[64] Sociologists of law have also been criticized for not paying close enough attention to race in their research. My own work in this area has shown that race scholarship within the field (using the *Law & Society Review* as a proxy) is not nearly as progressive as its scholars might think. An eighteen-year quantitative and qualitative study of *Law & Society Review* articles showed "not only that law and society scholars publish on race with less regularity than their [legal] colleagues, but also that, as a substantive matter, their race articles suffer from significant theoretical shortcomings insofar as they frame race (1) as an instrumentality (2) as taxonomic categories rooted principally in phenotype and (3) as a social problem constituted anterior to the law."[65] Laura Gómez came to a similar conclusion, arguing that law and society scholars' failure to incorporate insights from Critical Race Theory has led its race scholarship to be not as well rounded as it could be.[66] This point is well taken. Critical Race Theory can provide an important context from which to think seriously about the relationship law has with race. More importantly, it can help us situate the role of law in structuring race as primarily a visual experience in terms of the rules and precedents that condition how we see race, what we see racially, and what race means.

Important efforts are being made in fields outside of but related to sociology, such as within disability studies, to broaden perspectives within mainstream sociology. However, the relationship between disability studies and sociology has been tenuous at best. Colin Barnes, Geoff Mercer, and Tom Shakespeare have observed: "Where sociologists have taken an interest in the process of disablement, they have typically not addressed this as an example of social exclusion or oppression, but followed instead what has variously been referred to as an 'individual,' 'medical,' or 'personal tragedy,' model of disability."[67] At the cutting edge of disability studies is an effort to situate disablement as a socially constructed phenomenon not unlike race and sex. The argument is that disability shares the same sociological identity as race or sex in that it is constructed through social processes whereby groups of people are "(1) named, (2) aggregated and disaggregated, (3) dichotomized and stigmatized, and (4) denied the attributes valued in culture."[68] While disability rights activism has its own distinct history, this framing was and continues to be an important aspect of the modern disability rights movement.[69] Like many other social movements in the mid- to late twentieth century, disability rights activists leveraged the gains made by the civil rights movement to bolster their own claims about equality: access to education and employment, rights to independent living, and legal remedies for discrimination.[70]

Efforts at situating disability as a social construction share much with similar conversations regarding the social construction of race and gender in that they are an attempt to take the emphasis off of "good" or "bad" bodies (be they Black or White, male or female, disabled or abled) and to question how society produces the meanings and values placed on people and groups with shared characteristics.[71] More importantly, even less work has been done on how race interacts with blindness, or any disability for that matter. Deborah Sienstra argues that research in this area overemphasizes the need to provide culturally appropriate services in a manner that "isolates and seeks to treat the individual with impairments rather than addressing the broad context that creates disability."[72] As such, approaching disability research as a window through which to understand broader sociological processes affecting all persons is unique and may substantially contribute to our understanding of race.

What Can Blind People's Understanding of Race Contribute to the Race Literature?

Conceptual Interventions: Drawing Upon Art History for a Critique of Race and Vision

Vision has been a longtime concern within the humanities. Scholars in fields such as history, philosophy, and art history have explored what many call the pictorial turn—a moment not unlike previous deconstructive approaches to language—to examine "the constituted rather than the found quality of seemingly natural phenomenon."[73] Theories of perception—particularly in relation to visual cues associated with identity markers like gender and sexuality[74]—have become commonplace, "prob[ing] their disciplines' past and interrogat[ing] their present to unveil the hidden effects of visual metaphors and visual practices on their most fundamental assumptions."[75] The attention these scholars have paid to the constitutive nature of vision has brought great insight into historical and theoretical work concerning identity issues involving race, gender, and sexuality. Donna Haraway, a leading figure in the history of science, notes that "the rays from my optical device diffract rather than reflect. These diffracting rays compose interference patterns, not reflecting images. . . . A diffraction pattern does not map where differences appear, but rather where the effects of differences appear."[76]

This idea that our eyes do not naturally see difference but only absorb the effects of difference produced by society is taken up by Joan W. Scott in *The Evidence of Experience*, where she takes a critical perspective on history and the historian: "When experience is taken as the origin of knowledge, the vision of the individual subject (the person who had the experience or the historian who recounts it) becomes the bedrock of evidence on which explanation is built. Questions about the constructed nature of experience, about how one's vision is structured . . . are left aside."[77] This point regarding the ways in which experience structures visual observation has been most eloquently expressed by a small group of art historians. Jonathan Crary's *Techniques of the Observer: On Vision and Modernity in the Nineteenth Century* provides a fascinating history of vision, with a particular focus on the turn to modernity that made new ways of seeing possible. While Crary is most interested in the nineteenth century optical devices that began to mediate the relationship between observer and observed, his insights into how underlying social forces shape the possibilities of what we see and how this brought a new type of attention to bodies is instrumental for this book's underlying theory.[78] This is particularly important in how Crary explores the ways in which vision is not simply historically contingent, but contingent upon social relations:

> Whether perception or vision actually change is irrelevant, for they have no autonomous history. What changes are the plural forces and rules composing the field in which perception occurs. And what determines vision at any given historical moment is not some deep structure, economic base, or world view, but rather the functioning of a collective assemblage of disparate parts on a single social surface. It may even be necessary to consider the observer as a distribution of events located in many different places. There never was or will be a self-present beholder to whom a world is transparently evident. Instead there are more or less powerful arrangements of forces out of which the capacities of an observer are possible.[79]

Thus, this focus on how social relations and forces produce visual experiences is a much richer articulation of how particular cues become visually significant. It takes account of the iterative practices that shape a learned behavior without privileging history as a unilateral deterministic force—a tendency that can be seen in many constructionist writings.

Crary's second book, *Suspensions of Perception: Attention, Spectacle, and Modern Culture*, focuses on the historical nature of human attention in terms of how modernity constructs the way humans disengage from broader fields to fix their attention on a particular thing. This project gives Crary license to once again parse the relationship between vision and bodies by bringing in an analysis that takes power seriously: "What is important to institutional power, since the late nineteenth century, is simply that perception function in a way that insures a subject is productive, manageable, and predictable, and is able to be socially integrated and adaptive."[80]

This link between vision, bodies, modernity, and power relations is taken up by other art historians specifically interested in the way social practices shape perceptions of race. Patricia Johnston's *Seeing High and Low: Representing Social Conflict in American Visual Culture* offers a conceptual bridge between Crary's broad comments on the effects of modernity on individuals' perception and the particular social circumstances that lead artists to reproduce social conflict in their work for observers to internalize (and in a sense naturalize) as "art." Johnston notes that the fifteen essays in this volume "argue implicitly that all visual productions and experiences can be read as social as well as aesthetic documents—whether or not the maker intended them to be. The visual is an essential part of the cultural."[81] This idea is given more specificity with regard to race in Kymberly Pinder's *Race-ing Art History: Critical Readings in Race and Art History,* an engaging twenty-two-essay anthology spanning critiques of art from antiquity to the twentieth century with a shared theme: how "art produced by non-Europeans has naturally been compared to Western art and its study, which refers to a binary way of viewing both. Each essay . . . respon[ds] to this vision, to the distant mirror of looking at the other."[82] At the crux of each essay is an exploration into how visual interactions between the West and non-European art is constituted by broader political and economic struggles in the region.[83] Put another way, visually engaging with art pieces identified as racial in character is not neutral or objective, but is a product of social conditions.

Martin A. Berger makes this point most emphatically in *Sight Unseen: Whiteness and American Visual Culture,* in which he "takes[s] seriously the importance of situating racial identities in social context." Berger explores art history to make the main point about race and human vision that this book, in part, is trying to empirically demonstrate through interviewing blind people about race:

> Despite the human propensity to privilege sight, and the long standing Western tendency to root racial designations in observable traits, images do not persuade us to internalize racial values embedded within them, so much as they confirm meanings for which the discourses and structures of our society have predisposed us. Instead of selling us on racial systems we do not already own, the visual field powerfully confirms previously internalized beliefs.[84]

This is a compelling point that works from social constructionist writings showing that race does not reflect any natural or biological boundaries, yet goes beyond this to suggest that the very cues that have come to visually mark racial boundaries are not as self-evidently salient as widely believed. This is separate from the broader idea that race is socially constructed and suggests that an important research agenda awaits to examine the micromechanics that lead social understandings of race to orient around particular visual differences in skin color and other visible body traits. Yet understanding how what we "see" is constituted by broader cultural and social practices has largely evaded the work of scholars examining the social construction of race across disciplines. This book attempts to extend the constructionist project by blending it with the constitutive sensibility found in art history to fill this gap within legal and social science research to empirically investigate how visual cues associated with race come to be socially salient.

Empirical Significance

Now that important "gaps" in race scholarship have been exposed, it is time to start the process of filling them. On the theoretical side, the social constructionist approach has repeatedly decoupled the links made between social meanings and racialized bodies to demonstrate the social forces that make these linkages seem like a naturally occurring racial hierarchy. The social constructionist approach in general, and race theory in law and the social sciences in particular, have largely looked at how meanings attach to bodies without spending much time on how these racialized bodies become visually salient in the first place. On the empirical side, qualitative and quantitative scholarship on race has not engaged constructionist approaches as thoroughly as one might expect, leading race to be conceptualized even more rudimentarily as a visually obvious and relatively stable trait.[85] What connects both the standard theoretical and empirical approaches to race is that its salience—in terms of how racial difference is known and why it is thought to be visually striking—is thought to be self-evident: race is what you see.

Interviewing blind people provides an opportunity to peer beneath these theoretical and empirical shortcomings to examine the social interactions that make racial difference visible. By detailing the ways in which blind people have a visual understanding of race that is as robust as sighted people's, this research is able to leverage blind and sighted people's shared social experience as an influence giving rise to visual understandings of race. The social aspect of the visual salience of race is transparent to sighted individuals since the primacy given to visual perception leads racial difference to seem like a natural division of humankind. But since blind people cannot be seduced by the immediacy of visual perception, their visual understanding of race is inculcated in a more deliberate fashion that is part of the very same social forces that produce the visual salience of race for those who are sighted. Thus, blind

people are uniquely capable of discussing the social practices that at once produce the visually self-evident character of race and hide themselves so that
race is experienced at an individual level as mere observation of a fact-in-
the-world—akin to the way individuals visually engage a rock or tree. Thus,
what will become apparent throughout this book is that sighted people are
in a sense *blinded by their sight*: their visual perception prevents them from
"seeing" the social practices that produce the saliency and coherency of their
visual understanding of race. And, as will be discussed in the second part
of the book, there can be serious legal and policy implications when society
orders its understandings of race around the idea that its significance stems
from its visually obvious character.

In terms of this book's intervention and intended contribution, it is important to note from the outset what it is not trying to do. This research is not an
effort to rehash the well-established fact that race implicates multiple variables such as language, culture, and religion. Nor is it simply another attempt
to critique the idea that race somehow reflects natural differences between
groups by showing that it is socially constructed. As described in this chapter,
these are important contributions already made by social constructionists.[86]
Rather, this book is a *second-generation effort* in this tradition that seeks to
question a fundamental aspect of race epistemology—that race is what we
see—and to empirically demonstrate the social interactions that construct
the visual significance given to race. Moreover, this project challenges the
notion that vision is necessary to having a full understanding of race. The first
generation of scholarship on the social construction of race has productively
focused on historical evidence, doctrinal critiques, and postmodern theory—
a macro level contribution to understanding how broad social forces (not
nature or human evolution) give meaning to race. *Blinded by Sight*'s second-
generation contribution is to move from macro to micro—from history, legal
doctrine, and theory to an empirical analysis—to offer qualitative data that
flesh out the particular types of social interactions that constitute the visual
significance given to race by examining how social practices give rise to visual
understandings of race and how visual cues come to matter for blind people.

Piecing together the significance of vision to race is an area of first impression for sociological, legal, and law and society research. This research is likely
to allow us to add a qualitatively different credence to the claim that race is
a social construction and, at the same time, move this conversation in new
directions by highlighting the social processes outside of vision that constitute

racial categories and their meanings. Without a doubt, racial formation is an interactive process between what we see in the world and the categories created by social convention. Yet the overreliance on vision as racial truth may also limit deeper understandings of how, for example, law and society produce the significance we attach to what we see. It is one thing to say that race is a social construction in that its stratified meaning system is not supported by natural or biological differences. It is quite another to demonstrate empirically that the conventional body markings used to differentiate races are not as significant to the racial belief system as one might initially think. A clearer delineation between first-generation critiques of "race as nature" from this proposed second-generation critique of "race as visual cues" may offer insight into how to best approach remedies to racial injustices.

2 Theory, Methods, and Initial Findings

A REVOLUTION IN CONSUMER ELECTRONICS HAS RECENTLY BEEN ushered in without much fanfare. Gadgets that are a part of our everyday lives have seamlessly incorporated a new generation of optical devices and software that can detect faces and track body motions in a manner that personalizes users' experiences beyond anything imaginable just a few years ago. This is all part of an emerging new field called computer vision, which gives computers the ability to "see" and recognize objects in a manner that many considered to be uniquely human.[1]

Walk into your local Best Buy or Radio Shack and you will see this new technology in many products—digital cameras, gaming systems, and more. These developments are part of an amazing technological shift pushing the limits of human/computer interaction that demonstrate the extent to which object recognition and visuality are no longer the province of sentient beings. Rather, this can be increasingly replicated with a high degree of precision through computer hardware and software. But there seems to be just one problem: it is not uncommon for this new technology to have a hard time "seeing" people of color.

Take, for example, a controversy involving Hewlett Packard (HP) computer web cameras and face-tracking software, which are designed to follow users' faces and track movements so that images remain centered and in focus. In December 2009, two coworkers at a camping supply store in Waller, Texas—Wanda Zamen and Desi Cryer—noticed something peculiar about the HP computer: while the computer had no problem identifying and following Wanda, who is White, it could not detect Desi, who is Black (see

FIGURE 5. An image from the YouTube video uploaded by Zaman and Cryer demonstrating the difficulties that HP's face-tracking software's has with "seeing" Black people. Photo by Wanda Zamen and Desi Cryer.

Figure 5). In a YouTube video, the duo demonstrated this odd glitch by repeatedly showing the HP webcam's ability to "see" and track Wanda while Desi remained undetectable and virtually invisible. Cryer narrates the YouTube video, viewed over 2.9 million times: "As you can see, the camera is panning to show Wanda's face. It's following her around. But as soon as my blackness enters the frame, . . . [the camera] stops. . . . As soon White Wanda appears, the camera moves. Black Desi gets in there—nope. No face recognition anymore, buddy."[2]

There have also been reports of an issue with digital cameras that implement a similar face detection technology designed to thwart the timeless problem of taking someone's picture while that person is blinking. The camera detects the faces of targeted individuals and signals a warning that someone might be blinking if it senses closed eyelids (see Figure 6). While this may be a useful innovation, it seems to have difficulties with Asians. Joz Wang, a young Taiwanese woman from Los Angeles, purchased the Nikon Coolpix S630 digital camera with this anti-blink technology as a Mother's Day present. But she soon noticed that every picture that she took of her family elicited the

FIGURE 6. Photograph taken by Joz Wang showing the camera's difficulty with people of Asian descent. Photo by Joz Wang of jozjozjoz.com.

same error message: Did someone blink? To which Wang responded in a blog post, "No, I did not blink. I'm just Asian.[3]

Problems have also been reported with Microsoft Kinect, which is part of the popular Xbox 360 video game system. Kinect features a camera that connects to the Xbox 360 that detects users' faces and body motions so that they can physically interact with virtual gaming systems. On-screen avatars mimic users' motions to enable full body-motion game play—a futuristic upgrade from using traditional joysticks or other hand held controllers. But, akin to the HP webcam, Kinect also has had difficulties "seeing" people of color. In reviewing the system, the magazine *Gamespot* noted: "While testing out the Kinect, two dark-skinned GameSpot employees experienced problems with the system's facial recognition abilities. The system recognized one employee inconsistently, while it was never able to properly identify the other despite repeated calibration attempts. However, Kinect had no problems identifying a third dark-skinned *GameSpot* employee, recognizing his face after a single calibration. Lighter-skinned employees were also consistently picked up on the first try."[4] What's going on here? Taken together, how do we explain computer vision's repeated difficulties with racial minorities? If vision—computer or human—is merely an objective engagement with one's surroundings that is unmediated by broader social phenomena, why would a particular *type* of person be less recognizable than any other?

Here is where we can begin to understand the importance of putting not only what we see, but also the ability to see certain things in a social context. Despite our tendency to treat vision as a series of neutral interactions with the world, social conditions and practices can produce the very ability to see human difference. For example, part of the explanation regarding difficulties that face recognition technologies have with detecting racially diverse attributes is that the software, like voice recognition software, needs to be trained to perceive different types of human features. The software's accuracy improves with increased exposure to different types of human traits.

Here lies the rub between computer vision and its ability to "see" people of color. Finding a wide range of test subjects to serve as reference points to develop the algorithms used to detect facial characteristics can be tremendously expensive. The most comprehensive approaches involve taking test subjects' pictures several times over an extended period—ideally years—in order to properly calibrate the software to the subtle nuances of human characteristics. The data elicited from this training at the software development stage are crucial; the diversity of the data pool affects the range of people that the face detection software will accurately work with. Patrick Flynn, a computer science professor at Notre Dame, notes that having a diverse pool at this early stage is particularly important because the software "can't generalize. . . . It's proven extremely difficult to develop systems with flexible enough learning capabilities that they recognize eye shapes of people from Europe and not just of people from Northern Europe."[5]

Since it would be expensive to recruit and compensate a wide range of subjects, companies have typically relied upon employees, family members, or third-party databases. Yet, these pools tend to reflect the stunning lack of racial diversity in the high-tech industry. For example, an article by the *San Jose Mercury News* on racial diversity in Silicon Valley concluded:

> The combined work force of 10 of the valley's largest companies—including Hewlett-Packard, Intel, Cisco Systems, eBay and AMD—shows that while the collective work force of those 10 companies grew by 16 percent between 1999 and 2005, an already small population of black workers dropped by 16 percent,

while the number of Hispanic workers declined by 11 percent. By 2005, only about 2,200 of the 30,000 Silicon Valley–based workers at those 10 companies were black or Hispanic.[6]

While these data reflect only a segment of the industry, they mirror long-standing concerns over racial diversity in high-tech sectors. And to the extent that this demographic imbalance is the context from which software companies choose test subjects that are the basis from which face detection algorithms are created, it becomes apparent how Whiteness becomes the norm that leads computer vision to, in a sense, be blind to the diverse range of human features found in consumers that use these products. To computers using this new technology, people of color are often invisible.

These dynamics draw attention to the critique of race being visually self-evident in at least two regards. First, they provide a backdrop from which to conceptualize the constitutive theory of race as both an extension of and distinct from social constructionism. In this instance, social factors—such as a lack of diversity in the high-tech industry—can shape the underlying algorithms that constitute computer vision and these devices' difficulty with perceiving racial minorities. Like human vision, computer vision is often thought to be simply an objective engagement with the environment. Yet the difficulties that HP webcams, Nikon cameras, and Microsoft gaming systems have with seeing certain racialized bodies demonstrates how social practices might limit computers' visuality. What is seen and the ability to see are not merely mechanical phenomena but distinctly social ones tied to the lack of diversity in this industry.

But this critique of computer vision also highlights the critical importance of methods in ascertaining and surveying the social world—particularly when it comes to matters of race. That is, rather than taking the social world at face value and assuming that the salience of visual phenomena is merely self-evident, closer attention needs to be paid to the ways in which we operationalize modes of inquiry regarding race, how these inquiries are designed, and how such methods affect the way race is understood. For example, the racial limitations of computer vision are largely a methodological problem; the algorithmic shortcomings that obscure computers' ability to delineate racial difference are a function of programmers' lack of attention to human diversity as a crucial methodological criterion from which to build an image database that can "see" the wide range of human traits that both constitute and reflect their user base. Just as observations regarding computer vision elucidate the ways in which social contexts produce the ability of computer software to see or not see certain types of human difference, I argue that race (in the context of human vision) is not simply an obvious or objectively known trait that is self-evidently visually salient. Instead, social practices—the proverbial "algorithms" underlying human interaction—produce the visual salience of race just as mathematical algorithms shape the boundaries of computers' ability to "see."

This draws attention to how the theories and methods that we use to design our inquiries—such as computer algorithms to detect faces or empirical research studies—matter in having an accurate and meaningful engagement with the social world. Algorithms that cannot account for the diversity of human traits are just as flawed and limited as research studies that are theoretically or methodologically one-dimensional in their approach to understanding social dynamics. This chapter is a self-conscious attempt to acknowledge the interconnectedness of theory, method, and research outcomes by exploring the linkages between the methodological innovation that I advance—merging Critical Race Theory with empirical research methods—and the proposed substantive contribution of unearthing the previously unexplored perceptions of race among blind people. This approach highlights the opportunities for greater insight and deeper critiques facilitated by joining two areas of scholarship that many consider to be incompatible. For example, critical race scholars may be concerned that empirical research that takes a presumably objective and value-neutral approach to understanding the social world may not fit well with their normative commitments to racial justice.[7] Similarly, empirical scholars may be concerned that Critical Race Theory's explicit normative commitments may blur any attempt at a competent and objective assessment of data.

Despite such tensions, this chapter provides a path for theoretical and methodological reconciliation that is demonstrated in this book's inquiry into blind people's racial sensibilities and their implications for law and society. This chapter begins by first discussing the contributions that flow from the methodological intervention of joining empiricism—in this case, qualitative research methods—with Critical Race Theory and then goes on to describe the ways in which this approach frames this book's research design and data collection. I then describe the data and the initial findings stemming from this inquiry into blind people's understanding of race. What I find is rather remarkable: blind people understand race visually just like anyone else. Precisely how they come to this visual understanding of race is the subject of Chapter 3.

Critical Race Theory and Empirical Methods: Discontinuities and Synergies

Critical Race Theory and empirical methods each take different approaches to race scholarship. Critical Race Theory is not only distinguished by demonstrating the varied ways in which race is socially constructed, but also has put a finer point on the constructionist thesis by showing the ways in which law and other institutions construct race. From this perspective, law plays a central role in creating and solidifying racial meanings that attach to racialized bodies in a manner that reproduces a racial common sense that sustains racial hierarchies. Critical Race Theory has also been instrumental in offering a critique that racial subordination is not a series of detached episodes or unfortunate events that are an aberration to norms of fairness and equality. Instead, racial subordination is seen as being central to the organization of law and society. (Appendix A offers an extended discussion of Critical Race Theory's origins and goals.) Empirical methods, on the other hand, are distinguished by using the scientific method in both its quantitative and qualitative iterations to collect and analyze data to better understand human relations as well as the causes and consequences of various social outcomes.

While both Critical Race Theorists and social scientists using empirical methods have produced remarkable scholarship with groundbreaking insights, each approach has been criticized for its inability to, on its own account, offer robust articulations of how race operates in society. For example, Critical Race Theory has been chastised for prioritizing what its scholars understand to be social and racial justice over dispassionate data analysis. For some, this approach puts the cart before the horse and confuses politics with scholarship; claims are driven by norms rather than objective evidence. Others have criticized Critical Race Theory's methods, particularly the use of narratives and stories to provide meaningful and generalizable insight into racial dynamics. Those concerned with the ostensibly hyperpolitical nature of Critical Race Theory see narratives and storytelling as a method that is at best irrelevant to scholarly analysis and, at worst, a form of emotional blackmail that gives too much weight to isolated instances of malfeasance that (without further proof) may bear no resemblance to ordinary life experiences. Race scholarship using empirical methods has also been critiqued for its limitations—namely for allowing the inflexibilities of the scientific method to obscure the nuances of social life and racial interactions. For example, treating race as a coherent and internally consistent variable that can be placed into a survey or statistical analysis without any sophisticated discussion of what these categories mean and how they became significant can reify social categories of race as reflecting inherent human differences and ultimately undermine the social constructionist thesis.

However, with these criticisms comes an opportunity. With few exceptions, Critical Race Theory and empirical methods have largely remained conceptually and methodologically disconnected.[8] Social scientists rarely draw upon Critical Race Theory to inform their collection and analysis of data, and Critical Race Theorists have not engaged empirical methods as much as they could.[9] The reasons for this may vary. It may be as simple as many Critical Race Theorists not having had advanced training in empirical methods and merely not using what they do not know. Similarly, those whose training is in statistics and other empirical methods may simply not be aware of how Critical Race Theory may affect research design. Yet there may be other conceptual barriers to integrating both of these approaches in race scholarship. For example, one tension between Critical Race Theory and empirical methods is the role of positivism, or the idea that knowledge is best garnered through observation and collecting data through the scientific method. While this idea is the lifeblood of any and all empiricists, Critical Race Theorists may find the idea to be a tough pill to swallow if only because some aspects of the scientific method are historically contingent devices oriented toward promoting racial subordination.[10] To be sure, this anti-positivist sentiment is at the heart of Critical Race Theory's intellectual precursor, Critical Legal Studies,[11] and gives rise to their shared progressive critique of mainstream legalisms.[12]

Despite these discontinuities, blending Critical Race Theory and empirical methods can advance race scholarship. This approach can lead to important new insights into the contemporary nature of race and racism that are not only theoretically sophisticated in being sensitive to Critical Race Theory's critiques of status quo race dynamics, but also empirically robust in offering evidence of these dynamics' prevalence and centrality in law and society. The promise of this joint approach is highlighted by at least three synergies between Critical Race Theory and empirical methods that transcend the articulated tensions and discontinuities. First, their critiques give rise to an important synergy in that the shortcomings of each approach can be fruitfully addressed by leveraging each other's strengths. The major criticism of Critical Race Theory is that its claims are as broad as its supporting evidence is thin and that the methods used to sustain these arguments are far from vigorous. At the same time, race scholarship that primarily utilizes empirical methods is often criticized for being theoretically flat and deploying race in a manner that reifies it as a real rather than constructed category. Research questions designed to be sensitive to each approach can provide mutual support; critical race claims enhanced by empiricism and empirical approaches influenced by critical race sensibilities can yield race scholarship that is capable of capturing dynamics that might otherwise go unacknowledged.

A second synergy can be found in the very methods themselves. Despite tensions between the two approaches, there are important moments when the methods used by Critical Race Theorists and those used by empiricists dovetail in a manner that gives rise to new possibilities for thinking about race and racism. For example, this book is premised upon the synergies between narrative storytelling and qualitative research methods, specifically interviews. Critical Race Theory has embraced the use of narratives and storytelling as a way to give voice to the experiences and perspectives often marginalized by mainstream discourses. As Mari Matsuda suggests, Critical Race Theory's narrativity can provide an oppositional or antithetical voice that challenges the status quo and highlights the unique insights that may come from looking at social and legal institutions "from the bottom."[13] But this approach to uncovering some type of truth about law and society has also spurred a backlash by some for focusing on narratives' emotional purchase and aesthetic contours rather than demonstrating that these narratives are generalizable to a point of reflecting some type of meaningful social experience beyond that of the storyteller.[14] From a positivist perspective, such narratives and stories offer little in scholarly credibility in that they reflect an N=1. However, qualitative methods (such as the interviews used in this book) provide the opportunity to examine the narratives and stories of multiple Ns in a manner that is both scientifically rigorous and sensitive to giving voice to experiences and insights that are typically marginalized. With the proper research question and design, critical race sensibilities can merge seamlessly with empirical methods to offer a perspective on race that each approach might not be able to provide separately.

Lastly, there are important moral synergies between Critical Race Theory and empirical methods. Empirical methods and Critical Race Theory are committed to one simple pursuit: uncovering the truth and accurately describing social phenomena. To be sure, there may be significant disagreements on how to do this. But this shared commitment is nonetheless a synergy that can be the moral basis of a joint effort to rethink race scholarship in a way that is sensitive to the concerns and approaches taken by both fields.

Taken as a whole, the research question at the heart of this book compellingly demonstrates the synergies between Critical Race Theory and empirical methods and the opportunities for rethinking race scholarship that come from this joint effort. By empirically investigating how the visibility of race operates and the social practices that give rise to visual understandings of race, the resulting data can be interpreted through a critical race perspective that puts race front and center. Using empirical methods to push Critical Race Theory beyond descriptive accounts of the social construction of race to have a constitutive understanding of how visual cues become meaningful can be a substantial step forward for both approaches. From a critical race standpoint, it broadens the methodological repertoire of a relatively young field to provide the Matsudian "voice from the bottom" that reflects the perspectives of many. For empiricists engaged in the sociology of law, this approach can demonstrate how empirical studies can go beyond reductionist accounts of race, offering an example of how race studies can be empirically robust without sacrificing theoretical sophistication. Thus, as this chapter shifts from discussing methods to examining research design and the resulting data, it is important to keep these various tensions and opportunities in mind.

Methods Generating Theory: Toward a Constitutive Theory of Race

The approach discussed here is important because it may open up new possibilities for thinking about race and how it becomes visually salient. This book is part of a broader effort to fill the gap produced by the presumption spanning across multiple literatures: that the prominence of race comes from it being visually obvious, that race is an exogenous part of the social world whose perceptibility, visual coherence, and salience exist apart from any other social process, and that its boundaries are uniquely known by what is seen. This research is motivated by the hypothesis that the visual cues that have come to define race are not obvious in any objective sense, but capture our attention through constitutive social practices that treat race as a visually obvious part of the social world. From this constitutive approach, "seeing race" is far from a neutral or objective engagement with human variation. Rather, race becomes visually significant only as a product of these social practices.

I use the term *constitutive* as it is used in the law and society tradition. Rather than seeking a causal relationship between independent and dependent variables that are presumed to be discrete and external to human interaction, constitutive analyses take a more interpretive approach to understanding "the ways that our actions are at once delimited and enabled by a complex mix of partial, dialectically interactive knowledge-based (or discursive) factors."[15] Put differently, rather than examining how cause X leads to outcome Y, constitutive analyses empirically situate the social practices and interactions that make certain outcomes possible. For example, Susan Silbey describes the constitutive analysis of legal consciousness as follows:

> Emphasiz[ing] the role of consciousness and cultural practice as communicating factors between individual agency and social structure rather than expressions of one or the other. . . . [Constitutive] analysts try to describe how the taken-for-granted aspects of social relations, including the legal aspects, are produced, enacted, and reproduced. They document situations in which local processes reproduce macro social structures and institutions recursively, and at the same time provide openings for creativity in reshaping those structures. In particular, these constitutive/cultural analyses of legal consciousness describe the processes by which law contributes to the articulation of meanings and values in daily life. Attention is directed to the local contests to create controlling meanings from competing discourses within most aspects of ordinary life. . . . In these analyses, researchers observe both the orchestration of the local contest and the systematic outcome, in this way mediating micro and macro perspectives. Within this framework, consciousness is understood to be part of a reciprocal process in which the meanings given by individuals to their world become patterned, stabilized and objectified. These meanings, once institutionalized, become part of the material and discursive systems that limit and constrain future meaning making. In this constitutive conception of legal consciousness, law does more than reflect or encode what is otherwise normatively constructed. Law enables as well as constrains the possibilities of social interaction.[16]

Other examples of constitutive analyses of legal consciousness have explored how the discriminatory experiences of women and racial minorities relate to civil rights remedies, how people understand and deploy law in different ways in their day-to-day interactions, and how litigation—outside of the question of who wins or loses—can provide advocates with the language to mobilize and advance their cause.[17] While each of these projects has a constructionist component that looks at how meaning comes to attach to particular social phenomena, the key empirical aspect is a separate constitutive inquiry that pays close attention to the iterative social practices that make certain ways of thinking and being possible. My work follows in this vein. But rather than engaging in a constitutive analyses of legal consciousness, I pursue a constitutive analysis of racial consciousness by way of examining how race becomes visually salient and its significance for law and society. I seek to understand how we come to know what race is, the assumptions made about this process, and how the iterative relationship between these lay assumptions and legal developments can produce outcomes that systematically disfavor racial minorities in legal processes by obscuring how race operates and becomes visible in society.

The constitutive theory of race developed here is that race is not a visually obvious or objective engagement with, for example, variations in skin tone or body types. Rather, social practices produce the objectivity that we ascribe to racial boundaries while also masking their own existence. Social practices at once constitute the ability to see race while, at the same time, hiding themselves so that race is experienced at an individual level as visually obvious; race becomes simply what is seen.

Part of the difficulty in "revealing" these practices is the seductive nature of vision and the significant role it plays in how we understand the social world. Seeing is believing, so to speak, which often leaves race analyses to go no further than what is superficially observed. But given the emotive and commonsensical strength of taking what we see as objective truth, it is difficult to get beyond people's surface-level perceptions of race to explore the role of social practices in shaping racial consciousness. This is where interviews with people who have been totally blind since birth can be useful.

Much of this question deals with cognition in terms of how difference is socially communicated and individually comprehended. In terms of the current race literature, visual cues play a crucial role in this cognitive process in that meanings are constructed around certain groups' phenotypic appearances that, once visually perceived, convey particular notions about these groups' worth to individuals. This is a rough version of the constructionist thesis; social, political, and economic circumstances construct meanings that attach to certain types of bodies that, when perceived, affect how individuals react to people on a one-to-one basis. As previously discussed, this is also the starting point for much sociological and social psychological research on race, which ultimately frames its race conversations around the threshold issue of being able to see. By asking totally blind respondents how they understand and experience race, I attempt to examine the presumption that the salience of race comes from what is seen.

Blind people's understanding of and experience with race should tell us something about this presumption. If blind respondents report that they have a diminished understanding of race or that race does not significantly impact their lives compared to their sighted counterparts, then this might suggest a certain obviousness about race in that the inability to see reduces one's ability to fully comprehend or engage with a racial belief system thought to depend largely on visual cues. If, however, blind people's understandings of race are similar to those of sighted individuals in that race is thought to be primarily a visual experience, then this suggests that something other than the visually obvious nature of these cues creates this visual sensibility. An analysis of the shared social practices that give context to visual understandings of race might suggest that social practices constitute the visual salience in which we experience race. This might offer empirical evidence that supports the proposed constitutive theory of race and questions the prevailing theoretical framework underlying modern legal regimes that largely define race by what is seen.

Vision is obviously an important aspect of race and racial formation. Yet failing to interrogate how these cues became visually significant may prevent more sophisticated understandings of race as well as obstruct more fruitful remedies to race-related social problems. A research project that investigates blind respondents' understandings of race (in comparison to sighted individuals' perspectives) to explore race and racialization outside of vision is distinctively sociological in its construction and research design. Yet this project's attempt to subvert mainstream thinking on race through assembling the narratives of marginalized voices and demonstrating how their obfuscation furthers the conceptual basis of racial subordination makes this work sensitive to Critical Race Theory. A closer look at the research design and initial results from blind and sighted respondents further demonstrates the interconnectedness and fluidity of these critical race and empirical approaches.

Research Design

The empirical component of this project consists of approximately eighty hours of interviews conducted with blind and sighted individuals about their understanding of and experiences with race. This project has a comparative research design, where the bulk of the qualifying respondents (106) are blind while a smaller number of respondents are sighted (25). This numerical asymmetry allowed for a deeper exploration into the racial lives of blind individuals, which is an area of first impression for race scholarship and therefore the main research interest. Sighted respondents' racial experiences are documented at great length in the research literature. However, the inclusion of a smaller number of interviews with this group allows for a critical examination of the role of vision in blind people's understanding of race by comparing their responses to the responses of those who can see. If blind people have fundamentally different understandings of race than those of sighted individuals or if race is deemed to be less salient among them, that might suggest that vision plays a central role shaping the strength and contours of individuals' racial experiences. If, however, blind and sighted individuals have similar understandings of race, then it suggests that something else gives race its visibility and visual coherence.

It was conceptually important to focus on blind people who have been totally blind since birth (or shortly afterward) as opposed to individuals who became blind later in life. Since race is strongly associated with visual cues, a central aim is to understand how individuals who cannot see visual cues understand race. Those who became blind later in life may have visually experienced race as sighted individuals do, and therefore their experiences may compromise any attempt to empirically distinguish the racial experiences of those with and without vision. People who have been totally blind since birth cannot speak to the visual obviousness of race; therefore the self-evident nature that race has in the sighted community is not and cannot be part of their experience. However, people whose only disability is their blindness have the same cognitive mechanisms as sighted individuals, and thus have the same mental capacity to process and respond to race. Moreover, blind people are part of the same social and cultural milieu that interacts with these cognitive mechanisms, but in a manner that is not mediated by vision. Blind respondents may be able to speak to the social practices that inform their racial consciousness without firsthand experience with vision or visual cues.

TABLE 1. Sample Information.

	Total Number Interviewed	Qualifying Respondents	White	Non-White	Average Age	Male/Female	States
Blind	161	106	89 (83.9%)*	17 (16%)*	44.5	51/55 (48.1%/ 51.8%)	34
Sighted	25	25	17 (68%)*	8 (32%)*	47.08	7/18 (28%/72%)	6

* of qualifying respondents

These are practices that similarly affect the racial consciousness of sighted individuals but are less accessible to them due to the obviousness that attaches to race from being able to see.

Therefore, a comparative research design that isolates the visual component of race can help us reconsider traditional race paradigms to get at how individuals are socialized into thinking racially—in many ways, regardless of what they see. As a result, only those respondents that qualified as being totally blind since birth and have never seen anything—let alone the physical cues associated with race—were included in the sample. This approach may clarify the social process through which visual understandings of race become salient for all. (More details on the research design and methods can be found in Appendix B.) Demographic information can be found in Table 1.

The people who were interviewed were diverse in many regards. Although most of the non-White respondents were Black, other races and ethnicities were represented including South Asians, Latinos, and Asian Americans. Respondents were on average in their mid- to late forties, but some respondents were as young as eighteen and twenty while others were in their seventies. More than half of the states were represented, giving the data a geographical diversity that included individuals from every major region. Roughly speaking, the same set of interview questions was used for both blind and sighted respondents so that answers and experiences could be compared and analyzed for similarities and differences. In the next section, I examine the initial results from the data collected through these methods by discussing blind and sighted people's response to a rather simple question: what is race?

"It's a Visual Society": Sighted and Blind
People's Perspectives on Race

Visual Cues and Sighted Respondents:
Documenting the Seemingly Obvious

Before exploring blind people's understanding of race, I start with a discussion of the extent to which visual understandings of race are empirically observable within the sighted community. Each sighted person who was interviewed defined race primarily by what they perceived to be obvious visual cues. For example, when asked if there is anything that she associates with race, Layla noted: "Well, their physical characteristics would be how I would probably think. It would be whether they were Black or whether they were Asian looking, whether they were Hispanic looking. . . . I guess that's how I would kind of first make general assumptions. . . . The physical basis, basically skin color or [other] characteristics. Certain characteristics of the face, for instance the Asian eyes. That kind of thing."[18] This was a common response among sighted respondents. For example, Levett said, "When I think of race, I think of skin color. . . . I think of it more of a biological [characteristic] . . . more to do with skin type, body type, facial features." Melvin noted that he understands race as being "mostly based on physical appearance. . . . Everything like skin color and the sort of fold of the eye that Asians have and those type of characteristics." Mario took a similar stance, saying that "it's the color of people's skin that comes to mind first, and maybe the distinctions between how people look visually." He said that he knows someone's race "by looking at them, [although] sometimes it's harder to tell whether somebody is a mixed race. But I guess for me it's just by looking at them." Nancy, as well as many others, talked explicitly about the obviousness of knowing race, saying that she knows people's races simply "by looking at them. Usually I can tell. Most people are not ambiguous. Most people are clearly light or . . . clearly Black. You know, most people are very obvious."

Sighted respondents certainly had subtle understandings of the way race concepts interact with and are influenced by other identity characteristics such as ethnicity, nationality, and language. Nevertheless, what is interesting is the resilience of the visual cues that attach to race; the subtleties that may seem to complicate things quickly became insignificant to respondents' descriptions and subordinate to the primary idea that race is a concept known by visually obvious physical cues. For example, when asked to define race, Joey quickly conflated race, ethnicity, and visual traits:

Generally, I think of race as being of a certain ethnic background, and when I say ethnic background, I mean differences that are very obvious, such as skin color, eye color, hair color. . . . So, I guess, I think of it as, probably, ethnicity. And where people are from, where their parents are from, how those things influence who they are, and how they are reflected in that person.

This respondent defined ethnicity by race, which in turn is defined by visible physical differences between bodies. This move was not uncommon; other sighted respondents similarly acknowledged the many factors such as geography and nationality that inform our racial consciousness yet nonetheless settled upon visual cues as the definitive marker. Janice, for example, initially defined race as "people of different nationalities, different skin colors, different backgrounds," but then came to the conclusion that "as far as race is concerned, it's primarily facial features and skin color," that is, traits linked to visual cues.

To be sure, these non-visual characteristics emerged during the interviews to give more substance to sighted respondents' primary description of race as a visual entity. These characteristics played important secondary roles, meaning that visual cues dominated their understanding of race but were also informed by other types of collateral information. For example, ancestry played a noticeable role in these secondary characterizations, with several sighted respondents making reference to it as part of their understanding of race. When asked how to define race, David said, "I guess you can just say it's a physical difference in appearance of people based on where they originally came from." Similarly, Eli based his own racial identity, in part, on ancestry, noting that he identifies as African American "because my ancestors came from Africa and now I live in America." Emily said that she defines race as "people from different parts of the world who have different characteristics," and noted that she identified as Hispanic "because my grandparents came here from Mexico and because I have dark hair and I look Hispanic." This shows the way that various understandings of race vacillate between visual cues and secondary measures such as ancestry, but nonetheless sediment around the former to give meaning to the latter. Ezzie gives a bit more insight into this, noting that "the most obvious answer [to defining race] is heritage and skin color. It's one of the earliest things that you learn when noticing people are different and your parents will say 'these people are from a different area, so their skin color is different.' This is sort of what race is, I think." This draws attention to how even those respondents with more sophisticated understandings of race that try to incorporate the role of other variables nonetheless use visual cues to frame the relevance of secondary characteristics—in large part because the visual is most immediate. People are aware of these secondary understandings yet nevertheless continue to think of race in visual terms, as that is what is most directly impressionable in their everyday lives.

Another secondary understanding of race among sighted respondents is that race reflects biological differences between human groups. Levett was particularly explicit in making this point: "I think of [race] more as biological, more to do with maybe skin type, a body type, facial features, regions of the world where people originated from." This draws attention to the idea that the visually observable phenotypical differences that define racial groups reflect some type of deeper difference beyond mere skin color. Vicky explicitly took this point of view in defining race as "a breed of people." Cynthia drew a similar conclusion, noting that her definition of race "goes back to an anthropology class, years and years ago, and talking about there being basically three to four races: Caucasian, African Black, Asian, and then there was always a question whether Native Americans were Asian or whether they were [another] race." This suggests that visual distinctions stand in for a whole host of secondary meanings—such as biological differences and even ancestry—that constitute race as a concept but are nonetheless thought to be known by visual observation. It also suggests that the visual distinctions that are heavily relied upon to define race are thought to be biologically significant and, implicitly, reflect biological differences between racial groups. This suggestion might draw attention to how visual cues are often understood as more than aesthetic differences between human groups and are used as a proxy for understanding differences "under the skin" that cannot be directly perceived.

Race and Vision as Common Sense

Taken as a whole, sighted respondents articulated a certain common sense about race that is tied to their primary association of race with visual body markings. Ian Haney López introduces the idea of race as common sense to suggest that "what we think we know often takes the form of common sense—a complex set of background ideas that people draw upon but rarely question in their daily affairs."[19] With regard to race, Haney López suggests that these background ideas include uncritically allowing the surface-level, typological distinctions to orient our racial consciousness, which ultimately defers to visual cues as a primary mechanism for knowing what race is.[20] This explains the simplistic and at times confused responses offered by some sighted respondents when asked to define race. For example, when asked "how do you define race?" or "what characteristics do you associate with race?" several sighted respondents were somewhat puzzled by what they believed to be questions with obvious answers. Eli succinctly replied that race is "one's color . . . either Black, White, or yellow." Similarly, Sherry quipped that race is just "the color of your skin." Along the same commonsensical lines, Terry matter-of-factly said that race is "basically the color of a person, White versus Black, the color of a person's skin." For these sighted respondents, race needed no other explanation than the obvious: race is what you see. It is common sense. The resilience of this commonsense association of race with visual cues even shapes those who have participated in what they describe as advanced race conversations. Levett said that even though "I've had a lot of instruction and workshops on ethnic race [and] all that[,] when I think about race I think of skin color." This suggests that the common sense of race continues to over-power the training she has received.

This commonsense approach to race also manifested itself in the long pauses between questions and some of their responses. Questions such as "how do you define race?" often elicited extended periods of silence before the beginning of a response in a tone that implied the answer is obvious. These questions often led to tautological answers that highlighted the confu-sion experienced by many sighted respondents faced with what seemed like an obvious question. For example, when asked why they identified as Caucasian, Vicky replied, "Because I am." Tina replied similarly: "Because I think that's what I am. I think I am Caucasian White."

It is also interesting to note that most of the non-White sighted respon-dents gave declarative answers to the question "how do you define race" (e.g., short and unambiguous, such as "race is skin color"), while the respondents identifying as White often provided slightly longer answers with a little more ambiguity (e.g., "I think that's what I am"). These answers were function-ally equivalent to one another in that they reaffirmed the shared theme that race is what you see. This may at least partially reflect what Barbara Flagg has termed White transparency, or the idea that Whites tend to think that race is something that people of color have—not themselves.[21] For example, when asked what types of things she associates with race, Vicky (who identifies as White) said:

Well obviously, color of skin can come into play. Just physical characteristics of a race. Hispanics typically have jet-black hair. Asians have . . . —and I know it's different between Asians—but you know the almond slanted eye. Just those types of things. Again dark hair. Black, obviously color of skin. *White to me is a little bit more unclear. Because they all come from kind of a melting pot background. I don't know of any true White person.* [emphasis added]

This is in stark contrast to respondents identifying as non-White, who answered similar questions with short quips, such as Sherry, who said that race is "the color of your skin," or Terry, who repeatedly said that race is simply "the color of a person, White versus Black." For these sighted minority respondents, race is something that everyone has, including (if not especially) themselves.

How Do Sighted People Think Blind People Understand Race?

This commonsense approach to race that characterizes its salience as a function of its visual obviousness shapes how sighted people think blind people understand race. It is important to investigate sighted respondents' perspectives on how they think blind people understand and experience race in order to establish (1) sighted people's assumption that race is of diminished importance for blind people, (2) its link to the dominant role that vision plays for understandings of race in the sighted community, and (3) how this assumption frames broader social and legal ideas, such as colorblindness (discussed in Chapter 4) and Equal Protection's *"race" ipsa loquitur* trope (discussed in Chapter 5).

Given sighted respondents' tendency to view race through commonsensical visual cues, it is not surprising that some sighted respondents thought that blind people had no understanding of race whatsoever. When asked whether she thought race is an issue for blind people, Cynthia said, "No, I don't. I guess, because I identify race by physical characteristics." Other sighted respondents shared this thought: that since race—both in terms of identification and significance—is largely defined by visually observable physical characteristics, it therefore cannot be relevant to those unable to appreciate distinctions only knowable through visual perception. Bobbi shared this opinion, saying that "race shouldn't be [an issue]. I don't think so. No. I don't see how it could be." Benji stated that race "probably isn't something that they notice . . . and probably not something that really matters to them."

But some sighted respondents thought that blind people might have a limited sense of race that does not find visual markers meaningful but draws distinctions based on voice and accent. Joey thought that race can still matter to blind people "because people sound different, and people act differently. [If] they've been taught to fear [this distinction], then they'll fear it." This idea that voice or accent can serve as a meaningful proxy for blind people to understand racial differences that are more meaningfully known through observing visual cues was not uncommon among sighted respondents. For example, Layla thought that race could be an issue for blind people "because I would think [they] could just maybe identify somebody by an accent or the way they talk." David noted that blind people may understand race because "there is a cultural difference [such as accents] that can be identified more so than the pure color." Some sighted respondents attributed this ability to understand race despite not being able to see to the idea that diminished capacity with one sense (such as vision) heightens the perceptiveness of other senses. Terry explained this by noting, "when your eyes are down, your other senses become stronger. So just because they can't see, they can still tell by the voice whether they're a Black person or White person or Japanese or Chinese." Vicky corroborated this sentiment, saying that she thought race is still a part of blind people's lives "because they still have all their [other] senses about them. . . . Even though somebody is blind, if their language detects that someone is Hispanic, they're still going to be cognizant of race. They may not understand the color of skin thing. But they know."

While sighted respondents as a whole did not have any one singular view, the variety of answers nonetheless reassert the central understanding of race as "pure color" that can only be significant (if at all) to blind people in a diminished sense by proxy: language, behavior, food, and other racialized characteristics linked to senses other than sight. Taken together, the sighted respondents appear to believe that race is not as salient for blind people since they cannot directly perceive visual distinctions in human bodies. Those respondents who thought it might be important to blind individuals largely limited this significance to ancillary aspects of race such as detecting racialized voices or smelling racialized foods. But for the most part, they maintained that blind people had little appreciation for the primary significance of race: visible physical differences.

How Do Blind People Understand Race?

Put simply, race is understood and experienced by blind people as it is by those who are sighted: visually. The vast majority of blind respondents in this study primarily associate race with skin color and other visual traits. This visual association goes beyond a general awareness of how sighted individuals approach race. Rather, this visual understanding of race profoundly shapes the way blind respondents think about race. It also affects their response to race at deeply emotional levels, the way they organize their lives around the fact that groups differ phenotypically, and the social meanings they attach to visual differences.

When asked what is the first thing that comes to mind when hearing the word *race*, Carrie said, "I think of colors. Varying colors in people's skin colors." Most blind respondents answered this way, offering responses like that of James, who said that race is a "scheme of dividing people based on the color of their skin." Or Janice, who said that race is "the pigment of the skin or lack thereof." And Perry, who said that race is "primarily skin color." What quickly emerges from these interviews is that blind people think about race in terms of skin color and other visual attributes. For example, Pam discussed the first thing that comes to mind when hearing the word *race:* "Oddly I guess I would say skin color. Even though that's not really relevant to me. But that's the first thing that comes to mind. I guess that's a distinguishing factor that society uses and I acknowledge just like I acknowledge a lot of visual things that might not be particularly relevant to me. But, it's the way that it's done in our culture." Other blind respondents acknowledged the apparent irony in having a primarily visual understanding of race. Jerry noted that "the [racial] classification for most people tends to be a visual one because they see before they perceive any other information, and I think that applies just as well to blind people." Paul explained this tension between his blindness and visual understandings of race: "I think society, and in particular American society, has come to be very visual. It's a visual society. It's a visual set of stereotypes and people are always looking at things. . . . The reason I use skin color so much [to racially identify people] is because I think that's how society identifies it with different races." Pat simply noted that race "is color. Even though I can't see, that's what I tend to think of."

Several blind respondents shared this sentiment. When asked what race is, the matter-of-fact emphasis on skin color and other visual cues mirrored the commonsensical understandings of race in the sighted community. Blind respondents like Tim made blunt, straightforward statements such as race "is more what most folks [use to] refer to skin color. Color of one's pigmentation." Barry also noted in a commonsensical tone that "race [is used] to distinguish Black, White, Asian, Hispanic . . . [based on] skin color." When asked what comes to mind when hearing the word *race*, he responded: "Pretty much totally skin color." This visual understanding of race not only shaped how blind respondents thought about race in the abstract, but also how they thought about their own racial identities. For example, Dennis said, "I'm White . . . [because] I was created with White skin. That's just the fact of life." Tara similarly noted: "I am Caucasian, but I don't know if that has anything but skin meaning to me. Only the fact that I am." Serena also based her own racial identity on a skin color that she had no direct ability to see, saying that she identifies as White: "I guess because that's what I am. I mean, that's the color of my skin. . . . I mean, I'm not American Indian. I'm not Asian; I'm not Hispanic. I'm not Black." Blind respondents that identified as members of racial minorities also tended to base their own racial identity on visual cues, some of which (like skin color) they cannot directly perceive. Amy says she identifies as African American because "I have the attributes . . . you know, I definitely have the thick hair and dark skin myself." When asked why he identified as Black, Tim laughed in acknowledging the irony of his response, and said "skin color."

But this visual understanding of race often went beyond mere skin color to incorporate a rather sophisticated conceptualization of the range of visual cues that can make one race different from another. Roger defines race "more as the physical attributes that make people different from each other. Skin color, maybe type of hair, maybe some of the physical features that make people different from one another." Nell gave a bit more specificity to this sentiment:

> It's not only skin color because it's also [other] characteristics. . . . I know that various races like the Negroid race have the characteristic of [different] bone structure [and] facial structure. Asians [also] have [different] facial structure [and] body structure. I know that each race has its own set of characteristics to go with it. Color can be a defining characteristic. But [race] is not only based on color.

There was some variation in blind respondents' perspectives. A handful of individuals articulated a diminished understanding of race due to their blindness. Tara, who is quoted above as saying she identifies as White because of her skin color, also described the difficulty she has in fully understanding race: "I think most sighted people see the difference in race first, and they have preconceived notions about it for that reason, and I don't think that I have those, as much. I don't know how to ascribe a meaning to it. It just means a very insignificant difference to me." But despite limited variations such as this, the interview data suggest that race is first and foremost known to blind respondents in visual terms.

These data begin to demonstrate a theme that will be repeated throughout this chapter: how the visual salience of race comes less from any obvious physical differences and more from how social practices train individuals to look differently on certain bodies. This is a subtle point that will become clearer as the data present themselves. But what has emerged thus far is that in general both blind and sighted people understand race in visual terms, suggesting that there is a significant shared social experience that not only *constructs* its meaning and attaches it to bodies, but *constitutes* the very ability to visually apprehend these differences in the first place. This leads to a key finding: the very presumption that race is self-evident is part of a constitutive social process that produces a visual understanding of race at the same time it masks its own existence by making race seem obvious. Dale provides a bit more insight:

> I think a lot of what people don't understand is that blindness—the simple lack of sight—is not a very important factor in these things. Blind people, first of all, have other means of acquiring information than by sight. They are exposed to the same kinds of influences anybody else has, and it's not unusual to find that blind people are the same as their sighted peers, in regard to any of these issues, and the only thing that draws attention to the blindness is the fact that in America, the race issue is so identified with color. I know blind people who, before they decide how they're going to treat somebody, are going to find out, "Is this person a Black person, or is he a White person?"

If blind people understand race in the same visual terms as their sighted counterparts, how is it that something such as skin color—a concept whose coherency is inextricably tied to vision—becomes meaningful to people who cannot see it? What does skin color mean to a blind person and how does it affect judgments placed upon other groups?

These examples begin to show how visual understandings of race are not simply self-evidently known, but that they are much more the result of

a social process whereby the visual salience of race becomes knowable to blind and sighted alike. It is important to keep in mind that the mere physical inability to see does not mitigate the cognitive ability to think visually. The attention paid to visual distinctions reflects the broader human capacity to create difference—a process that invites meanings to attach to labels. Skin color and other visual cues become shorthand for difference, meaning individuals or groups that are either like or unlike oneself.[22] With regard to blind people's understanding of race, these categories of difference need not take on a positive character that can be directly perceived; difference as a label signifying something unlike the self is enough to fill those categories with a value that then becomes known as "race" for both blind and sighted people. Blind respondent Molly explains:

> Black means . . . I don't know what that exactly means. But it means they're not White or they're not Asian. . . . That's what makes them different races. But I don't know how different they are. From a technical point of view . . . their appearance, their skin color, some facial features, and other things that I'm not aware of [distinguishes races]. [There are] physical characteristics that are typical or definitive for one race over another.

Race labels and their social meanings can still cohere to shape racial consciousness in ways that are no less profound than they are for the sighted community while also retaining a visual importance. Janice, a blind woman, described the relationship between race labels and their substantive meanings:

> You know, a lot of people ask about color, whether it's skin or clothing or anything else. And they want to know whether it has meaning. And it doesn't in the sense that if I all of a sudden got my sight back today and saw, I'd know one color was different from another, but I might not know what [each color] was. The only way people have of describing color is with other colors. But I know it has meaning because people say some colors are light [and] some colors are dark. . . . [With regard to race] I think whether we see it or not, we all live in a society that has stereotypes. And we can't avoid them. We can try and mitigate them if we hopefully have some sense. But our society is too attuned to them and that's why I think it's important to people. It goes somewhat with the culture.

Matthew put it a different way: "I don't believe that prejudice is a visual concept. I don't think it's because of what you see that you're racist or that you have strong racial feelings. I think it's more of what you learn and then you use your eyes to identify it. I don't think it's from the physical out. I think it's more inward. I think it's more inside you, if that makes any sense."

Blind Respondents' Use of Secondary Characteristics of Race

Like the sighted respondents in this study, other sensory experiences also affirm the salience of race for blind people without displacing the primacy of its visual significance. Voice is probably the most significant of these experiences. Most blind respondents reported using accents, tones, and speech patterns loosely as a way to estimate a person's race. This should not be surprising. What is surprising, however, is that these audible clues do not stand in for the visual cues a sighted person might rely upon, nor do they become primary in how blind respondents conceive race. Rather, voice and accent remain secondary identifiers that "point to" what is thought to be the primary characteristic of race: visual cues. Tara makes a point that reflects blind respondents' sentiments, noting that differences in voice and accent do not "really mean anything to me, except that I know that they have a different skin color." Abe corroborates this sentiment by noting that voice and accent allow him to "make inferences as to what your skin color may be and then all these other things fall in line, behind it. Whereas, if you can see, . . . then you do it the other way around." Findings such as these suggest that differences in voice do not make up the substance of race for blind respondents, but rather provide a way to mark a racial difference that is most often understood in visual terms. Perhaps Laura says it most succinctly in noting that secondary characteristics of race such as voice are helpful in that they help her answer the question: "what would I see if I looked at you?"

While most blind respondents reported relying upon voice as a secondary characteristic, it is important to note that many of them also distrusted it as an unreliable proxy for determining an unknown person's race. Rachel said, "As I got older, I learned that [voice] is not a good way to identify someone— . . . like using someone's accent or way of speaking to identify them as a particular race—because it's not reliable." Respondents quickly recalled embarrassing moments when an unknown person's speech patterns led them to assume they were a certain race, only to find out that this assumption was wrong. Tammy recalled an experience from the summer before when she was a classroom teacher:

> I didn't know until maybe three weeks into the class that me and the two
> [other] teachers were the only White people in the room. My heuristic of judg-

ing people just didn't work. There were a couple of people who I really thought were White, and they weren't. My heuristic was unable to take [a certain] kind of voice [and conclude] "that's a Black man talking" or "that's a Latino talking." So, I was wrong. And so, [voice is] not a foolproof way of guessing. . . . I wouldn't even say it's pretty reliable.

Other blind respondents like Demi said, "You may think you know by the voice, you know, inflections of certain phrases or words they use. But you're not always right." Some, like Jack, simply said that "I never assume because the minute you assume, then you get into trouble." Despite this distrust, these interviewees continue to use voice as a way to guess a person's race. It is just that they distrust voice as reliable; it informs without being determinative. Nevertheless, the data suggest that sighted respondents' assumptions that voice *displaces* visual cues in blind people's understanding of race is largely inaccurate. To the contrary, voice and accents confirm the centrality of visual understandings of race within the blind community by serving as a proxy for the visual cues that are more meaningful to their racial conceptualizations.

Blind respondents also occasionally mentioned secondary characteristics that are detectable by their other senses as a way to perceive racial differences, yet they were not as important as voice or accent. For example, hair was cited as a telltale sign of racial difference. This may reinforce mainstream sentiments in that if these distinctions are perceptible through other means, some blind people may conclude that they must also be visually striking. Molly recalled the first time she touched a Black person's head while at a camp for blind children at the age of twelve: "We were swimming and I happened to touch his hair. And I didn't know that many Black people have kinky hair." Barry had a similar introduction to race as a child, saying that in fourth grade he "felt [my Black friend's] hair once, and I guess they call it kinky. I have no idea what that means, but it just felt strange compared to my hair because it felt different. The texture was different. I can actually feel it in my mind, right now. . . . And I was just like, 'Wow, everything is different about this guy!' " Rough skin was also mentioned by a few blind respondents as a defining characteristic for Blacks. Gerry said that "Black people's skin is usually just a bit rougher," and thus tips him off to race if, for example, he is shaking hands with a new acquaintance. Jim reported this as well: "I've felt some of them and there is kind of a difference in their skin. I don't know about their color. But just the way their skin feels. . . . I don't know how to describe it. Those who are Caucasian, or White, tend to have a little smoother skin. Black people tend to have rough skin. Or if they're women, they're not exactly as smooth as White women."

Though only mentioned a few times by blind respondents, the most intriguing sense used to detect racial difference was smell. Perhaps these few respondents have unusually discriminating noses, but they brought up smell as a racially distinguishing factor without any prompting. Timothy, for one, noted: "Some Black people have an odor about them that you know they cannot help. . . . The odor is like a perspiration type thing is what it reminds me of." Madge also drew tight connections between race and smell: "The first experiences [with race] I had was [with] a girl in my school who was Black. And I remember her. And the thing that I remembered about her, I hate to say this, was that she had a smell about her, an odor about her." And Connie, a White male, said:

> People from different races to me tend to smell different. Now, usually the way I can identify someone of a different race is that they smell different than a Caucasian person. Hispanic people smell different than Black people. And Asians have their own odor. But I'm not as familiar with it because I haven't really been exposed to that many Asians. But I'm sure if I had been that I'd be able to distinguish between the various Asians. But what most comes to mind is Hispanic people smell very different than Caucasian people and Black people.
>
> But Hispanics to me and even amongst the different Hispanics, like the Central American group tends to smell different from Mexicans. But it's a distinct odor. And I don't think it's related to diet either because . . . second- and third-generation Hispanics smell more similar to the first-generation ones than White people would. And they're following an American diet. There's one particular case that I distinctly remember when I was in high school. We had this one girl who was blonde and blue-eyed. And she spoke perfect English. And everybody thought that she was Caucasian. And I would say no, she is Mexican obviously. And then it came up in conversation that her father was born in Mexico. And even though she was blonde and blue eyed, she was half Hispanic. To me, she smelled Hispanic. So I knew she was Hispanic even though everybody else thought she was completely Caucasian.

Surely we all know individuals that emanate unique odors. But to associate particular smells with an entire group of people seems peculiar, at least to a sighted person. This may be an example of how being taught to think racially plays out differently for some blind people, who are socialized to draw tight connections between race and nonvisual sensory perceptions to give significance to race as a visual entity. It is interesting to point briefly to the experiences of Carrie, a blind White female, who said, "Sometimes I can tell [a person's race] by their smell." Carrie detailed the unique smells that she associated with Blackness, yet when asked what smells are typical of Whites, she could not describe any. This example of White racial transparency via olfaction will be discussed later on. Nevertheless, it highlights the extent to which race labels and their social meanings can interact with other senses to reconstitute the idea that racial differences are real, concrete, and obvious—concepts that are also prevalent within sighted communities. For example, Connie, who professed an ability to sniff out ethnic and generational differences among Latinos, attributed this unique ability to "genetically distinct oils that we make in our skin."

In addition to the secondary characteristics detectable by other senses, blind respondents also mentioned certain concepts that served as secondary indicators of the visual distinctions that primarily defined their understandings of race. Biology, or the idea that race reflects natural differences between racial groups, is one example. Some sighted respondents also mentioned biology. But what is striking is that while sighted respondents mentioned biology in rather broad anthropological terms that emphasized the existence of four or five different types of human groups, blind respondents who discussed biology did so through the specific language of genetics. For example, Jon defined race first by skin color and second by genetics: "There's Caucasian, African American, Hispanic, and Asian. And that's in terms of skin color—[the] different skin pigmentations. And there may be some genetic markers of some specific race." Molly defined race as "large groups of people with some sort of identifying trait. I guess it's genetic." And Matthew noted that he "think[s] of [race] as one of several gene pools that we all spring from." This genetic understanding of race even affected some blind respondents' own identity, with Timothy saying that he identified as Caucasian "because that's what I am. Biologically and forensically, that is an established fact. And you cannot deny an established fact."

The fact that biology plays a secondary role in understanding race is not surprising; biological understandings of racial difference have a long history in the United States that persist despite the popularity of social constructionism.[23] But why this has expressed itself specifically as genetics among blind respondents in a way that is not observed in the data from sighted respondents is puzzling. Perhaps it reflects a tendency among blind respondents to point to evidence of biological difference at the molecular level that no one can easily observe, while sighted respondents might assume that visual cues are self-evident proof of biological difference and thus need no further explaining.

Ancestry emerged as another conceptual secondary characteristic of race that both blind and sighted respondents share. While visual cues shape their concept of race, geography and ancestry help give race a bit more substance. Rachel discussed the relationship between skin color and ancestry: "I think skin color is attached to an underlying group of people. So, people with darker skin are typically from Africa, that sort of thing." Note the primary association of race with skin color—a visual cue—and then ancestry as a secondary matter. Amanda took a similar approach: "It seems like what most people think of as races are national ethnic distinctions that are marked by skin color differences, so Caucasians as a general rule tend to have a different skin color than people of African descent and then people of Asian descent are classified as being in a different category." More importantly, ancestry played a significant role for several blind respondents' own racial identity. Kitty, in a commonsensical manner, said that she identifies as Caucasian because "well, that's what I am. . . . All of my family that I know is of European ancestry, so that was just natural to label me as White." Benny identified as White for the same reasons: "Because that's what I've been told that my parents and all our ancestors were." Similar dynamics were present for blind racial minorities, as Tim said that he identified as Black "because my family is of African descent." But again, it is important to understand that despite such strong ties to ancestry or geography in respondents' own racial identity, the visual aspects of race were often embedded in these articulations and continued to play a primary role. For example, Crystal said that she identifies as Caucasian "because my family is light-skinned and is from Poland—Polish, Irish, and English descent."

As we tie these threads together, what becomes apparent is that the ability to see the markings that define racial boundaries is neither necessary nor sufficient in explaining the strong association of race with visual cues. If blind people define and react to race in primarily visual terms, then the empirical evidence begins to poke holes in the assumption that the salience of race—its striking nature, its perceptibility, and its importance—stem from its obvious or self-evident character. Something much deeper is at play. Rather than being obvious, could there be an underlying social process that gives visual understandings of race their significance?

Are There Any Differences Between the Way Blind
Minorities and Blind Whites Understand Race?
For the most part, the racial identity of respondents played a more important role in how they understood race than the ability to see. Specifically, the perspectives of minority respondents were quite similar regardless of whether they were blind or sighted, as was the same for White respondents. For example, blind White respondents and sighted White respondents both shared a high degree of transparency in their concept of race. Similar to the previously discussed transparency found among sighted White respondents, blind White respondents also understood race to be something that people of color had, not themselves. That is, White is the default while race is something that applies only to people of color. For example, Kitty, a blind White female, said, "to me, being White is fairly meaningless." Kenneth, a blind White male, similarly noted that the first thing that comes to mind when he thinks of race "is probably a Black person," suggesting that race is an attribute that minorities have and not Whites. Many blind White respondents voiced a similar perspective about being White, in that they did not think much about it and did not afford it much meaning. Race only became meaningful when talking about racial minorities. Steve, a blind White male, offers a typical example: "I don't think of the White race as much or the Caucasians [as a race]. If I hear the word *race,* I would picture an African American." Similarly, Wanda (also blind and White) said that she thinks of race as "a group of people who have a different background from White people." White blind respondent Roger shared this sentiment, saying that when he hears the word *race,* "I think of individuals who are different from myself. I'm Caucasian. And I think of African Americans, Hispanics, and Asians. . . . I think of people who are different from myself in terms of the color of their skin." Therefore, being blind does not mitigate the tendency, identified by Barbara Flagg, for Whites to think transparently about their race. On the contrary, both blind and sighted minorities largely viewed themselves as having a distinct racial identity. Far from being something that other people had, race, in terms of being a minority, is who they are.

Another perceptible difference between the responses from blind Whites and blind minorities is the extent to which blind Whites would use their physical disability to analogize to the social disabilities often faced by racial minorities as a result of their skin color or other visible traits. Several blind respondents who identified as White made this analogy, compared to zero blind respondents of color. For example, Alexis, a blind White female, said,

> You know that there were people in this world who actually thought that the color of somebody's skin was significant enough for them to make life difficult for people. Which I thought was terribly unfair. And I identified with this because people made life difficult for me because I was blind. And I think that's mainly why I identify with the struggle for civil rights. Because the struggle to have an identity as a person who's blind and the struggle to have identity and rights and so forth as an African American or as a person of color [are] somewhat the same.

Many White blind respondents shared this perspective. Denise, a White female, said, "I can really identify with somebody who is racially different because a lot of blind people, especially totally blind people, have a lot of stereotypical assumptions associated with them." Manny, a White male, similarly said, "I think that the blindness thing lets me understand what it is like to be in a minority group. Because being blinded, there aren't that many blind people in this country, so I can identify with folks that aren't necessarily in a major societal group." For some, this seemingly parallel discrimination faced by racial minorities and disabled individuals affected how they expressed their own racial identity. Crystal said, "I identify as Caucasian. But I don't feel like I fit in the classification of the Caucasian middle-class woman. Because of my own . . . oppression as a blind person. I had a [White blind] friend say that he identifies and calls himself a third-world Caucasian. And maybe that's how I feel." In this sense, being blind limited the sense of privilege that Crystal associated with Whiteness as a racial identity, leading her to feel "less White" and to assume a mitigated White racial identity that she articulates through an assumed third-world status. Duke, a White male, shared this feeling of mitigated Whiteness:

> I've never felt really a part of [the White] group. I've never felt like I was really empowered because I was blind. I have a job, I support my family, I do all right, but I never felt like I was making as much money as I might have if I'd been able to see. And I also think that really that's not the big issue. The big issue for me is that, as a blind person I think that I encounter a lot of the preconceptions, prejudices, and assumptions in my life that a Black person would encounter. And in terms of people assuming, "Oh, they're going to rob me"

or "Oh, they're poor," or "they're homeless," or "they're mean"—that might be the kind of assumptions that might come to mind when I think about the stereotypical assumptions about a Black person. Whereas me, it's like, "Oh, that blind guy can't do a thing. I don't even know how he can walk down the street. He must not have a job. How does he get dressed in the morning? Who feeds him?" Those would be the kind of assumptions that people have about me. . . . So, I guess in some ways I can identify with people that tend to have issues around race in terms of blindness, if that makes any kind of sense.

This is a striking comment in that it highlights how blindness can lead some White people to disengage from their racial identity because they do not feel that they are able to partake in the full privileges of being White; blindness confers a discriminatory experience akin to being a racial minority. Steve, a White male, even notes that "some [blind] people call sighted people sighties," which is a seemingly derogatory term to refer to sighted individuals that mimics some of the derogatory terms some racial minorities use to refer to what they see as their oppressor. Yet it is important to acknowledge the presence of variation in the sample, as some White respondents used their disability to support a colorblind approach to race. Tara, as an example, said, "It's hard for me to understand that skin color could be such a huge thing, because my attitude is that blindness is not a huge thing at all. Blindness is a nuisance. And if blindness is just a nuisance and not anything more—which I don't think it's more than just a daily problem—how could skin color be such a huge thing?" Nevertheless, while this "blindness as a racial experience" analogy was a sentiment expressed by some blind White respondents, none of the blind minority respondents equated their racial identity with their disability. Indeed, the trend among blind minorities is that they talked about race and blindness as completely separate experiences and identities.

These data provide the initial contours of a point that contradicts prevailing theories of race: individuals who have been totally blind since birth have just as strong a visual understanding of race as sighted people. This point demonstrates that the capacity to understand race—*and to have a visual understanding of it*—does not depend upon the ability to see. This calls into question the self-evident nature of vision to prevailing theories of race and suggests that broader practices outside of vision play a significant role in shaping its visual salience. But what types of practices constitute a visual understanding of race for blind individuals? This question is explored in the next chapter.

3   Visualizing Race, Racializing Vision

ULY 8, 2010. AS A BLACK MAN BORN AND RAISED IN OHIO AND LIVING
in the San Francisco Bay Area, I found this day to be momentous.
At 4:00 P.M. local time, I turned on the television to listen to the Johannes
Mehserle verdict. Mehserle is a White former police officer for Bay Area Rapid
Transit (BART) who shot and killed Oscar Grant, a young Black male. In the
early hours of New Year's Day 2009, Mehserle, along with a few other BART
officers, responded to reports of a fight at the Fruitvale BART station. Grant
and a few others were dragged off the train by BART officers and subdued.
According to filings by the Oakland police, Grant was placed face down on
the platform with both hands behind his back; one officer had his knee on
Grant's head and back. After a brief struggle to contain Grant, Mehserle stood
up and straddled the young man, pulled his pistol, and shot Grant in the back.
Grant was pronounced dead a few hours later at a local hospital.

Several bystanders captured Grant's detainment and shooting on video
(see Figure 7), which played on an endless loop in the days following the
shooting. In many ways, this was the twenty-first-century version of the Rodney King beating, where video evidence showed a uniformed police officer
treating a young Black male with violence and force that, on its own terms,
seem disproportionate to any threat or resistance put forth by the victim. But,
this time there was no "can't we all just get along moment." Though it was
brutal, King survived his beating. Grant, on the other hand, was dead.

Days later, Mehserle was arrested and charged with murder. The Alam-
eda County prosecutor's decision to charge Mehserle with murder came as a

FIGURE 7. Image from bystander video of the Oscar Grant shooting. Source: KTVU-TV.

surprise to many. *The San Francisco Chronicle* noted that the murder charges represented "an extraordinary decision[,] several legal experts said they could recall no other instance of a police officer in California being charged with murder for an on-duty incident."[1] During the trial, Mehserle's defense relied heavily upon an unusual claim: that he meant to reach for his Taser gun to subdue an uncooperative Grant yet somehow accidently drew and fired his pistol, leading to the fatality. The jury ultimately rejected the prosecutor's murder charges and only convicted Mehserle of involuntary manslaughter. This was a clear sign that they accepted the defense's argument that the shooting was simply an unfortunate accident.

Mehserle's jury did not include any African Americans. But sentiments in the Black community were quite clear. While many Whites and non-Blacks readily accepted Mehserle's claim that this was all one terrible mistake in the otherwise legitimate pursuit of law enforcement, Blacks were more likely to see something different. They saw an execution, one that was captured on video for the world to see on YouTube. Yet twelve jurors were blind to it in

FIGURE 8. "The Decision." Photo by Larry Busacca, Getty Images Sport.

their deliberation. Within minutes of the verdict's announcement that July afternoon, thousands of frustrated people began gathering in downtown Oakland for what would eventually erupt into protests and rioting unlike anything since the Rodney King verdict.

Shortly after the verdict's announcement, another race-infused melodrama was taking place on the other side of the country in the affluent Greenwich, Connecticut, suburbs. LeBron James, the self-proclaimed "King James" and world's greatest basketball player, entered free agency at the end of the 2010 season. Raised in Akron, Ohio, and having gone straight from high school to play professional basketball for the nearby Cleveland Cavaliers for seven seasons, the sports world had waited for months with baited breath for James to make what has become infamously known as "The Decision": whether to stay in Cleveland or join another NBA team. James decided to announce his decision in a remarkably unorthodox way: a live, one-hour primetime special on ESPN (see Figure 8). As helicopters began showing crowds gathering at 14th and Broadway in downtown Oakland to protest "The Verdict," I switched channels to watch how "The Decision" would unfold.

With the now iconic phrase "I'm taking my talents to South Beach," LeBron James turned the sports world upside down. Having spurned his hometown, blue-collar Cleveland fan base for Miami's glitz and glamour, James became what many then-called the most hated man in professional sports. James's Q score (a measure of professional athletes' popularity) plummeted: only 14 percent of people viewed him positively (a 41 percent drop from a January 2010 poll), while 39 percent viewed him negatively, which represents a 77 percent drop from before "The Decision."[2] But in Cleveland, "The Decision" not only took the narcissism and self-indulgence of reality television to unprecedented levels, it was experienced as a personal affront. One of "their own" had essentially jilted them in front of nearly 10 million viewers. ("The Decision" was the third-most watched television show of 2010; one in four homes in Cleveland tuned in.[3]) James was viewed as having given up on bringing Cleveland a championship and deciding that he was better off in a big city, which, in the midst of an economic recession that has been particularly challenging for midwestern post-industrial towns, made a bad situation even worse. In short, Cleveland fans felt angry and humiliated. This partly explains the images coming out of Cleveland in the hours following the broadcast that had a borderline lynch mob sentiment: women screaming, burnings in effigy, and people milling around the streets in anger (see Figures 9 and 10). But all because a man decided to switch basketball teams?

Outside of being young Black males, Oscar Grant and LeBron James have little in common. Grant was a twenty-two-year-old supermarket butcher struggling to stay afloat on the streets of Oakland, while James is a global icon with aspirations of becoming the world's first billionaire athlete. But on this summer day in July, their public images—ESPN's coverage of "The Decision" and the subsequent fallout in Cleveland along with the Mehserle verdict, its reiteration of the Grant shooting video, and the postverdict Oakland riots—intertwined as melodramatic race spectacles that speak volumes about the state of race and race relations in what many have claimed to be a post-racial society.[4] Jonathan Markovitz describes racial spectacles as follows:

> Massive media events in which virtually every type of communication technology and every sector of popular culture is involved in disseminating influential representations of race to national audiences [that] function as instruments of socialization: they provide the occasion for the closest thing we have to national dialogues about race, and therefore play a central role in national processes of "racial formation," in which categories of race are continually contested and reconstructed.[5]

FIGURE 9. Cavaliers fan screaming after hearing James' "Decision."
Source: Plain Dealer/ Landov.

Thinking about "The Verdict" and "The Decision" as parallel race spectacles is important for understanding how such media images reflect racial attitudes that often go unspoken in a modern world where norms of political correctness often bury such conversations. But they also reproduce these sentiments by imbuing the public with racial images that act as a shared narrative that congeals a collective racial consciousness while providing a common reference

FIGURE 10. Fans burning James's jersey after "The Decision." AP Photo/Akron Beacon Journal, Phil Masturzo.

point for public understandings of race.[6] As isolated instances, "The Verdict" and "The Decision" appear as disjoined phenomena in two wholly separate social and political spheres with no relation to one another. But viewed together as spectacles of racial formation, we begin to see how each outcome—Grant's killing and the jury's unwillingness to convict Mehserle for murder, as well as James's status as a villain for essentially changing jobs—are both mediated by and understood through particular understandings of race.

Markovitz reminds us that "spectacles do not have inherent meaning, but can be interpreted in varying ways and used for contradictory political purposes."[7] The fascinating thing about the race spectacles stemming from "The Verdict" and "The Decision," and the point of connection with this book, is that individuals' perception of these spectacles—the Grant shooting as an accident versus an execution, LeBron James as a villain versus being just another guy switching employers—depends heavily upon their racial subject position. And with regard to these twin spectacles, Blacks and Whites viewed these two sets of images in profoundly different ways. For example, a poll conducted by a Bay Area television station showed that Blacks were more likely to think that Mehserle should have been convicted of a more serious crime.[8] Yet shortly after "The Verdict," hundreds gathered in the largely White Bay Area suburb of Walnut Creek to protest Mehserle's involuntary manslaughter conviction as unduly harsh; they believed that Mehserle was innocent of all charges.[9] The same type of divide exists for "The Decision." Remember James's plummeting Q scores? Things look a little different when you break the numbers down by race: among Blacks; his negative Q score declined only slightly, from 14 to 15 percent, after "The Decision." While many Blacks did not care for how James announced his departure in a reality-TV, "look at me" manner, they did not necessarily hold it against him. In discussing the relevance of race to the harsh criticism pointed at James, sports journalist Michael Wilbon notes:

> Race is a factor in everything, or virtually everything. Black folks and white folks—this shouldn't come as a great shock—don't see this in the same way. For the most part, black folks who don't even like the way that LeBron went about this, see young black men deciding where they are going to play. Their futures. As opposed to older white executives trading them around, moving them around like pieces on a chess board. [Blacks] see that as a good thing. Maybe not all white fans . . . see it that way. But race is definitely involved. . . . This is what a lot of black folks like. *We* have control over this process now, not exclusively you [i.e., Whites]. . . . The vitriol, some of the ugliness that has been directed at LeBron is so over the top. What goes into this? What goes into this reaction? Not "I'm disappointed." Not "I'm angry." But "I hate you"? There's something else there.[10]

Wilbon's comments allow us to see the racially formative symmetry between these two seemingly unconnected spectacles as being the perceived legitimacy of power, control, and authority exercised by and denied to Black males. The reasonableness of these actions—literally, whether one *sees* these series of publicly disseminated images as legitimate or not—is experienced as objectively knowable, measured by characteristics external to the racialized subjects. The surface level conversation pertaining to the Grant and James spectacles is that Mehserle's actions would have been just as legitimate had Grant been a White Silicon Valley engineer and that Steve Nash would have received the same treatment as James did if he announced the end of his free agency in the same way. But, "The Verdict" and "The Decision" highlight how individuals' racial positioning shapes how they understand the legitimacy of the power *exercised over* Grant and the power *exercised by* James. For example, Mehserle's supporters often point to Oscar Grant's past criminal record—which includes resisting arrest—as evidence that Grant had a history of not obeying police authority, that he was resisting arrest at the time of the shooting (despite any contrary evidence presented by the video), and that he put himself in the position for this accident to happen in the midst of a chaotic moment that Mehserle and other officers were trying to control.[11] From this perspective, the authority exercised over Grant leading to the shooting was not illegitimate because Grant was a "thug." And those who support James often point to the implicit and, at times, explicit attitude among Cleveland Cavaliers executives and fans that James's decision to leave Cleveland was illegitimate because they somehow owned him. In the hours following "The Decision," Cavaliers owner Dan Gilbert posted an open letter on the team website using terms such as "disloyal," "cowardly betrayal," and "deserted," suggesting that the authority that James took to choose a different team was an illegitimate breach despite James's status as a free agent.[12] For many Blacks, such as Jesse Jackson, Gilbert's "feelings of betrayal personify a slave master mentality, LeBron as a runaway slave."[13] Thus, what can be seen through these two race spectacles is a consistent narrative of racial subordination that reflects and produces a mainstream sentiment legitimizing police brutality and delegitimizing Black self-empowerment, further rendering the Black male as a social pariah.

Less than a year later, on the evening of June 11, 2011, LeBron James and the Miami Heat lost in game six of the NBA finals, leading much of the sports world to delight in his failure. Just a few hours later, Johannes Mehserle was released from prison.

*   *   *

Analyzing visual spectacles such as "The Verdict" and "The Decision" helps us understand how the racial meanings taken from these images depend significantly on one's racial positioning; individuals' racial background and experiences literally shaped what they saw. The spectacles coming out of this one day in July 2010 highlight how a seemingly post-racial society is still imbued with certain ideas concerning Black male authority that trace back to the days of slavery. Akin to what Russell Robinson describes in a different context as perceptual segregation, images that on their surface appear as objective renderings of some freestanding reality gain meaning, coherence, and perceptibility *through* a lens constituted by individuals' own racial subjectivity.[14] This is consistent with the social construction of race literature to the extent that it highlights how race is not a stable entity, buts shifts across time, place, and social context. But only by jointly analyzing the social dynamics coming from these spectacles can we distill a deeper narrative on race, authority, and legitimacy embedded in yet often hidden from mainstream racial discourses.

But let's push this idea a bit further. What about the very basic ability to see race? Probably the most fundamental and least examined aspect of American conceptions of race is that it is what we see, and that mere visual perception provides an obvious, objective, and unmediated way to ascertain human difference. Visual cues are seen as the glue that gives race its coherency. Indeed, this is part of the common sense of race: regardless of whether we attribute meaning to racial categories (and we often do), they are thought to be self-evidently known and defined by what is seen. The inordinate attention we pay to rather fine distinctions in skin tone, hair color, or body shape are thought to be obvious, objective, and thus "evidence" of basic human difference. This perspective strongly implies that race could not be as significant an organizing principle in society *but for* these perceived stark differences in human bodies.

However, just as the salience and perceptibility of race spectacles such as "The Decision" and "The Verdict" are produced by social contexts of past and ongoing race relations, so too is the rudimentary and often overlooked process of seeing race. The preceding chapter discussed interview data collected from blind and sighted individuals showing that blind people have a visual understanding of race. Contrary to widespread presumptions that race can only be visually salient and meaningful to those with sight, these data show that blind people have a visual sensibility regarding race that is not unlike that of sighted individuals. This chapter delves deeper into the data to uncover the social contexts and practices that, akin to yet distinct from the meaning making and attachment processes latent in constructionism, produce this visual understanding of race. Qualitative research with blind people regarding their understanding of and experiences with race fleshes out the micromechanics of race, in terms of the everyday social interactions that give rise to the very ability to see and experience race as a coherent, obvious, and stable trait. This comparative approach utilizing blind and sighted respondents provides the methodological backdrop from which to go beyond the presumed visual obviousness of race to piece together the social and human interactions that produce this visual salience rather than assuming that it is merely observed. In short, just as social practices produce different racial meanings as exhibited in "The Verdict" and "The Decision," this chapter shows how similar social dynamics also produce the very ability to see race in particular ways. This raises significant challenges for social and legal conventions premised upon the assumption that race is visually obvious. These consequences are the subject of Part 2. But for now let's examine the productive forces that constitute and give rise to the visual salience of race.

"There Was a Line There That You Shouldn't Cross": How Blind People Come to Understand Race Visually

Social Practices

In addition to showing that blind people understand and experience race primarily through visual cues, the interview data also highlight the key role played by social interactions in giving rise to blind respondents' visual sense of race. The blind respondents who articulated a visual understanding of race linked it to early socializations during childhood and adolescence by friends and family members. These people went out of their way to not only make sure blind people knew the social importance of race and all of the rules, norms, and meanings that go along with it, but also that they thought visually about race so that human difference would be experienced as a fundamental lens through which to view the world. But the practices behind this race socialization are not unique to blind people. Everyone is subjected to them. Blind and sighted people are part of the same social fabric that directs individuals to pay inordinate attention to visual markers such as skin color, through which people organize their lives. This process is effortlessly transparent for sighted people, whereby racial knowledge becomes articulated as visually obvious. But the process takes a bit more work for blind people, who are detached from the ability of vision to entice them into uncritically reducing race to what is seen. Blind people are uniquely capable of discussing the social practices that give the visual cues associated with race an obvious feel. These are the same social forces that give visual understandings of race their coherency to the sighted, yet they remain hidden due to sighted individuals' overemphasis on visual fields. It is in this sense that sighted people are *blinded by their sight.*

Interviews with blind people help describe the social practices that produce their visual understanding of race and, at the same time, unearth the same type of practices that give salience to sighted individuals' understandings as well. Mitchell said that despite being totally blind since birth, the first thing that comes to mind when he hears the word *race* is "people of different skin colors." He said that the visual aspect of race became significant for him through learning: "I guess it's learned. You learn the differences; you learned that there were different races, that there is a Black race and there's a White race." Thus, as Mitchell emphasizes, race became visually striking for learned rather than self-evident reasons. Pat described this process a bit further, saying that skin color became a defining characteristic for her as a blind person because "that's what people talked about when I was little and [when] I was first introduced to people of races other than my own. They used terms that had to do with skin color." Visual cues transmuted through friends and family became part of the respondent's racial lexicon, where visual cues were linguistically prioritized over other aspects of race in early childhood conversations. But socialization does not only impact language. It also shapes the underlying meanings that are given to these racial labels. Maurice recalled the first time he began to understand race differences at around age four:

> We owned a farm and raised some livestock on it. And so we would go down there to feed the animals and do work around the property. And there was a lady that I would see sometimes down there talking to my parents, and she sometimes would talk to me. And I don't remember not knowing her. But I always . . . I remembered thinking she talks differently. She talks different from me, or there's something unusual about her voice. And I didn't associate her voice with being Black until I was maybe four years old. And the way that happened is that I was at a neighbor's house one day. And that neighbor had a [maid] who was a Black woman. I didn't know this at the time. But she was helping her in her kitchen. And she had some plumbing work done. And in the process of that, they had removed the little drain springs and so forth from the sink.
>
> And you had to be careful to not let things—utensils or whatever—go down the drain because there's this big hole there. They've left it that way so she could use it until they came back to finish. But anyway, the lady that was helping my neighbor let a dishrag go down the drain. And the neighbor said "that lame"—and she used the N word—"let my dish rag go down the drain." Well, as I say, I'm four years old, and I had heard that particular word. But I didn't really know [what it meant]. . . . At that time, I did not relate a racial name or a given name to any given race. So at that time, I'm sure I did not know the meaning of the word *race*. I just didn't know that.
>
> I left my neighbor's house and I went home, and I did not know that this

woman that lived next door to our property at that time had come up to help mother do some things. And so when I went in, I repeated what I had heard my neighbor say about the person that let the dishrag go down the drain. And of course my mother just goes into a [fit, telling me] "don't say that." Well, the lady who lived next to us very quietly said to me "nobody ever told you that that's the name that some people call me?" And that's how I found out that [she] was Black. *And that's what I associated . . . that's when I first associated the way that she talked with what other people saw.* . . . . That's my first memory of associating that what I was hearing as an unusual speech pattern and so forth with a person being Black. . . . It did make me aware of that difference. . . . I've always been told that I was White. And [this experience] sort of magnified some of those differences for me.

This narrative highlights how a racial slur and its subordinating meanings shaped the respondent's notion of racial difference in a manner that started to give value to the visual distinctions separating the races. Socialization occurs when a person's behavior—here, cursing a Black person through use of a racial slur for letting a rag go down the drain—connects with a distinction that Maurice could perceive (voice) in understanding the subordinating relationship between members of his own race and Blacks that is typically governed by the visual appearances of these groups. His initial perception that a group of people talked differently is subsequently racialized in a manner that denigrates the group through a slur that presupposes their inferiority. And this experience connects with the ever present notion communicated to him by other social interactions that visually obvious physical differences are what separate "us" from "them." He notes that "it was about that same time that I began to notice some of the other barriers that were there for non-White people in the area that I was growing up."

Being able to identify society's poor treatment of racial minorities and recognizing that this pejorative attitude is rooted in visual differences is a key means through which the distinctions that blind people can detect (voice, smell, etc.) are changed into a visual significance that they cannot directly perceive but recognize due to other people's behaviors. Cognitively, race therefore takes on a visual significance for them too. Liam provided an example of how this process works:

I began to be educated by people around me. For example, I might be talking to someone, and I would not necessarily know [their race] because I'm not looking at them. As far as I was concerned this was just a person, and someone would then come to me, and let me know that this person had been of a certain race, or color, or obvious ethnic origin which I would not have known. Sometimes [they would] impart information about their assumptions about that person, and how I should or should not behave, or who I should or should not be talking to.

These rules of engagement between different races—how to act, what to say, and what not to say—allow the visual distinctions between races to play a primary role in determining the type of treatment given to various people. This process is strongly tied to notions of status, which are similarly communicated to blind individuals through race. As this chapter discusses some of the social interactions that gave content to these understandings of race, it is imperative to keep in mind that socializing the visual significance of race is an ongoing process that requires maintenance and reinforcement in order to elicit a continued "buy in" from blind people that race is visually significant. Through these social practices, the visual salience of race ultimately sediments as an objective reality for blind people as much as it does for sighted individuals.

Even where race is not explicitly discussed, difference is being asserted in a context where the importance of visual distinctions has already been established and is used to filter social experiences with racial content. An example of this comes from Matthew, who recalls a harrowing moment as a child when norms around racial status (in terms of who can do what to whom and when) were bestowed upon him—almost at the expense of his mother's life:

From about third to seventh grade, one of my friends was this girl [Jane Smith] that was Black. And her mother and my mother worked together on many of the school fundraisers, the fashion shows and these kinds of things. And her husband was a doctor. He was a surgeon. Very fine surgeon. Well, it was around Christmas 1969, and in those days there were no HMOs. There were no twenty-four-hour automated emergency response doctors. You had your local doctor who had his local office. And if he went on vacation, he was on vacation. We never went to the emergency room or something. There was no sort of backup. So we had this family doctor who'd been our doctor.

My mother had what we thought was the flu and she had been sick for several days and the doctor was on vacation. And we were having a Christmas party, and my mom said we should still have the party even though she couldn't [participate]. To make a long story short, somebody took a look at her and said to my father, "She's in bad shape. There's something more wrong than just having the flu. She needs a doctor." And my dad said, well [our doctor] is away. Who am I going to call? So my mom said, "Call Dr. [Smith]." And my Dad said, "Well I can't call him. What would people think if this Black," . . . you know. So finally I got the phone and I called and I spoke to Mrs. [Smith]. And I told her what happened. She said, "Dr. [Smith] will be over there in five minutes." And sure enough, he comes in. He takes one look at my mother and starts calling an ambulance. And he says to my Dad, "If I'm right, she's got some kind of bowel obstruction. She's got to be operated on."

And so they take her to the hospital. And we go in. And most of the people who are waiting on her are Black, you know the attendants and [others]. I got this from conversations with my Dad. Their skin color. But there was some anger. There was this weird thing. My mother was always treated very well by people. People liked her. She's very attractive. She's very outgoing. And my Dad is very well liked. [Yet] there was this really weird kind of tension. And I couldn't figure out why. And at one point I'm sitting and I overheard this woman, I think she was a nurse or an orderly, saying, "Imagine that! Imagine a White woman having a Black man cut her down there!" The operation had to be just below, you know, sort of in a private area. And [the nurses and orderlies] were all sort of agreeing about this. And it was just weird because it was almost like Dr. [Smith] was doing the wrong thing. You know what I mean? He is saving my mother's life. It really stuck with me.

Sure enough, there was an obstruction and he'd saved her life. And when our family doctor came back, he said the same thing. He said, "You know, if [Dr. Smith] wasn't such a good surgeon, [things might have turned out differently.]" In fact, my Mom died for a minute [during the operation]. They thought they lost her. And they got her back. So anyway, [this] became just a very, very pivotal event in my life.

The father's hesitancy and discomfort with a Black man operating on Matthew's mother, along with the staff's shock by the intimacy of this operation, reaffirmed a notion of racial status on what was then a very young and impressionable mind: Black people do not operate on Whites, and White women certainly do not expose their private parts to a Black man—even if he is a surgeon trying to save her life. This is the function of Matthew's father telling him that the nurses and attendants were Black; the tension he felt was due to a crossing of visually significant racial boundaries that confer important status relationships. Their rigidity reflects the harshness of race socialization and the salience that a racial code of decorum based on phenotype can have on society—even for those who are blind. When such drastic circumstances are barely capable of breaking through a code where race defined by visual appearance structures how people relate to one another, it quickly becomes apparent as a broader sociological point that the significance of these racial markings do not depend on the ability to see them. What we learn about race and vision from instances such as this is the subtle ways in which preexisting social arrangements structured by race are imparted to blind individuals to shape their developing visual sense of race.

Yet this was not the only life-and-death story connected to race and blindness conveyed by a blind respondent. Pauline recalled an experience from a camp that she went to as a young adult:

> There was a [blind] person named [Viola]. She went swimming in the pool and she started drowning. Apparently she couldn't swim that well or whatever. And she was Jewish and there was this [blind] Black fellow named [Jamal]. He was a very nice person. He was always helping people, and he jumped in and went to save her and get her out of the pool. . . . Her head [is going] in and out of the water. You could hear her having trouble. And she's saying "I don't want you to touch me. I want you to get away from me." And it turned out that she knew he was Black, and she didn't want to have any contact with him even though he [was] about to save her life.

Viola was ultimately rescued by other camp counselors. But what we have here is a blind White person who would, quite literally, rather die before being touched by a Black person who could rescue her. How does this happen? How do racial boundaries, premised upon visual differences that Viola could not directly appreciate, nonetheless become salient to the point where someone would risk death before crossing racial boundaries in what is perceived as a socially unacceptable and personally revolting manner? The actual "work" of race socialization does not simply happen through dramatic experiences such as Matthew's or randomly express themselves in situations such as those recalled by Pauline. Rather, they are produced through everyday social interactions that largely go unnoticed yet accumulate over time to shape the racial perspectives of individuals and give rise to visual understandings of racial difference. Although blind people cannot directly perceive these visual cues, social practices inculcate a "faith"—reminiscent of 2 Corinthians 5:7, discussed in the Preface—in their existence, salience, and significance that orients how they "walk," so to speak, in their lives. It is this social process producing the visual significance of race that is parallel to those who are sighted, yet remains hidden from them due to the seemingly self-evident salience of visually perceived differences.

Yet the reach of these types of race socializations also extended to the realm of defining appropriate day-to-day behaviors, in terms of creating boundaries pertaining to "what White people do" and "what Black people do." Walter provides an illuminating yet subtle example: "I'll never forget the first time that my grandmother decided to cut a watermelon round, instead of in wedges. Great-grandma wouldn't touch it, and we asked her 'Why won't you eat it?' [She responded:] 'Oh, White people don't cut it that way.' " This is a particularly interesting example in that Walter, as a blind person, could not directly perceive the visual distinction between Whites and non-Whites but could feel the difference between round watermelons and wedges, which can then reaffirm the salience of the visual (and seemingly behavioral) differences underlying his great-grandmother's refusal to consume watermelon slices of the wrong shape. Thus, even the routine daily practices of how to eat food can become racialized to give substance to blind people's visual understanding of race.

Much of the "boundary work" regarding the types of interactions that are appropriate between people of different races happened through romantic relationships and the prospects of interracial dating. Several blind respondents recalled intense experiences when friends and family members went through extraordinary measures to ensure that they understood that certain types of relationships were off-limits due in large part to a racial difference that is visually striking. Much of this "work" occurred at an early age. Crystal said:

> I never really thought about skin color until I was about eight years old. I kept talking to my family about my boyfriend. And I brought home a picture of Vince. And my parents said "Crystal, he's colored." I said, "that's colored film." So they sat down and told me about the races and the differences. And I was very, very angry and cried and scraped off all the gloss and obliterated the pictures. And I went back the next week to talk to Vince and told him we can't be boyfriend and girlfriend anymore.

Based solely on a picture of Vince, Crystal's parents enforced this boundary to instill a racial sensibility that is particularly sensitive to the visual distinctions between races and how it is inappropriate to project that image socially—a

White girl with a Black boy—even though she has no direct appreciation of the visual difference or why such an image is troubling. Crystal was far from the only blind respondent to come to a visual understanding of race through family members patrolling interracial intimacy. Heidi recalled a particularly interesting interaction with her mother:

> I met this boy in school and I decided—I was like in second grade—[that] I was going to marry him. So I told my mother that I was going to marry him, and she said, "Well, do you know what color he is?" I said, "Well, no. What difference does that make?" She says, "Well, because you're White and he's Black, then you'd have polka-dotted children." Which is probably an absurd thing to say, but she would say anything to a blind kid, I guess. And I still couldn't understand why that mattered, but I guess it stuck with me because *it told me that there was a line there that you shouldn't cross.* I was on one side of it and Black people were on the other side, and I didn't feel anything bad about them. I just knew that there was that line there, *that sort of invisible separation.* [emphasis added]

The separation that was invisible to Crystal suddenly became visible in terms of significance and salience through this social interaction. This boundary work with regard to interracial relationships often continued into adolescence and young adulthood, similarly reproducing a visual sensibility of the salience of race among blind respondents. Such boundary crossing becomes a more serious social threat as individuals age, approach adulthood, and increasingly have more adult-like romantic relationships. Shauna recalled this instance from middle school:

> A boy actually asked me to go to a dance and I was thrilled. I was like, wow, you know. And I went up to my mom and I was like, "Darien asked me to the dance," and she was like "Darien who?" And I told her Darien somebody or other, and there was this long pause. Not a long pause but a pause. And she was like, "Well, Shauna, you don't want to go with him." And I asked why. I don't remember her reply, but it was just something like I knew that she highly disapproved of me going with Darien and I didn't go.

Molly had a similar experience with her mother:

> The first time I went out on a date, it was with another blind person. We'd met. And I didn't know if he was Black. It hadn't come up. And we talked on the phone. And so he invited me out to go to a movie with him and his brother

and his brother's wife. So they had a car. And my mom wants to know if the guy is Black. I'm like, "I don't know. Never asked him. It didn't come up." And she said, "Well, if he's Black, you're not going." I'm like, "Well, wait a minute. You mean this guy is going to come to the door and you're not going to let me go if you see he's Black?" And she goes, "Yup." And it didn't come up because he turned out to be White. So, I mean [my mother] definitely had some lines that she didn't want crossed. And that was one of them.

But what is particularly interesting is how this type of boundary work extends into the adult lives of some blind people, with complete strangers often trying to maintain what they see as the appropriate relationship between Blacks and Whites. Pauline, a White woman, recalled an example of how the boundaries are monitored and patrolled by random people who are neither friends nor family:

> One time I had a Black friend visiting my house. . . . The superintendent of our building who lived next door to me, rang the bell, came over, and says, "Are you all right?" And I said, "What do you mean, am I all right?" He says, "They saw a Negro come into your house." I was so embarrassed. I mean, it was so traumatic to know that this person was hearing this question being addressed in this nasty way. I said [to the superintendent], "This person happens to be somebody that I love, and you have a lot of nerve to question it in any way. I want you to get out of my house."

It is tempting to think that such intense boundary work from a relative stranger that reconstitutes and reaffirms the visual significance of race is a product of the distant past. But Brianne offered an example that occurred six months prior to this 2009 interview:

> I was at the mall and the person that was with me [to help with shopping] happened to be Black, and some lady came up to me. The guy went down the aisle to get something for me, and this lady walked up to me and said, "Pardon me, but do you know your husband is Black?" And I said, "My husband is not Black." And I said, "How would you know that? My husband is not even here!"

But in addition to daily practices such as eating watermelon and patrolling the boundaries of appropriate human relationships, other aspects of everyday life were filled with racial content so that blind respondents could sense the significance of the visual distinctions they could not immediately perceive.

Space and property became important boundaries of racial decorum, in terms of conveying notions of racial difference by emphasizing the spatial distinctions of each group's residence and reconstructing this difference as a function of racial minorities' inherent inferiority that is typically known through visual mechanisms. For example, Matthew, who sensed the tension around his White mother being operated on by a Black surgeon, also remembers "being told by adults in my neighborhood that Black people in the projects defecated on the floors and put it under their beds." Gerry provided an interesting sketch of how his father drew upon his other senses to instill a race sensibility that drew sharp contrasts between Whites and Blacks:

> I was brought up to learn that I was White, of course. And unfortunately I learned that I was White so that White could be contrasted with Black. One of the first memories I have of learning about race was driving with my father downtown. And he said, "Do you smell that smell?" and indeed there was a smell. And I said yes. And he said, "That's the smell of nigger town." And I didn't know what that meant. But he was perfectly glad to tell me. That is where the Negro lived. And then he began to describe all the stereotypes with being a nigger, or Negro. At that time, there was supposed to be this difference. If you were pretty good, you were a Negro. Otherwise you were a nigger.
>
> But it didn't matter. You still weren't a White person, and that's the way it was. He would say things like "you know what you smell is partly the way that they keep their houses and their yards and there's just trash laying all around. But then part of what you smell is just them. They can't help it." And then he would go on: "Well, they talk differently because they're less educated, and they're less educated because they're less capable of being educated." So pretty soon you begin to develop a race identity that kind of says, wow, this is sad for them and sad for us too.

Gerry's father went out of his way to compensate for his child's inability to see racial differences by using spatial distinctions (driving from his suburban home to the inner city) and drawing upon other senses (the smell of trash and poverty in urban environments, differences in speech patterns, etc.) to paint a picture that obscures the discriminatory social forces leading many Blacks to inhabit poor social conditions. This casts these outcomes as a function of Blacks' natural racial tendencies in order to justify Whites' spatial isolation—typically known as White flight. Timothy had a similar experience, where, as a child, anytime his family would travel from their suburban home into the main city, "They'd say, 'Well, we're entering nigger heaven.' And I thought, 'What is nigger heaven?' That was something that just [didn't immediately register]. . . . What is a nigger? Why are you calling [them] niggers? Why? What's the deal? I thought, ok [Black people] talked a little different. [But] I just don't understand this." Leveraging this sensibility of spatial isolation to convey the significance of maintaining racial boundaries was not limited to curtailing travel outside of one's own segregated enclave, but also asserted the importance of keeping racial minorities from coming in. Kenneth notes:

> My parents, we would be considered probably lower middle income when I was growing up, and the biggest asset that they had was a house. And they were always afraid that Black people were going to move in to our neighborhood, and consequently their major and only asset would lose value. . . . Although my parents were not the kind of people that were vindictive about [race] or were constantly outspoken about it like many of my neighbors were. But, that was my initial concept of race, and it always goes around Black people, since that's what they were concerned with. . . . I'd like to think that I adopted the demeanor of my parents, and that was to be polite and cordial *but not to get too close.* [emphasis added]

Vincent was also exposed to understanding the social and visual significance of race through spatial mechanisms:

> My parents belonged to a group called [South Sequoyah] Neighbors. And all I knew about them as a little kid was that they put on these nifty picnics every year. They had barbeque and stuff, and I got to eat hamburgers and beans and stuff like that. But the purpose of the [South Sequoyah] Neighbors was to keep Black people from moving into our neighborhood. . . . I asked my Dad, "Why did we join up with these neighbors?" And the answer came, you know, "We got to keep the niggers out of here."

This notion of tying family wealth and well-being to spatial separation from Blacks was also discussed by other blind respondents as an important mechanism through which their racial sensibilities were shaped. For example, Pam recounted this memory:

> I remember this one joke that I heard, and I didn't understand it, and I just pondered and pondered. One of my dad's friends . . . I might have been about ten, said, "What's the most horrible thing that a homeowner wants to hear?" and the punch line was, *"Hi! I's yo new neighbor."* And I didn't get that joke.

But they all thought it was hilarious. And I just remember thinking "I don't get it." So I must have asked someone who told me well, that's because you know that means that the new neighbor was a Black person. And so I just thought . . . *wow, you know there's a real distinction.* [emphasis added]

Thus, for Pam as well as many other blind respondents, informal interactions such as these work to constitute this notion of a "real distinction" existing that, in turn, orients their lives. It is through these types of repeated social interactions that visual differences can become fantastically and vividly real—even for those who cannot see. Socialization along other lines of perceptible difference can make imperceptible ones (such as those based on visual cues) seem like common sense. *A belief system that race is visually obvious is being structured;* its underlying architecture is the aspect of race that is hidden from yet nonetheless binds the sighted community, where race is simplistically experienced as it is seen. The experiences relayed by these blind respondents are not unique to the blind community. Rather, they reveal how all individuals are trained to seek and acknowledge the salience of the visual distinctions that society deems important. Laura offered an example of how she was socialized to "smell" differences between races:

> We had this babysitter [named Ellen], and I came down one morning and said [to my Mother], "What are you doing?" She said, "I'm washing the counters." And I asked, "Why are you washing the counters?" She said, "Well, because Black people smell, and your babysitter was here last night." And I said, "That's interesting" and filed that away. So, [Ellen] came the next week, and she was standing with her arm on the counter, and I walked up to the counter, and I sniffed it, and [Ellen] said, "What are you doing?" and I said, "Oh, I'm sniffing the counter, because my mom said you guys smell, and she's right. There's a smell that's different from ours on the counter."

This example illustrates how difference did not make a difference until the difference was pointed out and racialized, becoming a seemingly intrinsic part of who Black people are as a group in the young mind of this respondent and feeding into the socialization process that the visual significance of race (which remains primary) is perceptible through other means. It would be a folly to limit this experience to the young, impressionable mind of a child; recall Connie's ostensible ability to smell even the slightest hint of racial difference as an adult. These efforts to construct a race consciousness in which differences are striking and pervasive suggests that it does not take a fantastic leap of logic for these social practices to inculcate a visual sense of racial difference among blind people and make visual cues seem like obvious boundaries among the sighted.

Institutional Practices

Another recurring theme from the data is the way institutions become part of the social practices that constitute visual understandings of race for blind people. Institutional forces have a different scope and effect than the previously described socialization that flows through friends and family members. Institutions provide a broader and more depersonalized context that, when synchronized with the intimate socializations initiated by relatives and friends, can establish a robust mechanism for thinking a certain way about the world.

The example that stands out the most from the data is that of segregated schools for the blind. This is only relevant to the relatively small number of respondents who went to primary and secondary schools in the South prior to widespread desegregation in the 1960s and 1970s. Yet these cases powerfully demonstrate the lengths society goes to express racial ideas. School segregation was part of a broader system of Jim Crow that forced Blacks and Whites to live separately across a number of areas in civic life.[15] This had the purpose and effect of relegating Blacks to second-class citizenship. For those who were sighted, separate facilities (such as restaurants and water fountains) were a way to visually and spatially express Blacks' presumed racial inferiority. "Colored only" and "Whites only" signs, residential segregation, and school segregation were ways to reaffirm the color line—a visual and spatial separation of these groups' day-to-day lives. Imparting the significance of these visual lines of separation to blind children who could not see them was so important that it was thought to be necessary to have segregated schools for the blind. Dennis, a blind White respondent, described how transparent and unremarkable segregation seemed when he was a child:

> I went to a school for the blind [and] we didn't give it a matter of thought. This was before Brown v. Board of Education in '54, and the Civil Rights Bill in '57. There was the White Side and what was called the Colored Side, and I knew that there were some of them who spoke differently from the way White folks spoke, but I didn't know that it's White as color. I just assumed there was one side of the school called White, because we were on the White side. The other side they called the colored side, nobody told us why.

This experience highlights how institutional segregation kept this respondent ignorant of race and racial difference during his primary school years. While his awareness of race as a visually significant entity developed later in his childhood, this separation served the purpose of only socializing him around other Whites—to keep him among his own kind. Pam, who went to a segregated school for the blind in the same southern state as Dennis, talked about how this institutional separation affected her and other blind children's perceptions: "[School] segregation says a lot because you're telling the privileged race that basically they're better than the other guys. So I think that might have had a certain mind-set for a lot of people and probably myself included as a young person who wasn't able to ferret out what the real truth was early on." Institutional practices such as school segregation played a pivotal role in driving home the idea of racial difference and the type of treatment that should be afforded to each race. Often this was not explicitly visual, but it helped give cognitive content to blind people's understanding of race, in that they could not directly perceive the visual cues that typically frame one's racial consciousness. Maurice, a White respondent, recalled a way in which school segregation conferred disdain toward blind Black children because of their race:

> I also became aware of the limits that the separate system caused, and this was not just in terms of blindness. This was in terms of everything. I remember [asking] early in high school, "Why won't the rehabilitation people come out and talk to us?" . . . [The school] would send people to the rehab place to talk about possible jobs, summer employment, and other stuff. But the rehab people would not come onto the school campus. We had to go. We actually had to call ourselves and make an appointment and go talk to them. [The school] would take us down there. But [the rehabilitation people] wouldn't come on campus. And that was a racial thing. . . . I was told flat out [that] if [the rehabilitation people] come out here, they'll have to go over and talk to the Black school also. And I said, "So what?" . . . Well, I realized at some point what they were saying was that we don't want to do anything for [Blacks]. But in order to avoid doing something for them, we're not going to do it for you either.

This begins to demonstrate the way that institutions affirm the idea of racial difference first by separation and then deploying resources in a manner that further embeds a sense of privilege. Again, only a small number of respondents reported going to such formally segregated schools for the blind. But, at the very least, these accounts remain useful in highlighting the deeply embedded institutional mechanisms used to ensure that blind children were socialized in a manner that fostered a perceptible appreciation for how society treats people based upon visual cues such as skin color.

Another experience among the blind respondents was how institutions such as *integrated* schools for the blind enforced racial boundaries. Denise attended an integrated residential school for the blind and said that the school "did not want interracial dating. . . . People told me that houseparents would really lecture them and make sure that they knew [their dating interest] was Black, and that you stuck with your own kind." In some ways, houseparents who supervised blind children while they were away from home played the role that their parents would have played while they were away at school. But they also had an institutional role as school employees to look after students' welfare. Nevertheless, it was not uncommon for them to take it upon themselves to actively discourage interracial dating and to make sure that students understood that it was inappropriate by social and institutional standards to date someone who did not look like them, who was not one of "their kind." This, in turn, gave the visual cues associated with race greater significance to blind schoolchildren. Jillian attended a residential school for the blind and described an additional way in which the institution dealt with interracial intimacy:

[The school] tried to convince us that [a biracial] friend was Filipino. They would not admit that one parent was Black and one parent was White. . . . They hated the idea of Black and White people intermixing. And because they hated it so much, they just couldn't deal with it. And so it was easier to come up with the idea that these children were of some other [race]. They told another child that she was half Italian and half Indian. Which is ridiculous; she was mulatto too. But they told her, and she may still believe that she's Italian Indian. . . . Her mother was Italian. That's true. But her father was Black. And her mother never did say to her [that her] father wasn't an Indian. He was a Black man. Her mother was perfectly happy to say, "Oh well, gee, ok. So we'll call your dad an Indian." The school did. So she still might believe. . . . [The school] never did admit that any one of those people were mulatto. Not one of them.

Patrolling racial boundaries in this manner was a way of creating racial purity (with regard to denying interracial relationships between Blacks and Whites) where none existed. Again, this did not directly create a visual sense of race for blind people, but it was an attempt to convey that the visual racial boundaries that blind students could not see were nonetheless real and should shape how they organize their lives. Rachel, a White female respondent, described how her day school for the blind would collaborate with parents to ensure that these children understood the importance of race:

> There was a young boy that I befriended in my classroom. And his name was Calvin and he was Black. And he and I were really good friends. We played together. We played hopscotch together. I have fond memories of him. We talked to each other. We walked. . . . What happened was the school contacted my parents. And I don't know if we were maybe walking and holding hands or—you know how little kids are. They just will hug each other or do something like that. And I think that's what we must have done. And I really did like him. I considered him my best friend. The school called my parents and told them that I was playing with him or they were concerned about this. My parents sat me down and said that I could never talk to him again. [They said that] not only was I not allowed, [but] that the school had called. . . . I was not to play with him. I was not to have anything to do with him. And I just felt terrible. I was just really hurt. But I was more hurt in having to go to school and talk to him because nobody told [Calvin] that. Nobody said to him you can't talk to her. And so when I went [back to school], he didn't know. I mean he just came over to me, and he was ready to do what we did everyday. And I had to say to him, "I'm not allowed to do this. Something happened with the school, and all I know, Calvin, is I'm not allowed to do this anymore. And if I do, I'll get into a lot of trouble." And he was very sad and I was very sad.
>
> And [the school] separated us. We used to sit together. And they wouldn't let us sit together. They just separated us. And then by the end of the year, he was gone. And he never came back to the school.

Here, Rachel's parents drew upon and collaborated with an institutional authority to enforce the color line as an important barrier that cannot be crossed—even when their child cannot see it—to give importance to the visual cues and social meanings associated with race.

Another institutional mechanism blind respondents associated with shaping their visual understanding of race is the media. Descriptions of people on television, radio, and in books that focus on a person's visual description in relation to specific types of behavior were cited by a few respondents to influence their visual thinking about race. When asked how she learned that people had different skin colors, Laura (a blind White woman) said that she learned it

> from songs about different kinds of people and from "Little Black Sambo." It was a child's book. . . . It's really interesting now, to read the stuff about "Little Black Sambo" from other points of view, because, honest to God, and maybe it's because I'm blind, and I just didn't put together that he was different. That was just his name to me. I didn't even make a connection that he was Black. . . . It just didn't dawn on me, but I do know it means, on a subconscious level, I guess I found a way [to recognize] that he was Black.

Other blind respondents noted that Little Black Sambo was an important part of their early childhood recognition of racial difference. Laura remembers this book for introducing her to racial difference and the demeaning renditions of race that can occur in popular culture that are disseminated widely through media publications. Indeed, some unauthorized versions of the book that were more widely available in the United States took on aggressively racist overtones, "with gross, degrading caricatures that set Sambo down on the old plantation or, with equal distortiveness, deposited him in Darkest Africa. . . . [These] bootleg Sambos were much cheaper, more widely distributed, and vastly more numerous."[16] Kip recalled Little Black Sambo as being a part of his childhood, calling it a "degrading, irresponsible book. . . . I never really gave it too much thought, but I was thinking the other day of how irresponsible and naive [it is]. What a toxic poisonous thing to have a book like that in your home. To read a story like that is so degrading." It is not clear which version of the book these blind respondents read, but the book nonetheless had the effect of creating the social and cognitive conditions to give significance to visual cues of race.

Sharice noted the impact of Huckleberry Finn on shaping her own identity as a White person. When asked when she started to identify as a White or Caucasian, she replied, "I remember reading *Huckleberry Finn*. When I was a little girl, I had a tape, a dramatized version of *Huckleberry Finn*, and I remember realizing that we were people like Huck Finn, and then, there are people like Jim, and that we were the White people, and he was the Black person." News reporting also goes a long way in affirming the significance of race and its visual cues. Perry, a blind White female respondent, admitted that she had a deep fear of Black men because she thought they were rapists.

She said that she went through an extended period of self-reflection to try to understand where that perception came from, and she concluded, "a lot of it is the media. The media does it to a lot of people. . . . They'll say, for example, 'A Black [person] was cited for [a particular crime].' They don't ever say 'a White [person]. . . .' They are beginning to [now], but it was always a Black, an Asian, a Latino, a Mexican. . . . They always point out the minority." This type of media reporting significantly impacted the content of her visual understanding of race, leading her to connect men who looked a certain way to their propensity for committing rape.

These institutional practices can be seen as an interesting backdrop from which to understand the matrix of social and institutional interactions that can encode a visual understanding of race within many blind respondents. While social practices can create this visual sense of race and fill it with emotive content, institutional practices can play a broader, reaffirming role in giving them a sense of wider acceptance and propriety beyond one's immediate circle of family and friends. Thinking visually about race, seeking out the visual cues that define a person's race, and attaching meanings to them become solidified as the norm of social interaction. But how does this norm affect blind respondents' everyday lives?

"I'm Not Racist, But I Hate Niggers": Blind People's Visual Understanding of Race and Its Impact on Their Everyday Lives

It is tempting to think that the data presented thus far only show that blind people are simply repeating, or "parroting" the visual understanding of race conveyed to them by sighted individuals without this understanding having any real effect on their daily interactions. This response, which I term the parrot thesis, suggests that blind people are aware of what sighted people tell them about race but that this visual understanding of race is thin and insignificant to their social and interpersonal relations. The data show that this is demonstrably wrong. In many instances race was socialized to not only take on visual significance to blind people, but a visceral one that significantly impacted their everyday lives. Jillian, a blind White woman, provided an example of the remarkable effect this socialization can have:

> My first memory of race is when I was a little girl and probably about six years old, and I had a little [blind] friend and she was a Black girl. She used to come

home and visit. And at the time my mom used to conserve water, time, and energy by bathing kids together. She told [me and my black friend] to go upstairs and take a bath together, which is typically what she would do with me and my sister. And [my black friend] started to cry. She said that she couldn't do that.

Mom asked her why she couldn't do it and why she was so upset. But [she] just started to cry. I mean she became very, very distraught. My mom asked what the problem was, why she couldn't do it, and why she was upset. And she said that if she did her black would rub off on me. And that was such a weird thing. I mean, I didn't understand what in the world she was talking about. Because up until that point I didn't realize that [she] was any different than me. I thought [she] was just another blind kid in school, and we were all alike. At that time I didn't realize or didn't know that there was such a thing as Black, White, or different people. I thought people were people were people. . . . *I had no idea how real [race] really was.* [emphasis added]

The Black girl's houseparents were White and used this notion that her Blackness would rub off on White people as a socialization tool to keep her from intimate situations with White children (such as bathing) in order to enforce boundaries. This demonstrates the extent to which race is solidified as a visual or "real" entity to create a belief system among blind and sighted alike that race is an observable, tangible, and substantive trait.

Tim bluntly described the effects of being socialized into thinking about race visually, noting that "perception is everything. How something is perceived, or how one class of folks are perceived is everything." Put differently, to be part of a culture that thinks visually about racial meaning and to be subject to social practices by friends, family, and institutions that fill these labels with substantive content is to affect their perception of the racial world, which in turn becomes reality. Just because blind people cannot see the racial boundaries that people often organize their lives around does not mean that they do not find these lines useful in organizing their own lives. Jackson, a blind White man, recalled a conversation with a blind woman that he talked to "from time to time. We were talking about race one night. And her exact words were, I'll never forget this: 'I'm not racist, but I hate niggers.' "

To understand how this sensibility can be inculcated in a person that cannot see the very lines that mark the difference that she hates, Raymond notes: "Racism is a learned behavior, and so blind people are just as racist as the sighted. And we shouldn't be, because we can't see the color anyway.

But that's why I suggest that race is just not necessarily just the color of your skin. It's a philosophy. It's a school of thought. It's a prejudice that's taught, that's handed down through the generations." The interview data highlight numerous examples of how blind individuals' lives, decisions, and relationships revolve around race—a finding remarkably similar to what occurs in the lives of sighted individuals. As touched upon earlier in this chapter, dating and interracial intimacy provide a poignant example of how racial boundaries are patrolled and enforced to confer the visual salience of race to blind people. Thus, it is similarly interesting to look at how this boundary work and visual understandings of race can shape blind people's dating preferences. Tim, a blind Black male, talked about the difficulties he had with dating outside of his race: "I just love African-American women. I don't know why. I had White friends that I hung out with, and we went to class together, and worked on projects together. I just never had a desire to do that. . . . I tried it, but I just couldn't gravitate to it. I think I did it for about a week, and I was just like, 'No, I can't do this.'" He went on to talk about some of the cultural dissimilarities that made dating outside of his race difficult, such as different tastes in music. Cultural barriers can certainly be difficult for people to transcend, but this interview revealed an unvoiced difficulty with the race issue as it played out in terms of physical differences, not merely cultural ones. Other respondents voiced this hesitation as a desire to not disrupt social norms, knowing that interracial dating provides a visual image that they may not be able to perceive but is nonetheless looked down upon by others. Dale recalled a blind White friend's experience:

> He was going to college and he had started working with a reader. She was very attractive to him, and he started seeing her. Then, somebody told him that she was Black, and he broke it off. He broke off the relationship. He justified it by saying that it would not have worked, in the South, for a White man to be involved with a Black woman. But that's an incident that shows [how] once he learned that she was Black, the prejudice set in.

Keenan discussed how race, at least in his experience as a blind Black person, becomes a primary filter in dating:

> A lot of my Black blind friends have sort of a joke because when someone doesn't know our race—especially the males—they'll find some way to reach out and touch our hair. People want to know, and that's the one [racial clue] they can always get. . . . That's one thing that I've noticed. People always come

up with some kind of way to [touch our heads]. They'll massage you or do something. You know mostly you don't get too mad at blind people because a lot of them are touchy-feely or whatever. And so you don't think anything about it. The next thing [you know] they went for your hair. It's a way for them to figure out [your race] if they don't know. . . .

I think [this happens] mostly in dating. You know, if they're going to make some decisions. I've seen people that seem sort of interested in someone and then discover that they're Black and change their intentions. I go to a lot of the conventions now, the national conventions [for the blind]. And there are people trying to meet somebody [to date]. You can see that they're kind of pursuing somebody [that they find attractive]. And they'll go for the hair, and then they'll change their mind. They're always still friendly. I've never known anybody who just stopped talking to anybody altogether. They'll give themselves some time. But you're Black.

What stands out from this passage is how race is not simply a passive characteristic that blind people happen to find out and store away in their mental rolodexes as they meet people, but rather is information that is often actively sought to determine the nature and terms of any ongoing interaction. For example, Madge acknowledged the importance of race:

Race is important in terms of a date. I remember meeting this guy at a program for the blind at the university. And most of the guys there I wasn't really that impressed with. But this one guy, he really stood out. And I liked him and I enjoyed talking to him and stuff. And when I found out that he was Black, I knew it wasn't going to work for me. But I felt kind of bad then, because I was hoping that it would [work out]. But that's where [race] usually makes the most difference in my life.

But race plays this important role of structuring the terms of human interactions beyond the realm of dating. For example, Tammy said that knowing someone's race is useful because "it makes it easier to interact with them [so] I won't say a stupid thing . . . something like a statement that would be assuming that they're White. [It's also important] just so that I can have equal access to information. I can say it matches the information that the sighted person has. It's really important to me."

It is also important to acknowledge that the very fact that a blind person cannot see the basis upon which they are racialized does not seem to mitigate the ability of race to shape their own self-perceptions or relationship with the racial group they identify with. Paula, a blind Black female, talked about what it was like being a Black adolescent who went to school with Whites yet lived in a Black community where she was teased for not being "Black enough." She found herself "trying to like music that [she] didn't like, . . . trying to make sure [she] read certain books," in order to become "more Black," so that her outward actions would correspond with the expectations placed upon her due to her physical appearance. Ultimately, this led her to immerse herself in Black culture by consciously choosing to attend a historically Black university for graduate school, which reshaped her own racial identity and relationship with the Black community:

> I loved it. I loved it. I gained a whole new respect for, and knowledge of what people do. . . . I learned a lot about our history, I learned a lot about our people, and I marvel at the various fields [of Blacks'] accomplishments. This was a fascinating world for me, because it was different than what I was used to.
>
> I think [the experience developed a new side of me], and I think it was a good side, meaning that it was just one more thing to help bolster my confidence as a woman, as a person of color, even as a person who is blind. . . . The racial thing, it's a part of who I am. So, I try to treat it the same way I treat the other parts of who I am.

But the sense of support and racial solidarity that blind racial minorities might expect to have with sighted members of their communities can be lessened by their disability, leading them to endure *intra*racial discrimination that they experience as particularly hurtful. Tim, a blind Black male, said this:

> Particularly in terms of education, we had more White folks help us than my own people. My own people hurt me. I've had more Blacks hurt me more than help me. And that hurts. Black on Black discrimination hurts. And, I'll never forget when I went to public high school, which was predominantly Black. I was accepted, then rejected. I couldn't get a tour for the school, and they were asking me, like, "Could I walk up the steps?" What the hell does walking up the steps have to do with my capacity to learn? And the principal was Black, the teachers were Black, and I said, "Here I am, African American male, I'm not standing on a street corner, I'm not in the club, I'm not doing those stereotypical things. You following me, [in terms of] how some African American men are perceived? I'm not doing those things. The only thing I'm asking for is a quality education, and it just blew my mind. I said, "You talk about what

happened with civil rights in 1964. You talk about segregation. You talk about Blacks not having access to economic wealth, etc., etc., etc. But here it is, I sit, trying to get an education in a predominantly Black school system, and an African American male with a disability, and you're going to be discriminatory based on someone's disability. That's the same thing as a White person telling me you can't sit at their lunch counter, or you can't come to their church, or to their school, or whatever function. It's the same thing. Discrimination is discrimination no matter how you cut it.

For Tim, the sense of solidarity that he feels with other Blacks stems from a shared social experienced linked to their shared phenotype and cultural values. That is, he is disappointed that Blacks have not always supported him since he is one of them. Being blind does not alter his group affiliation. In fact, it aggravates the disappointment he feels from the lack of support. But after conveying these sentiments, Tim stated:

> I'm just sitting here, thinking about the situation now. We have some investment properties. It's funny that I'm about to say this, but I find myself being discriminatory in that I have an option of selecting people, people who are Section 8 [federal housing assistance for low income families]. And, what I have said is that's not my preference. And I'm sitting here now, and we're having this conversation, I'm like "Damn, is that discriminatory?" So, I need to rethink that.

This highlights the complexity of within-group race relations, as divides along disability status and class can rupture the sense of solidarity that one might expect. This exchange draws attention to the fact that blindness does not exempt blind people from these complications. Race—as a visual, conceptual, and aspirational practice—is just as coherent to blind people like Tim as anyone else and structures his relations with Blacks and people of other races.

The racial identity one builds through understanding one's physical appearance and group affiliation can also be a significant, if not wholly irrational barrier. The norms that people are socialized into affect how they view themselves and others for the rest of their lives. Pam, a blind White female, recalled a time as a child when she was at the beach:

> And my dad was on a rock . . . and he was fishing. . . . We were down in the water some little bit of distance from him. And a boy came. And we were talking with him. He sounded like he was my age. We were just fooling around

and having fun in the water. Turns out this was a Black boy. I did not know that. But my dad looked down and saw us and became so upset and agitated that he slipped coming down the rock. And [he] had a bottle of cough syrup in his pocket because he developed a cough. And it broke. And he cut his hip really badly because he was so upset that I was in the water talking to this Black boy.

Experiences such as these in which racial boundaries are patrolled and maintained to create a profound sense of difference between groups can have a lasting effect on how individuals relate to even ancillary aspects of racial difference. The same respondent described these effects through an experience several decades later, when she went to an estate sale for a recently deceased Black woman:

And so it turns out that the dead woman was my same size. And so I purchased a few of her dresses and things. And when I put them on, I felt really strange knowing that she was a Black person. And I really . . . I don't know where that feeling came from. And searching my soul about it, I think it was baggage from the way I was raised and how I had been indoctrinated as a child and a young person. And I think that just bubbled up and I had to say, ok, is this really me? Is this what I really think? . . . I was ashamed of that feeling.

The irrationality of this response is inextricably tied to the way in which a visual understanding of difference shaped by social interactions (such as her father forbidding Black playmates) affects how she as a White woman felt wearing something once owned by a Black person. The knowledge that the deceased lady was Black and belief that this difference mattered led to feelings of anxiety and shame. Whether or not Pam could actually see the difference leading to these feelings mattered very little.

This chapter goes beyond demonstrating blind people's visual understanding of race to show the constitutive social practices that give rise to this visual understanding and how it affects blind people's everyday social interactions. Although this mainstream understanding of race in the sighted community relies heavily on the ideas that (1) race is largely known by physical bodily differences such as skin color, (2) these cues are visually obvious, and (3) people without vision do not have a full understanding of race, the data provide evidence that race is not simply an ocular phenomenon. Its visual salience is produced rather than merely observed. Given that these constitutive social practices reveal themselves through examining blind people's experiences but nonetheless shape the racial consciousness of blind and sighted similarly, these data provide an empirical standpoint from which to rethink the presumption that the visual salience of race is self-evident—a presumption that is embedded in all areas of social life, particularly law. Part 2 starts from this point, whereby the empirical data discussed in Part 1 provide a grounded basis from which to rethink various social and legal ideals that orient around the notion that race is visually obvious.

PART II
"'TWAS BLIND BUT NOW I SEE":
SOCIAL AND LEGAL
IMPLICATIONS

4 Revisiting Colorblindness

THE 1967 RELEASE OF THE FILM *GUESS WHO'S COMING TO DINNER* generated a social discussion on race unlike anything else in the civil rights era. Rather than putting the issue of integration on the table by talking about schools or the workplace, *Guess Who's Coming To Dinner* tackled racial integration of the most intimate kind: sex, marriage, and family. The all-star cast featuring Academy Award winners Spencer Tracy and Katharine Hepburn—who won the Oscar for best actress in this movie—as well as a young Sidney Poitier forced Americans to grapple with love across the color line in an impeccably timed fashion: the film was released six months after the Supreme Court decided *Loving v. Virginia*, which unanimously held anti-miscegenation laws to be unconstitutional.

The movie's plot is fairly straightforward. Joanna Drayton (played by Hepburn's niece, Katharine Houghton), the daughter of an established White San Francisco family, comes home unexpectedly early from a trip to Hawaii newly engaged to a respected physician, John Prentice (played by Poitier), who just happens to be Black (see Figure 11). Being the liberal-minded child of a stereotypically progressive San Francisco family, Joanna assumes that her family will not have a problem with their marriage. As Prentice notes of his future bride, "It's not just that our color difference doesn't matter to her. It's that she doesn't seem to think there is any difference." Thus, Joanna gleefully presumes her parents (Matt and Christina Drayton, played by Tracy and

FIGURE 11. Joanna Drayton and John Prentice in the 1967 film *Guess Who's Coming to Dinner.* "GUESS WHO'S COMING TO DINNER" © 1967 Columbia Pictures Industries, Inc. All Rights Reserved. Courtesy of Columbia Pictures.

Hepburn) feel the same way and will approve their engagement before they fly off to Geneva later that evening.

However, the Draytons hesitate at the prospect of their daughter marrying Prentice, despite his stellar credentials and remarkable accomplishments. Some have criticized the filmmaker's crafting of Prentice as being *too perfect*—an almost inhuman amalgamation of achievements thrown together to force the race issue upon the Draytons and, by extension, the audience in a manner that is arguably cheap, contrived, and without nuance.[1] Then again, perhaps that was the point of making a film like this in 1967: to control for all meaningful variables in order to put race, and all of its superficial and substantive qualities, on cinematic trial in a manner that forces the audience to render a verdict as to whether race, in and of itself, mattered in affairs of the heart.

Christina Drayton comes to support her daughter's decision rather quickly. But the bulk of the film centers around Matt Drayton's careful deliberations on whether to give his approval to this proposed union. After voicing various reservations throughout the length of the film, he rationally concedes to the power of love right before the end credits roll: "The only thing that matters is what they feel, and how much they feel, for each other. And if it's half of what we [Matt and his wife] felt—that's everything. As for you two and the problems you're going to have, they seem almost unimaginable. But you'll have no problem with me."[2] Thus, in many ways, *Guess Who's Coming to Dinner* is a social and (given the timing of *Loving v. Virginia*) *political* statement on how reason, love, and courage can trump racial prejudice. Over time, however, the film's title has taken on a social significance much broader than this; in some circles it has come to signify the ongoing dissonance that some experience when seeing an interracial couple and its attendant social stigma as opposed to the reasoned acceptance of interracial coupling promoted by the film. While growing up in Ohio decades after the film's release, it was not uncommon to hear someone say, "Uh oh, guess who's coming to dinner?" when an interracial couple walked by, akin to how *Jungle Fever* became synonymous with interracial attraction after the 1991 release of Spike Lee's film.

Although interracial relationships are more common now than they were in the 1960s, the unease some experience when seeing an interracial couple persists in a manner not unlike the Draytons' initial reaction to meeting Dr. Prentice. This sentiment's resilience provides a context from which to think about the 2005 movie *Guess Who*—a loose remake of the original 1967 film. But *Guess Who* offers a twist to this social conversation on interracial relationships: rather than portraying a Black man going home to meet his White fiancé's family, the "who" is a White man going to the home of his Black fiancé (see Figure 12). *Guess Who's* plot centers around Simon Green (played by Ashton Kutcher), who is a rising star in the financial sector with a future

FIGURE 12. Simon Green and Theresa Jones in the 2005 film *Guess Who*. "GUESS WHO" © 2005 Columbia Pictures Industries, Inc. All Rights Reserved. Courtesy of Columbia Pictures.

as bright as Dr. Prentice's. Green travels to New Jersey to meet the family of his soon-to-be wife, Theresa (played by Zoë Saldana). Like *Guess Who's Coming to Dinner*, Theresa's mother quickly accepts her daughter's relationship after initially being surprised, while much of the movie centers around her father, Percy Jones (played by Bernie Mac). And, like Matt Drayton nearly four decades earlier, Jones works through his initial displeasure to finally accept the relationship.

There are certainly important differences between the movies that complicate efforts at making blunt comparisons. *Guess Who's Coming to Dinner* was created as a serious and dramatic social commentary on a form of human relationship that, at the time the movie was in development, was criminal in several states and faced harsh social rebuke in most others. *Guess Who* was developed as a relatively lighthearted romantic comedy—a genre shared by films such as *There's Something About Mary* and *My Big Fat Greek Wedding*—where the aim is to tell a story about *individual characters* rather than to engage in a broader *political* discussion. Yet there are also interesting parallels between the two films that make the 2005 version a recognizable if not altogether coherent remake of the 1967 original. For example, Simon Green is also constructed as an ideal partner to force the relevancy of his Whiteness on to the Black family and the audience. Indeed, Green's only "flaw" in the movie is that he is not forthcoming to his fiancée about quitting his job, which ultimately turns out to be a redeeming character trait: he quit because of his supervisor's bigoted statements about his decision to date a Black woman. Both Prentice and Green were raised by families that worked hard and sacrificed to give them professional opportunities. Both Matt Drayton and Percy Jones surreptitiously run background checks on their daughters' fiancés. Both Joanna and Theresa have supportive mothers who battle their husband's hesitancy to approve their daughter's relationship. Unlike their fiancés' assumptions that race is not an issue, both Prentice and Green are racial pragmatists concerning the difficulties that may follow from their relationship. And the list goes on.

To the extent that the race conversations in both films largely exempt Joanna and Theresa from any serious race deliberations and instead focus on their fiancés' struggles, *Guess Who* comes off as an intelligible remake of the original film through the unspoken yet ever-present sentiment that there is a moral parallel between Prentice's and Green's experiences with race. Those engaged in interracial relationships, regardless of their individual race, often face social hostilities. But the particularly brutal consequences that faced a Black man in the mid-twentieth century who dared to engage the sexualized color line—think Emmett Till, the fourteen-year-old Black boy lynched in Mississippi in 1955 for allegedly whistling at a White woman—somehow become morally equivalent to the difficulties faced by a twenty-first-century White man. The overarching sentiment espoused by *Guess Who* when read as an update of its 1967 namesake is that discrimination is discrimination is discrimination; *Guess Who's Coming to Dinner* as social and political commentary is retold in *Guess Who* as the story of an otherwise privileged White man being individually discriminated against at work and at home for his dating choices. The context that mattered so much in 1967 is now irrelevant; *Guess Who* shifts the conversation to individuals, drawing a moral equivalency between the prejudice experienced by Prentice and Green without acknowledging the fundamentally different social situations and contexts that they find themselves in. Just as *Guess Who's Coming to Dinner* was developed in the context of the civil rights movement and *Loving v. Virginia* to emphasize the social and political difficulties concerning interracial relationships, *Guess*

Who developed in a context that emphasized the individual nature of racial discrimination, which raises an important question: what facilitates *Guess Who*'s particular rendering of race and discrimination? What shifting social dynamics allow this approach to race—that a White man's discriminatory experiences in 2005 are meaningfully similar to a Black man's in 1967—to be thinkable and coherent?

Colorblindness.

*   *   *

In his 1999 HBO stand-up routine, Black comedian Chris Rock made the following observations about race relations: "Man, the White man thinks he's losing the country. You watch the news. [White people say] 'We're losing everything. We're fucking losing.' Affirmative action, and illegal aliens . . . and we're fucking losing the country.' Losing? White people ain't losing shit. If y'all losing, who's winning? It ain't us. It ain't us. Have you driven around this motherfucker? It ain't us."[3] What initially seems like typical comedic armchair sociology that might garner a chuckle yet can be easily dismissed actually found empirical backing in a 2011 study by Michael Norton and Samuel Sommers. They asked a large, nationally representative sample of Black and White Americans to use a ten-point scale (1 = not at all, 10 = very much) to describe the extent to which Blacks and Whites suffered from racial discrimination decade-by-decade, from 1950 to the 2000s. Surprisingly enough, Rock was on to something. Whites and Blacks had similar views on anti-Black and anti-White bias in the 1950s; both groups scored anti-Black bias high (between 9 and 10) and anti-White bias low (between 1 and 2). This should not be surprising. But what is surprising is the extent to which these perceptions have changed in recent years. Present-day Blacks continue to see anti-Black bias to be a substantial problem (6 out 10), but better than in the 1950s, while Blacks similarly perceive anti-White bias to be as negligible a problem as it was in the past (about 1.3 in 1950 versus roughly 1.9 in the 2000s). But White respondents saw today's discrimination against Whites (4.7) as *more of a problem* than prejudice against Blacks (3.6), with "some 11% of Whites [giving] anti-White bias the maximum rating on [the] scale in comparison with only 2% of Whites who did so for anti-Black bias."[4] Norton and Sommers identify this emerging perspective among Whites as "zero-sum racism": Whites see decreasing levels of anti-Black bias being tied to increasing levels of anti-White bias. Blacks' gains are thought to be linked to Whites' losses; when one group wins, the other must lose. But how is it possible that this sentiment is growing at the very same time that virtually all empirical evidence—from racial disparities in health to education to employment to wealth—continues to show that Black outcomes are significantly worse than White outcomes? For example, a 2011 study by the Pew Research Center shows that White households' median wealth is twenty times greater than the median wealth of Blacks and eighteen times higher than that for Hispanics, the widest gap in the twenty-five years that the data have been collected.[5] Norton and Sommers do not offer any clear answers for how Whites perceive increased discrimination against their own group at the very same time that their material privilege grows. But they do note that their data "suggest that rather than having different reference points for racism . . . the racial divergence we observe over time is likely due to *recent changes in how bias is conceptualized*. . . . Our data are the first to demonstrate that not only do Whites think more progress has been made toward equality than do Blacks, but Whites also now believe that this progress is linked to a new inequality—at their expense."[6]

I argue that the conceptualization of race that leads to this discordant perception of White inequality in the face of repeated empirical demonstrations of White privilege can be understood as a product of colorblindness. At its core, colorblindness represents a normative ideology of racial nonrecognition; individuals, organizations, and government bodies should give no special attention to individuals' race; decisions should not be made because of race, even to level the playing field; and resources should not be distributed along racial lines, even for remedial purposes. This ideology has entrenched itself in American law, politics, and social thought as a means to limit remedies to past racial injustices—most notably seen in the affirmative action debates of the 1990s, in which several state initiatives led to laws prohibiting state and local governments from taking race or ethnicity into consideration for school admissions, government contracting, and other areas.[7] But colorblindness is more than a passive ideology. It is an active, always present filter through which increasing numbers of people understand the social world. This filter is a prism through which the realities of race are viewed, which distorts an accurate understanding of race by making at least three problematic disassociations seem like a rational take on the social world and racial order.

What is Colorblindness?

First, colorblindness acknowledges that race is a social construction without any inherent biological significance.[8] Race is just skin color, without any more significance in and of itself than eye color or foot size. But it uses the constructed nature of race to conclude that since race has no biological meaning it therefore has no social meaning and therefore should not be recognized at all. Colorblindness encourages a *disassociation with the social significance of race*; it is an affirmative nonrecognition of how racial meanings, constructed as they may be, still impact social and legal decision making in a manner that fundamentally shapes everyday life. Secondly, colorblindness treats race as a superficial individual trait, disconnected from vertical understandings of group hierarchy to promote a horizontal conception of ethnicity that is devoid of any power dynamic. It embraces the idea that everybody is from somewhere; being Irish or German is no more significant than being Black or Latino. This race-as-ethnicity thread in colorblindness discourses produces a *disassociation with the group dynamics of race*, whereby everybody is part of a group deemed to be racially equal without acknowledging power relations that produce group-based disadvantages among racial minorities and group-based privileges among Whites.[9] Lastly, colorblindness has a temporal element that frames race relations as only about the present and future. It asserts that individuals should not be punished or disadvantaged because of previous generations' sins, creating a *disassociation with racial history and the inertia of social structure*. This is an affirmative nonrecognition that past disadvantages based upon race have consequences for present and future inequalities and injustices. Through this disassociation, colorblindness only has a moral commitment to leveling the playing field today and tomorrow by not acknowledging how centuries of unevenness between racial groups have fundamentally skewed opportunities and outcomes. Taken together, these three disassociations bolster the perspective that racial categories should not be used in law or public policy for either remedial or discriminatory purposes.

But colorblindness is more than about keeping race out of government decision making and the distribution of resources. It is also about producing social and legal theories in which race is a trite characteristic with an ugly history that should nonetheless have no bearing on the present. From this vantage point, racial discrimination is seen as being morally equivalent to race-conscious remedies to past injustices. Or, as Supreme Court Justice Clarence Thomas noted in *Adarand Constructors v. Peña*, in which the Supreme Court vacated and remanded a lower court's decision upholding the use of minority preferences in awarding government contracts, "government-sponsored racial discrimination based on benign prejudice is just as noxious as discrimination inspired by malicious prejudice. In each instance, it is racial discrimination, plain and simple."[10]

Scholars have repeatedly shown how colorblindness uses misguided notions of formal racial equality to maintain substantive racial inequality and White racial privilege.[11] By popularizing a theory of race and discrimination that disassociates race from its social significance, disassociates individual race from understandings of group privilege and group disadvantage, and disassociates the history of race relations from current and future group outcomes, colorblindness essentially freezes the status quo distribution of resources, wealth, and opportunities as the racial norm whereby even incremental upward mobility by a minority group—through affirmative action, humane immigration reform, and the like—is seen as a step backward to the majority. This explains the relevance of colorblindness to Norton and Sommers's zero-sum finding; incremental shifts in the racial landscape toward racial justice can disrupt the White racial norm so that they are perceived as a "loss" and thus indicative of increasing social hostility toward Whites in that things "aren't the way that they used to be," or as popularized by the Tea Party's opposition to President Obama, "I want my country back." This occurs despite empirical evidence showing that Whites are materially better off as a group. Therefore, colorblindness allows those in power to at once claim to be anti-racist while promoting policies that entrench status quo racial inequalities.

There has been much scholarly discussion on the politics of colorblindness, in terms of whether the normative vision of race that it espouses is good, bad, or even constitutional. But little thought has been given to a separate question: how is it that colorblindness, and its attendant disassociations, becomes a legitimate way to understand race relations? Is this simply the bad faith of racial politics? Perhaps. But that does not fully explain the sincerity with which many across the political spectrum advocate the racial nonrecognition promoted by colorblindness as the appropriate way for the country to move forward. In the face of growing racial inequalities, how do these disassociations come to be seen as a coherent and proper worldview? In this chapter, I explore the metaphorical significance of colorblindness in relation to how the term itself allows an otherwise unthinkable idea about race—that mere blindness and inattention to group difference can foster equality—to become an intelligible if not favored approach. Certainly, the rise of colorblindness only makes sense in a specific historical and political context. But, what has thus far gone unexplored is the ways in which metaphors can be leveraged to make broader ideas about the world more palatable. Thus, in this chapter, I place colorblindness's seeming palatability as a social, legal, and political strategy in conversation with the empirical evidence discussed in Part 1 to destabilize its discourses and practices so as to rethink the appropriateness of using colorblindness as a normative vision for race relations.

The Beginning

The idea that law should be blind to racial differences dates back to debates during the Civil War and Reconstruction periods.[12] However, Supreme Court Justice John Marshall Harlan gave the term *colorblindness* and its attendant ideals its first forceful public articulation in 1896 in his dissenting opinion in *Plessy v. Ferguson,* where he proclaimed: "Our Constitution is Colorblind, and neither knows nor tolerates classes among citizens."[13] In *Plessy,* the Supreme Court upheld the constitutionality of the "separate but equal" doctrine, which gave legitimacy to Jim Crow segregation until the Court's 1954 ruling in *Brown v. Broad of Education.* It is in the context of Justice Harlan's declaration that the Constitution is colorblind (and his prescience that the Court would eventually regret the holding in *Plessy* as much as its previous decision in *Dred Scott* to allow Blacks to be treated as chattel) that Harlan is often viewed as a maverick voice of moral clarity. Thus, it is not uncommon for modern advocates of colorblindness and even those who proclaim no particular affinities to colorblind politics to nonetheless view Harlan as a race progressive of his era. For example, Andrew Kull, author of what many consider to be the definitive legal history on colorblindness and American constitutionalism, notes that "Harlan's famous dissent in *Plessy* is customarily praised as a glowing affirmation of human rights."[14] Kull continues:

> *Plessy* embodies both our constitutional law of racial discrimination and its antithesis, crystallized in Justice Harlan's dissent; and the legacy of the case is the choice it presents us. With Justice Harlan's dissenting opinion, the colorblind Constitution became one of the available meanings of the Fourteenth Amendment. . . . Harlan's luminous opinion gave lasting form to the idea that might not otherwise have survived him. He did so, not least, by giving it a name.[15]

But what is interesting is how many commentators on colorblindness, even scholars like Kull, continue to praise the ideal of colorblindness articulated by Justice Harlan without mentioning—let alone taking seriously—the sentences in *Plessy directly preceding* those famous words:

> The White race deems itself to be the dominant race in this country. And so it is, in prestige, in achievements, in education, in wealth, and in power. So, I doubt not, it will continue to be for all time, if it remains true to its great heritage and holds fast to the principles of constitutional liberty. But, in view of the Constitution, in the eye of the law, there is in this country no superior, dominant, ruling class of citizens. There is no caste here. Our Constitution is color-blind, and neither knows nor tolerates classes among citizens.[16]

In his three-hundred-page book on the history of colorblind constitutionalism, Kull references this context of the birth of colorblindness only in a buried footnote, dismissively calling it the "preferred citation of [Harlan's] latter-day detractors."[17] But this approach to colorblindness obscures a rather obvious detail: the very idea of colorblindness originated in a context in which Harlan assumed—and indeed celebrated—White supremacy.[18] The distinction that Harlan drew in proposing that our Constitution is colorblind was not between racial discrimination and racial nonrecognition in absolute terms as suggested by Kull and many others. Rather, it was between formal legal equality—which, in Harlan's eyes, the Constitution mandated—and social equality, which was assumed to be outside of the law's purview. Law only had to give Blacks the same civil, political, and legal rights; Harlan's dissent from his colleagues in *Plessy* was over where to mark the boundary between legal and social realms. In his *Plessy* dissent, Harlan boils down his dispute with his judicial colleagues by saying this *immediately* after his colorblind proclamation:

> *In respect of civil rights*, all citizens are equal before the law. The humblest is the peer of the most powerful. The law regards man as man, and takes no account of his surroundings or of his color *when his civil rights* as guaranteed by the supreme law of the land are involved. It is therefore to be regretted that this high tribunal, the final expositor of the fundamental law of the land, has reached the conclusion that it is competent for a state to regulate the enjoyment by citizens *of their civil rights* solely upon the basis of race. [emphasis added]

This repeated emphasis on civil rights allows Harlan to bifurcate the social and civic realms, whereas the state can allow racial categorization in the former in furtherance of a Social Darwinist understanding of Whites' inherent superiority while at the same time limiting the state's ability to categorize by race with regard to the enjoyment of formal civil rights. This bifurcation between the social and civic realms of permissible and impermissible race categorization is further demonstrated, as Haney-López notes, in *Cumming v. County Board of Education*, in which "two years [after *Plessy*], Harlan would write for a unanimous Court in supporting a Whites-only high school, finding no 'clear and unmistakable disregard of rights secured by the supreme law of the land'—education, Harlan concluded, lay within the social sphere in which the state could mandate racial separation."[19]

Nevertheless, colorblindness as a term and an ideal has had an appeal beyond Harlan's initial conception that continues to entice the American public and has become the dominant perspective on Equal Protection within the United States Supreme Court. Much of the legal discussion on colorblindness has focused on the proper way for courts to read the Fourteenth Amendment's Equal Protection Clause in terms of an anti-subordination approach that protects groups by using a race-conscious strategy to remedy the current effects of past discrimination versus an anti-classification approach that adheres to colorblind principles in protecting individuals and treating all forms of discrimination as morally and constitutionally offensive. (This specific incarnation of colorblindness as *constitutional colorblindness* will be discussed further in Chapter 5.) Despite having its origins in *Plessy*, these debates in the public and jurisprudential realms regarding colorblindness did not become salient until the 1970s after *Brown* and the civil rights movement, when there were increasing demands on the State to amend for past wrongs through race-conscious programs such as affirmative action.[20] Therefore, one way to account for its dormancy and surging popularity is as a particular legal and political strategy to get the state out of the business of redistributing opportunities, resources, and wealth to provide remedies to historically disadvantaged racial groups. This account of colorblindness as political backlash has been well made.[21] Yet this is also an account that tends to frame the rise of colorblindness as a conscious practice developed specifically (and perhaps insincerely) to promote Whites' interests. Implicit in this narrative is an argument that advocates of colorblindness are at worst disingenuous in voicing a commitment to racial equality through racial nonrecognition and at best negligent in disregarding the ways in which colorblindness preserves the unequal status relationship between Whites and minorities by transforming the way equality is understood.[22]

But does this explain the intuitive, almost commonsensical appeal of colorblindness to many Americans? How is it that the three aforementioned disassociations, contestable to many on their face, somehow go without much scrutiny when folded under the umbrella of colorblindness? In order to fully understand the cognitive appeal and rationalization of the underlying legal and political claims, we have to take the term itself seriously. Scholars have only briefly discussed colorblindness's linguistic appeal, often in a dismissive manner that reduces it to mere rhetoric—a colorful phrase that is insignificant on its own terms that is used to label a political agenda. Yet this failure to take colorblindness seriously—not only on its own terms but specifically *as a term*—to understand the "work" that it does and how it makes otherwise unthinkable approaches to race thinkable ultimately impoverishes the overall critique of colorblindness and produces an overly deterministic understanding of political mobilization.

More Than Rhetoric: Metaphor's Cognitive Significance

It is well established that language shapes the way we think. Psychologist Lera Boroditsky has shown that people speaking languages that use gendered nouns ascribe masculine and feminine characteristics to inanimate objects. For example, "the word for key is masculine in German and feminine in Spanish. German speakers described keys as hard, heavy, jagged, metal, serrated and useful while Spanish speakers said they were golden, intricate, little, lovely, shiny, and tiny."[23] Similarly, the word for bridge is masculine in Spanish and feminine in German: "German speakers described bridges as beautiful, elegant, fragile, peaceful, pretty, and slender, while Spanish speakers said they were big, dangerous, long, strong, sturdy, and towering."[24]

Metaphors play a particular role in structuring human cognition. The traditional view of metaphors, prevalent among both advocates and critics of colorblindness, is that they are only a matter of figurative language—a mere figure of speech used to convey an idea without saying it literally. The point of metaphors, as literary devices, is to use a known concept to give meaning to an abstract or less tangible thing. Examples include "time is money," which gives substance to the abstract notion of time by comparing it to monetary value that we all appreciate, or "that person is as cold as ice," which conveys a stoic demeanor by comparing the person to a commonly known frozen substance. In this regard, metaphors are common literary tools that play an important role in spicing up the way that we communicate to quickly convey meaning to one another.

This traditional perspective places the utility and influence of metaphors squarely in the realm of language; their persuasiveness and coherence are thought to stem from the wit and eloquence with which they are delivered. But this understanding is becoming highly disfavored, as cognitive scientists have shown how "the locus of metaphor is thought, not language[;] metaphor is a major and indispensible part of our ordinary conventional way of conceptualizing the world[;] and that our everyday behavior reflects our metaphorical understanding of experience."[25] To the extent that "the essence of metaphor is understanding and experiencing one kind of thing in terms of another," metaphors are central to human cognition rather than peripheral speech acts.[26] Metaphors' commonsensical salience—such as an old joke or a stable economy—come from their ability to leverage fundamental aspects of human cognition that enable us to experience intangible concepts through tangible ones to make otherwise abstract concepts seem real. This transfer of materiality can then affect much of how we understand and experience intangibilities in the social world, from boiling anger to sunny happiness.

Thus, metaphors shape human perception of social reality at a deeply cognitive rather than merely textual level. They filter how information is processed and understood, and how reality subjectively appears. Metaphors play upon the underlying architecture of our cognitive systems to give cohesive force to individuals' ability to experience abstract concepts in terms of known tangible entities in a manner that organizes entire thought patterns.[27] Thus, metaphors allow us to seamlessly project one area of experiential knowledge that is directly perceptible to other areas that are merely conceptual or theoretical so as to give them substance.[28] Metaphors allow certain ideas about the world to become thinkable. But how?

This is an area of active research and debate among philosophers, linguists, and neuroscientists. Examining the neural basis of metaphors can help improve our understanding of how language shapes comprehension and the way humans interact with each other. Cognitive functions are typically described as being lateralized, meaning that particular processes are thought to be more heavily active in either the left or right brain hemisphere. Language, in both its literal and figurative incarnations, has traditionally been seen as a left-hemisphere function; early understandings of processing the abstractions embedded in metaphors were thus attributed to this side of the brain.[29] However, there is also a "right hemisphere theory of metaphor processing," suggesting that this hemisphere contributes to how non-literal language is understood. A key study from 1977 showed that patients with right hemisphere brain damage had more difficulty matching metaphors with pictures than those with brain damage to the left hemisphere, which "indicates that an intact left hemisphere does not itself ensure adequate comprehension of all linguistic messages."[30] It has also been shown that patients with damage to the right hemisphere have more difficulty understanding non-literal language and humor.[31] These findings are interesting as the right side of the brain has traditionally been associated with the processing and perception of other concepts, such as emotion.[32] Yet there has been some push back against the specificity of the right hemisphere theory of metaphor processing. Studies have shown that patients with right hemisphere damage had retained dexterity with metaphors, while damage to the left hemisphere is associated with decreased metaphor comprehension.[33] At the same time, studies involving functional magnetic resonance imaging (fMRI) of various parts of the brain—including the dorsolateral prefrontal cortex, the superior temporal gyrus, the middle temporal gyrus, the inferior temporal gyrus, the precuneus, the temporal pole, and the hippocampus—have not shown any statistically significant differences with regard to which brain hemisphere is most responsible for processing metaphors.[34] While much more research is needed, it is becoming increasingly likely that metaphor comprehension occurs bilaterally.

It is difficult to draw any hard and fast conclusions from these hypotheses and (at times) conflicting empirical studies. While these are largely descriptive accounts of the mechanisms underlying metaphor comprehension rather than a substantive account of how these mechanisms produce their persuasive effects, they nonetheless suggest that there is an underlying physiology that shapes metaphor comprehension that explains its salience. This cognitive structure allows attributes from one tangible concept to be persuasively—even unconsciously—mapped onto an intangible concept as a way to understand its character in a manner that is significant beyond the cognition of mere literal language. At the very least, this suggests that the remarkable cognitive framework in place that makes metaphoric reasoning possible and therefore a coherent way to understand the world should give pause to the dismissive manner in which most legal scholars treat colorblindness and other metaphors (see Chapter 5). Without taking metaphors literally, these initial findings suggest that they nonetheless ought to be taken seriously as a *cohesive force in discourse* that can make the otherwise unthinkable thinkable.[35]

The limited point being made through this neuroscientific evidence is simply that metaphors are not merely pretty language. Rather, there are complex neural and cognitive structures that give metaphors meaning and coherence beyond normal language that may uniquely impact and frame daily experiences, making certain ideas plausible and disparate concepts seem reasonable when they otherwise might not. Moreover, this research also substantiates an important yet until now unmade argument: just as the popularity of colorblindness can be partially explained by historical and political contexts, we must also take seriously the *cognitive* context that makes the perceived attributes of blindness seem like an accurate way to understand legal and political commitments to race. In other words, colorblindness by another name might not be quite the same. Given this cognitive context it becomes important to ask, without taking the metaphor literally, about the accuracy of the claims concerning race and blindness embedded in the metaphor. This can help us understand the work that is done when these perceived attributes of race in the blind community are mapped on to our normative commitments to racial justice.

Empirically Destabilizing Colorblindness as a Metaphor

While Justice Harlan is often credited with being the first to use colorblindness as a metaphor to describe the Constitution's normative commitment to racial nonrecognition, he likely borrowed the term from Homer Plessy's attorney, Albion Tourgée. Tourgée wrote in his brief to the Court: "The exemption of nurses shows that the real evil [for authors of the law] lies not in the color of skin but in the relation the colored person sustains to the White. If he is dependent it may be endured; if he is not, his presence is insufferable. Justice is pictured as blind and her daughter, the Law, ought at least be colorblind."[36] Both Harlan and Tourgée use colorblindness as a metaphor to suggest that law should neither make nor enforce status distinctions based upon race, a characteristic that is defined by skin color and other visual traits. Both of their usages work from an assumption that blindness, or the inability to see such visually obvious distinctions, is empowering with regard to notions of formal equality; implicit in their claims is the idea that blind people are unable or unwilling to racially discriminate due to their disability.[37] This is the metaphor's cognitive force: the twin assumptions that (a) race is salient because it is visually obvious and (b) the commonsensical intuition that blind people live pure lives of racial innocence and perfect equality since they are unable to see or react to these otherwise self-evident lines of human difference. As arguably the most salient human sense, the tangibility of vision (and its converse, blindness) as concepts are then metaphorically mapped onto the Constitution's rather intangible conceptions of equality to frame a normative commitment of racial nonrecognition thought to mimic the racial paradise inhabited by blind people. Colorblindness as a metaphor uses the seemingly concrete notions of vision and its absence—blindness—to give substance to the jurisprudence of nonrecognition and a general ethos that law's refusal to "see" race is the purest explication of its commitments to racial equality.

Therefore, the entire concept of colorblindness and its normative claims rest upon a particular understanding of how race actually plays out in the blind community: that it is irrelevant to blind people's day-to-day lives and does not play a significant role in their human interactions. While the social experience of being blind—that is, not having any vision—is not literally the same as the experience of being colorblind—that is, having vision but not being able to properly distinguish colors—the two concepts, in this context, share an overall framing that not being able to visually recognize or distinguish between racial groups—the conceptual and normative thrust behind colorblind claims—fosters racial equality. Indeed, the conceptual and normative appeal of colorblindness are only amplified in the context of blind individuals. For those unable to see racial difference, race is thought to simply be unknowable and meaningless; it is assumed that blind people can only judge people by their character—the racial utopia thought to be the goal of American constitutionalism.

Several sighted respondents from the data reported in Chapter 2 embraced the sentiments behind colorblindness as a metaphor—that blindness produces a diminished understanding of race—as an appropriate if not accurate representation of the role of race in the blind community. For example, when asked whether she thought blind people understood race, Bobbi (a sighted White woman) exclaimed, "Oh I hope not! Wouldn't it be wonderful if nobody knew!" This sentiment echoes colorblindness's normative vision of racial equality through nonrecognition; Bobbi's whimsical aspirations implied a desire to transcend the messy quagmire of race by envisioning a world where race is visually imperceptible. Although she did not use the term *colorblind*, the race utopia that she envisions is premised upon an

understanding of blindness that precludes the possibility of race being significant due to its visual characteristics. It is these types of beliefs that can cognitively prime individuals to buy into colorblindness as a distinctively political
endeavor through a metaphor that leverages the commonsense understanding of race and blindness to give coherence to the jurisprudence and politics
of racial nonrecognition. Sighted White respondent Cassy also shared these
sentiments regarding colorblindness without explicitly mentioning the metaphor in describing why she thought race was not meaningful for blind people: "No, I don't think race is an issue for anybody who looks at somebody
and [can't] see the color. You know what I mean? [Race] is not who they are.
They're not first a Black person; they're first a humanity. That's who they are.
And I think [blind people] are taking [others] at whatever value that human
being is." This draws attention to how the sighted community's commonsense
understandings of race and blindness align with colorblind politics along
another dimension: the idea that not recognizing race allows individuals to
be individuals, which is thought to be the epitome of fairness and equality in
a democracy. Even sighted people with blind children can underestimate the
relevance of race to blind people and allow this misperception to shape their
own normative conclusions. For example, Amanda, a blind White respondent, recalled a moment as an adolescent when she asked her sighted mother
what race she was:

> So, I went home and I asked my mom, just kind of at the dinner table, whether
> I was Black or White, and it was like this big deal. It took her a while to
> respond to me because she seemed really surprised and dumbfounded by it,
> that I would ask that. And then I heard her subsequently telling a lot of her
> friends about how beautiful it was, because I was blind I didn't know the dif-
> ference between Black people and White people, and it meant that I wouldn't
> be prejudiced, that those differences don't really matter, that I care more
> about what's on the inside, blah, blah, blah. And I think now in retrospect,
> because I've grown up and because I've met other blind people and I've also
> had experiences with people that are racist, I do think that it's possible for a
> blind person to develop the same kind of biases that sighted people have about
> members of other groups.

The intuition that blindness precludes a robust understanding of race as an
empirical matter and the politics of racial nonrecognition can mutually reinforce each other *through the metaphor of colorblindness* so as to embolden the

metaphor's cognitive force to make its underlying theory of race and norma-tive claims seem rational and unproblematic. This is not to suggest that this common understanding of blind people's racial experiences directly underlie the broader social, political, and legal discourse on colorblindness. The color-blindness phenomenon is much richer than this.[38] But this does highlight the attraction of colorblind rhetoric in terms of how individuals can read their own racial fantasies through other people's disabilities. From this perspective, blind people are seen as *better off* in some limited sense by not having to deal with race.

But in light of the findings presented in Chapters 2 and 3, the data make clear that this implicit claim about race and blindness giving rise to the color-blind metaphor's cognitive force and its intuitive appeal are simply indefen-sible as an empirical matter. Not only do blind people have the same visual understanding of race as their sighted peers, but this visual understanding of race also shapes their daily interactions as it does for sighted individuals. Visual understandings of race do not stem from their obviousness as much as they do from the social practices that shape the way we think about race. Moreover, the data also show that blind people's perspectives on the color-blind ideal often contradict the way their disability is leveraged by portions of the sighted community to portray them and their experiences as indicative of a racial utopia facilitated by a literal blindness that can be replicated through importing the colorblind metaphor into social, political, and legal discourses. Blind respondent Allison confirms this idea:

> A lot of sighted people like to think that because we can't see skin color, race doesn't matter to us. That's kind of a misconception that runs out there that if we can't see it, we can't judge by it. That's false because I definitely know blind people that do. So yeah, I do think that it's definitely an issue in the blindness community that most of the time the public thinks that it isn't, because they think that race doesn't matter to us.

Kip, another blind respondent, offered this perspective, arguing directly against colorblindness as a term that reflects blind people's experiences: "I definitely don't want to self-identify as being colorblind towards race because I think that would just be very ignorant on my part. I understand that there are differences between people and if I wanted to deny that, I would either be lying through my teeth or I would, in my mind, be pretty stupid." Ken-nedy, also a blind respondent, similarly objected to the ideas underlying colorblindness, particularly the notion that blind people only judge people by their character: "Some people think that blind people, you know, they can't see with their eyes, so they feel with their heart, and they think they don't judge people by their race, but you know what, we [do]." Some blind respondents, like Jack, acknowledged that sometimes "it's an asset to be blind and not judge someone visually right off the top of your head. So many of my sighted friends looking at someone and just judging the person immediately. I really have no way of doing that." But, this draws attention to how blindness might delay rather than preclude blind people's ability to apprehend race without making their substantive understanding of it any different from that of their sighted peers. In the end, Gerry provides the most comprehensive articulation of why the colorblind emperor, despite its intuitive appeal, has no clothes:

> Race probably plays just as important [a] part for blind people as it does for others. I wish we could be the societal model that would show every society who gives a damn how to be colorblind. But I don't think we can. Because there's a whole lot more to race than what's visually observed. We built [race] around whether it's there or not. And we can't live in a world without knowing all of this unless you're also blind and cognitively impaired.

The empirical data presented in this book begin to destabilize the coherence of colorblindness as both a metaphor and a normative aspiration. To the extent that colorblindness's metaphorical salience depends upon a seemingly tangible and intuitive claim about race and vision that has now been shown to be empirically inaccurate, the metaphor should simply be retired from social, legal, and political thought. This draws attention to the fragility and incoherence of a colorblind jurisprudence based upon a theory of racial nonrecognition that itself is confounded by the constitutive theory of race emanating out of this research. This crystallizes, from a different direction, a claim made by other scholars of race and colorblindness: that anti-classification approaches to Equal Protection further entrench racial subordination by failing to deal with the social, historical, political, and economic dimensions of inequality that can be overcome only through race-conscious remedies.

Colorblindness as a metaphor and the policy choices it supports must also be retired because they are offensive to blind people. The coherence and depth of this misperception concerning blind people's relationship to race is tied to long-standing stereotypes about blindness conferring superordinate powers.[39] In effect, colorblindness as a metaphor turns blind people into racial mascots in much the same way that some sports teams demean Native Americans by misappropriating their imagery and social experience. A distorted, misunderstood, and objectified understanding of group abilities and social dynamics is celebrated as a rallying cry at the very same time that it dehumanizes the group by denying full acknowledgment of their complex lives. Colorblindness has turned blind people against their will into a series of cartoonish representations of a racial utopia that fundamentally warps their human experiences. Tammy, a White blind respondent, discusses this further:

> People are always trying to make all these statements about how nonjudgmental the blind are. . . . People don't see me as an imperfect being, and that's how I want to be seen, imperfect and flawed, because the rest of the world is imperfect and flawed. That someone is seeing blindness as this utopia, as inspiration and nonjudgmental, that's such a horrible place to be stuck in. I hate it. And its not even real.

Empirically Destabilizing Metaphors: Why It Matters

Metaphors are a common aspect of law and legal reasoning; liens are held, law has a voice, and corporations are conceived as bodies, to name a few. But visual metaphors hold a special place for filtering the relationship between law and society. University of Pittsburgh law professor Bernard Hibberts notes:

> [Law] has long favored visual metaphors. We frequently consider law as a matter of looking: we "observe" it; we evaluate claims "in the eye of the law," our high courts "review" the decisions of inferior tribunals. Alternatively, we speak of law as something one would usually look at: it is a "body," a "text," a "structure," a "bulwark of freedom," a "seamless web," and even a "magic mirror." We identify particular legal concepts with striking visual images: property rights are a "bundle of sticks;" a long-standing constitutional principle is a "fixed star"; a sequence of ownership is a "chain of title." We associate legal reasoning with the manipulation of visible geometric forms: we try to "square" precedents with one another; we repeatedly agonize over "where the line [between different doctrines and situations] can be drawn." We discuss legality in terms of light and darkness: we search for "bright-line" tests; we consider an area of concurrent jurisdiction to be a "zone of twilight"; we seek to extend constitutional protections by probing the shadowy "penumbras" of

well-known guarantees. With the aid of metaphor, we go so far as to give law the visual quality of hue: we make a property claim under "color of title"; we discourage "yellow dog" contracts and make securities trading subject to "blue sky" laws; for good or ill, we frequently adhere to "black letter" rules.[40]

Given this emphasis on vision, it is not surprising that a visual metaphor like colorblindness would catch the legal imagination in coming to characterize claims on how to understand law's normative commitments. Indeed, the legal commitments associated with visual metaphors such as blindness are embodied in the iconic image of law in Western civilization—Lady Justice (see Figure 13). In their exhaustive study of the many representations of Lady Justice and their cultural significance, Judith Resnik and Dennis Curtis note:

> Throughout the twentieth century and into the twenty-first, Justice imagery has been used on government buildings and in representations of political personages in magazine articles, newspapers, advertisements, and cartoons. These various deployments all rely on the fact that we (people living in Europe, North and South America, Africa, Australia, and Asia) can "read" them. We recognize an oddly dressed woman with her various attributes (scales, sword, and sometimes a blindfold) as representing or referring to law and justice. Designers of contemporary courts, purveyors of goods and services, and cartoon artists know that placing this figure in front of their building or on a placard prompts viewers to make an immediate association with law. This linkage of state power with Justice images spans continents and differently constituted polities.[41]

While the presence and meaning of Lady Justice's vision has shifted over time, her blindfold has come to represent law's impartiality, objectivity, and fairness in a manner that allows colorblindness as a metaphor to have a strong resonance and normative appeal.[42] It becomes remarkably easy to think that if law is conceptualized and personified as blind to symbolize intolerance for unduly privileging or burdening any party, then surely law should also be colorblind with regard to not giving preferences to or discriminating against litigants due to their race.

But the problem with metaphors used in a legal capacity is that the cognitive force that they carry in persuading individuals to conceptualize intangible concepts in terms of tangible ones can distort, obscure, and oversimplify human experiences in a manner that can smooth over injustices that otherwise would

FIGURE 13. A common modern depiction of Lady Justice, blindfolded and with scales. © H. ARMSTRONG ROBERTS/ClassicStock/Corbis.

not be tolerated. Not all metaphors are created the same or run this risk in terms of their social impact. But some can grease the cognitive wheels in a manner that can corrupt deeper sensibilities concerning law's commitment to justice.

A new line of experimental research in linguistics is demonstrating this point. Lera Boroditsky and colleagues have examined how different metaphorical systems regarding crime can lead to people having fundamentally different ways of thinking about solving social problems.[43] Their experiment involved exposing participants to descriptions of otherwise neutral crime reports that were embedded with language either describing crime as a predator (stalking victims, hiding in shadows, etc.) or as a virus (an infection that spreads, risk factors that lead to disease, a containable problem, etc.).[44] They found that "when crime was compared to a virus, participants were more likely to suggest reforming the social environment of the infected community. When crime was compared to a predator, participants were more likely to suggest attacking the problem head on—hiring more police officers and building jails."[45] The authors also note that these experimental results

> suggest that metaphors can influence how people conceptualize and in turn hope to solve important social issues. It appears that even casually encountering one metaphor or another in discourse about crime can lead people to unwittingly propose different types of solutions for the crime problem. Importantly, it appears that the metaphors had a subconscious effect on people's reasoning. Very few of our participants thought that the metaphors influenced their crime-reducing suggestion.[46]

This is rather remarkable experimental evidence of how metaphors matter in shaping policy preferences and notions of justice. But there are also real life examples of how metaphors may unwittingly affect policy preferences in a manner that erodes civil liberties and social justice. Take the common metaphor in criminal forensics that "DNA is a gold standard" for identifying individuals that have committed crimes.[47] This metaphor is often used to suggest the virtual infallibility of criminal identification techniques that use DNA testing. Although the gold standard is no longer "the gold standard" in terms of defining monetary value, the term has a deep cultural resonance to convey a standard for excellence, that is, the best there is or possibly could be.[48] The association of the gold standard metaphor with DNA forensics is part of society's fascination with DNA as a "cultural icon, a symbol, almost a magical force," leading few to question the use of DNA forensic techniques to identify perpetrators.[49]

But in light of efforts at the federal and state level to radically expand DNA databases to include larger portions of the population, there is increasing evidence that the gold standard metaphor is obscuring a remarkable amount of tarnish that can lead to injustice. For example, the expansion of DNA databases is based upon the idea that it is nearly impossible for an innocent person to be falsely implicated in a crime, since no two people share the same genetic profile. Scientists examining database profiles typically look at thirteen areas on a chromosome called loci; matching a known and unknown sample at all thirteen regions is thought to be a full match in identifying a suspect, and some experts have argued that partial matches at nine or more loci are enough to determine someone's identity.[50] Yet data from Arizona's state DNA databases (containing over sixty-five thousand profiles at the time) showed that 122 pairs of profiles matched at nine loci, twenty at ten loci, and two pairs (each siblings) matched at eleven and twelve.[51] Maryland's database, with more than thirty thousand profiles, reportedly showed similar oddities, with thirty-two pairs matching at nine loci and three at thirteen; Illinois's database reportedly had 903 pairs matching at nine or more loci out of 220,000 profiles.[52] How is this possible, if DNA profiles matching at nine or more loci are supposedly unique? If DNA databases are part of this gold standard, how can there be such substantial confusion? No one quite knows, due in large part to federal and state governments' refusal to allow independent researchers to study these databases.[53] But there is evidence that this imprecision, obscured by metaphors of infallibility, may lead to innocent people being convicted of crimes they had nothing to do with.[54] And with the push to enact new laws to expand DNA databases by lowering the bar for inclusion—DNA databases were originally reserved for those convicted of heinous crimes and now in some states include those merely arrested for misdemeanors—more people are at risk of being on the short end of having their profiles coincidentally match evidence that may implicate them in a crime they did not commit.

This concern regarding the way that metaphors like gold standard can create the conditions for unjust outcomes is not simply theoretical. The case of John Puckett provides an instructive example. Puckett, a seventy-year-old disabled man, was arrested in 2005 for murdering a San Francisco woman in 1977. The case lay stagnant for decades until investigators ran the crime scene evidence against California's DNA database, which turned up a "cold hit" that partially matched Puckett's profile at 5½ loci. Given the decades in between the murder and the arrest, DNA provided the most significant evidence against Puckett. Jurors were told that there was a slim probability—1 in 1.1 million—that a randomly selected Caucasian-American would have this profile, implying that the link to Puckett was unlikely to be coincidental.[55] No other evidence connected Puckett to the crime, and he was convicted of murder based largely on this statistical claim. This points to a debate about whether population figures should be used as a reference point in calculating these statistics (as they were in the Puckett case) or the number of profiles in the relevant database. The problem in using population figures as a reference point is explained by William C. Thompson, professor of criminology, law, and society at the University of California, Irvine:

> Suppose that a partial DNA profile from a crime scene occurs with a frequency of 1 in 10 million in the general population. If this profile is compared to a single innocent suspect, the probability of a coincidental match is only 1 in 10 million. . . . By contrast, when searching through a database as large as the FBI's National DNA Index System (NDIS), which reportedly contains nearly 6 million profiles, there are literally millions of opportunities to find a match by coincidence. Even if everyone in the database is innocent, there is a substantial probability that one (or more) will have the 1-in-10 million profile. Hence, a match obtained in a database search might very well be coincidental.[56]

If the size of the database is taken into account in Puckett's case—a practice recommended by expert committees convened by the FBI and National Research Council but rarely followed—the probability that the database has at least one profile that might coincidentally match the crime scene evidence if the assailant's profile is not present becomes 1 in 3.[57] The Court only allowed the jury to hear the 1 in 1.1 million figure, and Puckett was convicted of first-degree murder. Afterward, when asked if the 1-in-3 statistic would have changed anything, juror Joe Deluca told the *Los Angeles Times,* "Of course it would have changed things. It would have changed a lot of things."[58]

The possible injustices lying behind DNA forensic techniques are concealed, in part, by culturally embedded metaphors that overstate its accuracy to give coherence to policing practices and prosecutorial conduct that might otherwise be deemed objectionable. The significance of the data from the state databases, along with examples like the prosecution of John Puckett, provide empirical and anecdotal evidence that can chip away at the cognitive force of "gold standard" metaphors. The language and metaphors of DNA forensics have justified the enactment of remarkable new policies that radically expand the size and inclusion criteria for DNA databases, all under the theories that (a) the more people in the pool, the more likely the police are to catch the right criminal, and (b) if you have not done anything wrong, you have nothing to worry about since the chance of being falsely implicated is infinitely small. But the empirical data and the questions they raise are leading increasing numbers of scientists, journalists, and advocates to challenge not only DNA databases as a technology, but the politics underneath this technology's growth.

Just as these empirical data points provide a foothold for cognitive (and therefore legal and political) pushback in DNA forensics to resist the commonsensical acceptance promoted by "gold standard" metaphors, so too can empirical data on blind people's visual understanding of race provide a foothold to push back on the colorblind metaphor that rationalizes injustices regarding the way law understands its commitments to racial equality. In both cases, empirical methods provide entrée to destabilizing the cognitive force behind these metaphors that give their underlying politics and perspectives undue salience. This creates opportunities for oppositional accounts that reflect the empirical realities of groups and individuals in furtherance of social and racial justice. The empirical findings in Part 1 allow our faculties of human reason to resist the implicit cognitive appeal of the colorblind metaphor and to deeply question the politics of nonrecognition that it supports. Therefore, destabilizing metaphors is a way to destabilize the logic of injustice and oppression.

The ongoing need for this empirical engagement with colorblindness as a metaphor and the logic it engenders can be seen in two recent Supreme Court cases. In *Parents Involved in Community Schools v. Seattle School District No. 1*, the Court held that using race to assign students to various schools for the purpose of racial integration and balancing violated Equal Protection. *Parents Involved* was decided together with *Meredith v. Jefferson County Board of Education*, whereby both cases involved plaintiffs that were part of a public school system that apportioned slots at desirable campuses through race-conscious efforts designed to promote diversity across the system by balancing the proportion of White and minority children in each school. The Court notes that "the plans are tied to each district's specific racial demographics," thus working from a theory of diversity that children's education improves when classroom demographics mirror community demographics.[59] The Court rejected this approach.[60] In a second case, from 2009, *Ricci v. DeStefano*, firefighters brought Title VII and Equal Protection claims against the City of New Haven for doing away with an examination for promotion since the results showed that Whites systematically outperformed Blacks; the defendants argued that basing promotions on these test results could expose the city to a disparate-impact lawsuit. In reaching only the Title VII claims, the Court held in favor of the White plaintiffs: "All the evidence demonstrates that the City chose not to certify the examination results because of the statistical disparity based on race—i.e., how minority candidates had performed when compared to white candidates. . . . Without some other justification, this express, race-based decisionmaking violates Title VII's command that employers cannot take adverse employment actions because of an individual's race."[61] The decisions in both cases are steeped deeply in a jurisprudence of nonrecognition—where states cannot use race-conscious efforts to ameliorate racial inequality—that is given coherence by a visual understanding of race that underlies colorblindness's three disassociations. Both *Parents Involved* and *Ricci* reflect a *disassociation of race from its social significance* by their failure to appreciate how socially constructed meanings that attach to race can still impact decision making in education and employment that can be mitigated by race-conscious efforts that increase minority representation. The decisions blur the social benefits of diversity by obscuring the ongoing social significance of race. Both holdings also demonstrate a *disassociation of race from its group dynamics*, whereby the discussion on discrimination is framed almost entirely in terms of individuals as opposed to the asymmetrical power relations that continue to make racial groupings significant. Lastly, the decisions reflect a *disassociation with the racial history and inertia of social structure* that produce the underrepresentation of minorities in desirable schools and promoted officers in fire departments. These three disassociations gain coherence through the colorblind metaphor and its logic in a manner that allows the Court to see the predominantly White plaintiffs' claims of discrimination in both cases as being morally and legally equivalent to racial minorities' discriminatory experiences. This produces a distorted application of Equal Protection and Title VII to protect the interests of the White majority in a manner that would have been incoherent decades before—despite substantial empirical evidence of persistent White privilege and discrimination against racial minorities with regard to educational and career advancement. Thus, just as colorblindness produces a racial logic that allows *Guess Who* to seem like a reasonable remake of the racial discourse in *Guess Who's Coming to Dinner,* so too does colorblindness produce a jurisprudential logic that reframes race as a socially insignificant, individual, and ahistorical trait with zero-sum sensibilities; race-conscious efforts to assist minorities are thought to specifically burden Whites and are thus morally and legally reprehensible. Similar to *Guess*

Who's reincarnation of Sidney Poitier as Ashton Kutcher, colorblindness operates in *Parents Involved* and *Ricci* to reframe Whites as the new Blacks; previous Equal Protection and Title VII claims asserted by Blacks in a socio-historical context of racial subordination are now framed as morally and legally equivalent to the claims of racial discrimination made by Whites, who, as a group, still enjoy remarkable advantages. This discourse is exemplified by Chief Justice Roberts at the end of his plurality opinion in *Parents Involved:* "Before *Brown,* schoolchildren were told where they could and could not go to school based on the color of their skin. The school districts in these cases have not carried the heavy burden of demonstrating that we should allow this once again. . . . The best way to stop discrimination on the basis of race is to stop discriminating on the basis of race."[62] Framing the harm in *Brown v. Board of Education* as morally and, at least in part, legally equivalent to the alleged harm in *Parents Involved* would be unthinkable without the cognitive work of the colorblind metaphor and its surrounding politics, which can ultimately warp commitments to social and racial justice. Therefore, the importance of empirically destabilizing this metaphor lies in the ability of empirical data to undermine the cross domain reasoning of the conceptual system that falsely maps what is perceived as blind people's nonrecognition of race onto a broader normative understanding of the Court's application of constitutional law and statutory rules. Using empirical data to destabilize this understanding of race draws attention back to the significance of social practices that produce the visual salience of race that cannot be transcended by simply becoming proverbial ostriches with our heads stuck into the ground. The emphasis on social practices and their cognitive impact on what we see promotes a conversation on engaging with these forces, which runs directly against a jurisprudence of nonrecognition. This is more than just a straw man exercise of showing that one domain does not literally apply to another. Rather, it is a way to intervene in an entrenched, damaging, and unjust thought process that nonrecognition of race leads to racial equality.

This intervention allows us to see how colorblindness uses an empirically inaccurate metaphor to make certain ideas about race that bear no relation to the real world seem rational and appropriate. That is the power of metaphor as a filter for how we see the world. The empirical data discussed in Part 1 help us see how colorblindness perpetrates a fraud on the American public in furtherance of racial subordination. We must therefore not only reject the language of colorblindness, but also the politics and jurisprudence that it supports.

5   Race, Vision, and Equal Protection

RACE SPECTACLES ARE NOT UNIQUE TO MODERN TALES SUCH AS those involving LeBron James, Oscar Grant, Rodney King, or even O. J. Simpson. Rather, the media-infused race melodrama is as American as apple pie and has been deeply rooted in social relations for quite some time. One of the more famous iterations from the early twentieth century came out of what seems like a relatively modest dispute: a marriage annulment. But the trial and outcome would characterize American race relations for years to come.

Leonard Rhinelander, the socialite son of a wealthy New York family, met Alice Jones through her sister Grace in the Fall of 1921, and the couple quickly became quite fond of each other. On at least two occasions during their first few months together, the couple—Alice, then twenty-two, four years Leonard's senior—secluded themselves in New York City hotels where they were intimate.[1] Over the next few years, Leonard took several extended trips at his father's request that separated the couple, but they remained in touch through frequent letters proclaiming their love for one another. Leonard returned to New York in May 1924, and the couple secretly married that October, as Leonard's family was none too fond of the former Miss Jones. The couple lived in secret with Alice's family for about a month, until the story hit the *New Rochelle Standard Star* titled: *Rhinelanders' Son Marries the Daughter of a Colored Man.*[2] Thus, a wealthy White man from 1920s New York high society committed one of the biggest social faux pas one could imagine at the time: marrying a Black woman.

Alice was the biracial daughter of an English mother and a father described as "a bent, dark complexioned man who is bald, except for a fringe of curly white hair" (see Figure 14).[3] A few days after the story broke, Leonard was shown a copy of Alice's birth certificate; it said she was Black. Less than a week later, Leonard filed suit for an annulment.[4] The reason? Fraud: Leonard alleged that Alice misrepresented that she was not colored to trick him into marrying her. The stage was now set for what some might characterize as (up until then) the race trial of the century: a legal determination of whether Alice committed fraud by "passing" as White or if Leonard knew Alice's race before their marriage. The questions at the center of the trial became, what did Leonard know and, more importantly, what *should* he have known?

The early twentieth century was a time of transition in social and legal understandings of race. *Rhinelander v. Rhinelander* was far from the first case in which a person's racial background was litigated. Legal historian Ariela Gross has painstakingly documented racial determination trials in the South during the antebellum era, when courts were used as a forum to resolve disputes concerning an individual's race.[5] She shows the variety of evidence used during this period to "prove" someone's race, including one's performance: "doing things white men or women did became the law's working definition of what it meant to be white, . . . [which] operated in a law-like fashion [to prescribe] certain rules of behavior for people of different races."[6] This was linked to early notions of biological race, in that "white blood" and "black blood" were thought to steer individuals' behavior and social performances. Thus, as Gross notes, "while the essence of white identity might have been white 'blood,' because blood could not be transparently known, the evidence that mattered most was evidence about the way people acted out their true nature."[7]

But by the turn of the century, notions of race determination were evolving. Two cases decided by the United States Supreme Court shortly before the Rhinelander trial highlight these changes. In *Ozawa v. United States*, Takao Ozawa (a person of Japanese ancestry) claimed that he was White under U.S. naturalization laws, in part because he had White skin. In a 1922 decision, the Supreme Court rejected this understanding of Whiteness as it related to naturalization: "The test afforded by the mere color of the skin of each individual is impracticable" and instead defined Whiteness by "what is popularly known as the Caucasian race."[8] The Court "ran together the rationales of common knowledge, evident in the reference to what was 'popularly known,'

FIGURE 14. Alice Jones with her mother and father. © Bettmann/CORBIS.

and scientific evidence, exemplified in the Court's reliance on the term 'Caucasian.' "[9] But three months later, in *United States v. Thind*, the Court took a different direction, one that moved away from the science of racial typologies and toward common knowledge, emphasizing the visual obviousness of one's racial membership. Bhagat Singh Thind, an Indian man, claimed to be eligible for naturalization since he fit the scientific categorization of Aryan, or Caucasian. The Court rejected this claim, emphasizing the visual cues associated with race as the primary determinant: "It is a matter of *familiar observation* and knowledge that the physical group characteristics of the Hindus render them *readily distinguishable* from the various groups of persons in this country commonly recognized as white"[10] (emphasis added).

Thus, the 1925 Rhinelander trial happened at a moment when law and society were struggling to define how to determine someone's race. These shifting notions of race determination do not mean that biological race was wholly discredited, as this very same time period marked the growth of the eugenics movement. Rather, they indicate that outward physical cues such as skin color were thought to reflect inherent biological differences (in ability, aptitude, etc.) that explained different group outcomes and justified racial hierarchy. Nevertheless, this shifting emphasis turned the specific legal question of whether Alice committed fraud in concealing her race into a broader race spectacle concerning race relations and the illicit crossing of racial boundaries.[11] This, in part, explains the front page coverage of the trial in the *New York Times* and other major newspapers, leading Alice to be for a "brief 14-month period . . . the most talked about, read-about, maligned Negro woman in American history."[12]

This tension between the blood, biology, and science of race on one hand and race as a self-evidently known visual trait on the other was reflected in the strategies of Alice's and Leonard's attorneys. The strategy developed by Isaac Mills, Leonard's attorney, portrayed him as mentally challenged and Alice's physical features as racially indeterminate. Given this racial uncertainty and Leonard's alleged cognitive disability, Mills claimed that the hypersexed nature of Alice's Blackness—a direct nod toward "black blood" producing certain behaviors—was able to aggressively take hold of Leonard and perpetrate a fraud against him. Mills argued: "She had him so, as I said in my opening [address], that he did not know Black from White, that he did not know or have control of himself," leading the biological substrate of a visually indeterminate Blackness to manifest itself through the aggressive sexuality then thought to be inherent to Black women.[13] The defense from Alice's counsel, Lee Parsons Davis, was quite simple: there was no fraud as Alice's Blackness was visually obvious. Davis mockingly said to the jury:

> I think the issue that Mills should have presented to you was not mental unsoundness but blindness. Blindness. . . . You are here to determine whether Alice Rhinelander before her marriage told this man Rhinelander that she was white and had no colored blood. You are here to determine next whether or not that fooled him. Whether or not he could not see with his own eyes that he was marrying into a colored family.[14]

After raising serious doubts about Leonard having a cognitive disability, much of Davis's defense rested on showing that Alice's race could be obviously known by simply looking at her body. This became a central theme in Davis's argument; he repeatedly asked Alice and her sisters to stand up and show the jury their hands and arms. But to hammer home this point, Davis wanted the jury to see all of Alice's body—not just hands and arms that might darken over time with routine exposure to sunlight. Given the couple's pre-marital sexual relations, Davis argued that Leonard had seen all of Alice before being married, and that it was crucial for the jury to see the same intimate details of Alice's body that Leonard did before marrying her. Against objections from Leonard's attorneys, the judge allowed it. And what transpired was one of the biggest race spectacles of the twentieth century (see Figure 15). From the Court record:

> The Court, Mr. Mills, Mr. Davis, Mr. Swinburne, the jury, the plaintiff, the defendant, her mother, George Jones, and the stenographer left the courtroom and entered the jury room. The defendant and Mrs. Jones then withdrew to the lavatory adjoining the jury room and, after a short time, again entered the jury room. The defendant, who was weeping, had on her underwear and a long coat. At Mr. Davis' direction she let down her coat, so that the upper portion of her body, as far down to her breast, was exposed. She then, again at Mr. Davis' direction, covered the upper part of her body and showed the jury her bare legs, up as far as her knees. The Court, counsel, the jury, and the plaintiff then re-entered the courtroom.[15]

This dramatic revealing of Alice's body to the jury, composed entirely of White married men, was stunning, especially for 1920s sensibilities. Once back in the courtroom, Davis asked Leonard: "Your wife's body is the same

FIGURE 15. Composite photograph of Alice Rhinelander revealing herself to the jury, which appeared in the New York Graphic, November 25, 1925. New York Graphic.

shade as it was when you saw her in the Marie Antoinette [hotel] with all of her clothing removed? Leonard responded affirmatively, to which Davis said, "That is all."[16]

Shortly after this display of Alice's body to the jury and Leonard's acknowledgment, the jury returned with a verdict in favor of Alice, finding that there was no fraud. To put a finer point on this: an all-White male jury in 1925 ruled against a wealthy White male socialite and in favor of a working-class Black woman because her race was found to be so obvious and self-evident that there could have been no deception. At a historical moment when theories of racial determination concerning blood and vision were competing in many regards, the jury found that Alice's body, and race in general, visually spoke for itself. Alice did not have to take the stand at any point during the trial. Her body, and the jury's ability to observe it, was all of the evidence that was necessary.

*   *   *

This idea that race visually speaks for itself—a notion that I call *"race" ipsa loquitur*—is not something that is marginally relevant to law, or an idea that pops up occasionally in cases such as *Rhinelander v. Rhinelander*. Rather, this notion that race is not only visually obvious but that its social salience, perceptibility, and visual significance stem from self-evident distinctions fundamentally shapes law's most robust mechanism for governing race and remedying racial injustice: Equal Protection. This dynamic can be seen in three areas of Equal Protection jurisprudence. The first is the court's scrutiny inquiry, or its determination of the analysis it will apply—strict scrutiny, intermediate scrutiny, or rational basis review—to individuals claiming to be the victim of an Equal Protection violation. Strict scrutiny (in which the state faces the highest bar to justify the use of explicit categorizations) is typically (though not exclusively) reserved for groups targeted by race and ethnicity, while laws targeting groups for other reasons are generally afforded lower forms of scrutiny and are more likely to pass constitutional muster.[17] While the court uses a few factors to determine which groups deserve heightened protections from burdensome classifications, the visibility of the trait that defines group membership plays a crucial role; racial minorities have become the model group deserving the strongest protections due in large part to the visual salience of group-defining difference: skin color and phenotypical characteristics. These groups are thought to deserve stronger protections because the discrimination that they face is based upon characteristics they have no control over and cannot be concealed. But given the findings in Part 1 of this book, how should we understand law's continued reliance on the idea that the salience of race stems from it being visually self-evident and obvious, when the empirical evidence suggests that this visual salience is socially produced rather than merely observed?

"Race" ipsa loquitur also shapes Equal Protection jurisprudence through the theories used to understand the scope of the Court's remedial powers. As discussed in the preceding chapter, colorblind ideologies have altered normative commitments to racial justice in law and public policy. In this chapter, I take a closer look at how the notion of *constitutional colorblindness*, as a specific articulation of colorblind ideology, has influenced this area of Equal Protection doctrine—all through an underlying logic perpetuated by the idea that race is salient because it is visually self-evident.

The third aspect of Equal Protection jurisprudence shaped by the *"race" ipsa loquitur* trope is the intent doctrine. This is a critical area where the court has held that in order for plaintiffs to demonstrate an Equal Protection violation, they must be able to show that the defendant *specifically intended* to discriminate against the person making the claim. This rule has limited the reach and scope of Equal Protection in devastating ways; outside of the most egregious and most blatant situations, it is nearly impossible to prove that any one actor specifically intended to discriminate against another person because of racial animus. But, the very idea that race operates in such a discrete manner is linked to an understanding that race is salient because it is visually obvious: a person with racial animus who looks out into the world sees an objectively knowable and visually self-evident racial difference that brings that animus to the forefront, and then discriminates according to this visual engagement. But the consciousness and discreteness implied by and embedded in the intent doctrine can be critiqued by the empirical evidence offered in Part 1 in a manner that may lead us to rethink the utility of this approach.

By examining these three areas of Equal Protection law, we can tease out the extent to which Equal Protection's race jurisprudence, as a whole, is driven by a particular theory of race: that its salience and therefore its significance in law and society comes from its visual obviousness. This illuminates a larger question: what are the implications when the theory of race distilled from this doctrinal analysis—that race is salient precisely because it is self-evident—is incongruent with empirical findings showing that the salience of race is socially produced rather than merely observed? If we take the empirical evidence discussed in Part 1 seriously and put it in conversation with the theory of race embedded in Equal Protections jurisprudence, it suggests that the current emphasis on race as a self-evident trait may warp Equal Protection inquiries by framing discrimination as something that starts with visual perception rather than the social practices that shape our visual sensibilities to make looking a certain way possible. This emphasis on visibility may prematurely exclude other groups facing discrimination from appropriate legal remedies, promote questionable normative theories to understand the boundaries of Equal Protection remedies and give rise to an analysis that farcically focuses on intent. It may also produce an impoverished understanding of racial discrimination that ultimately disserves racial minorities and inhibits any true efforts at creating a just society. Thus, putting the theory of race distilled by the doctrinal critique in conversation with the comparative empirical evidence concerning sighted and blind people's understanding of race destabilizes ideas about the salience of race simply being visually obvious and highlights its socially productive aspects. In all, the empirical research opens up alternative doctrinal possibilities for Equal Protection that can be reoriented around social practices rather than a presumption that race is salient for self-evident reasons.

"Race" Ipsa Loquitur and Equal Protection Doctrine

The Fourteenth Amendment to the United States Constitution was ratified in 1868 as part of an effort designed to transition the United States from a society that tolerated slavery to one in which all individuals enjoyed full citizenship and legal rights.[18] Section 1 notes: "No state shall . . . deny to any person within its jurisdiction the equal protection of the laws." Known as the Equal Protection Clause, its meaning, scope, and application have been a major subject for modern discussions concerning race and racism.

There is a long and extensive literature well told elsewhere on the origins of the Equal Protection Clause, its initial ambitions, and its evolution since its inception following the Civil War. While its initial purpose was to extend legal protections to newly freed slaves, Equal Protection evolved in the twentieth century to embrace a broader mandate: to provide more substantive legal protections to minority groups that may suffer from irrational forms of prejudice that cannot be remedied through the political process. The conceptual and doctrinal foundations of this transition began in the 1930s with *United States v. Carolene Products*—a rather pedestrian case concerning the interstate shipment of filled milk. Nevertheless, Justice Stone offered language in footnote four of this opinion that initiated Equal Protection's modern evolution to speak to failures in the political process that may foster forms of discrimination against minority groups that run counter to the spirit of the Fourteenth Amendment. Justice Stone wrote that the Court's standard of review may be stricter for laws "directed at particular religious or national or racial minorities . . . [since] *prejudice against discrete and insular minorities* may be a special condition, which tends seriously to curtail the operation of those political processes ordinarily to be relied upon to protect minorities."[19]

Former Supreme Court Justice Lewis F. Powell Jr. called this "the most celebrated footnote in constitutional law" in recognition of the seismic shifts it precipitated in the doctrinal and scholarly interpretation of Equal Protection.[20] Footnote four drew attention to how failed political processes may expose minority groups to forms of discrimination that belie any reasonable understanding of the Constitution's guarantee of Equal Protection of the laws. If minority or disempowered groups are subject to the prejudicial whims of majoritarian lawmaking that systematically exclude them from democratic processes, does this not require some type of judicial intervention? In light of these difficulties, footnote four suggests that the courts should interpret Equal Protection in a manner that gives greater protections to certain minorities. This protection does not extend to all minority groups; by definition, some political minorities must lose in a democratic society. Rather, Justice Stone suggests a certain type of sensitivity to minorities that are discrete and insular.

But what does this mean? Louis Lusky, who was Justice Stone's law clerk when *Carolene Products* was decided and is thought to be footnote four's author, provided some insight:

> As a matter of language, "discrete" means separate or distinct and "insular" means isolated or detached. The words do not describe aliens as such; many of them, who are Anglophones *pass unnoticed*, and many if not most others fit into the social scene with little difficulty. . . . In my opinion, the phrase "discrete and insular" applies to groups that are not embraced within the bond of community kinship but are held at arm's length by the group or groups that possess dominant political and economic power. . . . Justice Stone, I believe, would have agreed.[21] [emphasis added]

To the extent that Lusky juxtaposes "discrete and insular" to the ability to pass unnoticed and easily "fit" within society, one can reasonably conclude that Lusky (and, by inference, Justice Stone) was primarily concerned with groups with seemingly immutable traits that lead them to stand out in a manner that can generate irrational hostility, making these groups easy targets for discrimination. Thus, the inability to pass unnoticed—a rather direct nod to the visibility of groups' defining traits—is at the center of this turn in Equal Protection's modern development.

From this we can see how Equal Protection's transition from being primarily concerned with *slave status* to a minority experience warped by a failed political process was, from the very beginning, infused by the idea that race as a particularly salient category of human difference should be a special concern to the Court due to it being a visually obvious trait marking a minority existence. This jurisprudence may have developed this way for the understandably pragmatic reasons of providing a tool for the Court to protect minority groups facing the wrath of state-sponsored discrimination. Nevertheless, this

idea of race being visually self-evident—that is, salient, striking, and potentially divisive on its own terms—has become embedded in Equal Protection
jurisprudence in at least three different ways: the scrutiny inquiry, theories of
constitutional colorblindness, and the intent doctrine.

Equal Protection's Scrutiny Inquiry

Roughly a decade before the Supreme Court's decision in *Brown v. Board of
Education*, the idea that the Court should understand Equal Protection as providing stronger judicial oversight for minority groups made its first appearance in the main body of a Supreme Court opinion in *Korematsu v. United
States*—a 1944 case concerning the constitutionality of Japanese internment
during World War II. The Court wrote: "All legal restrictions which curtail
the civil rights of a single racial group are immediately suspect. . . . Courts
must subject them to the most rigid scrutiny."[22] Ironically, this first articulation of what is now known as strict scrutiny nonetheless led the Court to
uphold the executive order allowing the internment of Japanese Americans.[23]
Nevertheless, *Korematsu* established the now familiar constitutional structure
whereby courts deploy strict scrutiny—where a law must be narrowly tailored
to serve a compelling government interest—to laws implicating race, national
origin, and alienage while most other Equal Protection challenges (except
those implicating children born to unmarried parents, sex, and gender, which
receive intermediate scrutiny) are merely afforded rational basis review in
which courts will uphold their constitutionality as long as the law is rationally
related to a legitimate purpose.

While Equal Protection's doctrinal development has been robust since
Korematsu and *Brown*, there has been relatively little investigation into precisely how courts understand race in fulfilling their constitutional duty to use
judicial review to protect the rights of these groups. Moreover, there is even
less coherency in the court's jurisprudence on the principles that justify treating racial discrimination differently from other forms of group-based subordination, such as that based upon sexual orientation or class. This is important since Equal Protection jurisprudence dictates that a plaintiff's group
membership shapes the judicial determination of whether the state categorization is permissible. As Kenji Yoshino notes, the court has extended stronger
forms of scrutiny beyond mere rational review to classifications "based upon
race, sex, national origin, alienage, and illegitimacy . . . [without] provid[ing]
a clear overarching rationale for why these five classifications, and not others,

are particularly deserving of judicial solicitude."[24] Rather, the Court takes three factors (not necessarily requirements) into consideration: whether the plaintiff is a member of a group that (1) has historically been subjected to discrimination, (2) that is a politically powerless minority, and (3) "exhibits obvious, immutable, or distinguishing characteristics that define them as a discrete group."[25]

What appears first as a rather parsimonious three-pronged test is actually the product of several divergent jurisprudential threads coalescing around modern Equal Protection commitments. The first prong's concern with a group's history of discrimination emanates from the Court's post-*Brown* commitments to affirmatively use judicial review to go beyond overly formal notions of equality to engage in a more pragmatic understanding of how the social histories entwined with legally enforced discriminations can lead to apartheid. The second prong's concern for protecting politically powerless groups is an offshoot of footnote four in *Carolene Products*. The Court discusses the relevance of these first two prongs in *San Antonio Independent School District v. Rodriguez*, which concerns the constitutionality of funding schools through tax bases that systemically favor the wealthy. The Court held that the appellees residing in underfunded areas did not constitute a suspect class that could elicit a strict scrutiny analysis since they constituted "a large, diverse, and amorphous class, unified only by the common factor of residence in districts that happen to have less taxable wealth than other districts."[26] As such, the Court declined to exert its highest form of review typically reserved for claims of racial discrimination since "the system of alleged discrimination and the class it defines have none of the traditional indicia of suspectness: the class is not saddled with such disabilities, or subjected to such a history of purposeful unequal treatment, or relegated to such a position of political powerlessness as to command extraordinary protection from the majoritarian political process."[27]

The third prong's emphasis on obvious, immutable, or distinguishing characteristics provides the most direct articulation of how groups deemed visually distinct are granted the highest form of protection.[28] Yet there is doctrinal evidence that this prong's emphasis on granting groups with visually distinguishable markers higher protections also shapes how the Court thinks about the other two prongs. For example, in *Matthews v. Lucas*, the Court said that while law often treats children born to unmarried parents differently than those born in traditional families, "this discrimination against illegitimates has never approached the severity or pervasiveness of the historic legal and political discrimination against women and Negroes . . . perhaps in part because illegitimacy does not carry an obvious badge, as race and sex do."[29] Moreover, in *Frontiero v. Richardson*, the plurality extended strict scrutiny to sex-based discrimination (later revised as intermediate scrutiny in *Craig v. Boren*) based in part on a theory of political powerlessness linked to the visibility of women's sex difference: "It can hardly be doubted that, in part because of the high visibility of the sex characteristic, women still face pervasive, although at times more subtle, discrimination in our educational institutions, in the job market and, perhaps most conspicuously, in the political arena."[30] Therefore, the third prong's bluntness can be largely seen as a constitutive element of the other two prongs in terms of how visibility filters the way the Court understands the severity of groups' political powerlessness and history of discrimination. It can be argued that the visibility component was always already a prerequisite for higher judicial scrutiny, but only became articulated as a "prong" as a way to justify extending heightened scrutiny to sex-based classifications. The doctrinal justification for treating sex-based classifications more like race classifications in *Frontiero* is that sex discrimination, like race discrimination, orients around visible physical differences that trigger prejudices that are difficult to mitigate solely through political processes and therefore require stronger constitutional protections. The explicit articulation of a visibility prong post-*Frontiero* can be reasonably seen as restating what was up to then part of the obvious in Equal Protection: that the theory of discrimination (and, implicitly, theory of race, since racial minorities are conceived of as the model) driving this jurisprudence is one that treats phenotype and other human markers as visually obvious and self-evident triggers of potentially antagonistic social relations.[31] These markers' visibility and salience are thought to exist anterior to law and society rather than produced by social and legal relations. That is, *"race" ipsa loquitur*: race and its visual salience simply speak for themselves.

The Coherence of Constitutional Colorblindness
"Race" ipsa loquitur impacts Equal Protection jurisprudence beyond serving as a gateway concept that arbitrates the level of scrutiny afforded to various groups' claims of discrimination. It also plays a constitutive role in shaping the Court's normative vision for the appropriate role of government in using racial categories. This perspective, known as colorblindness, reflects a legal

ideology of racial nonrecognition; Equal Protection read through a colorblind framework has come to be understood as substantially limiting the state's ability to take race into consideration when allocating resources or benefits—even when done to remedy ongoing disadvantages linked to past harms.[32] Here lies a key question: how did this transition from a post-*Brown* era of race consciousness to a modern era of Equal Protection race-nonrecognition occur? What theories of race led to this changing perspective?

While some have maintained that constitutional colorblindness reflects a good faith application of its intellectual antecedents, scholars have traced the birth of modern colorblindness to the unique racial politics of the post–civil rights era that generated a backlash against efforts to use law and public policy to atone for the racial apartheid stemming from centuries of racial subordination.[33] It has been argued that "the proximate origins of contemporary colorblindness [can be located] in the effort by neoconservatives beginning in the 1960s to respond to an emerging structural understanding of racism by positing instead an ethnic reconceptualization of race."[34] The writings of Nathan Glazer and Daniel Moynihan, along with scholarship from the legal academy, challenged the wisdom of affirmative action as public policy during this period while also reconceptualizing the sociology of racial inequality as a phenomenon linked to personal or group failures rather than racial hierarchy.[35] Eduardo Bonilla-Silva similarly argues that colorblindness "became the dominant racial ideology as the mechanisms and practices for keeping blacks and other racial minorities 'at the bottom of the well' changed . . . [whereas] contemporary racial inequality is reproduced through 'new racism' practices that are subtle, institutional, and apparently nonracial."[36]

The colorblind approach to race is evident throughout the Court's modern Equal Protection jurisprudence, which has centered in large part around the issue of affirmative action. The Court began to head down this path in *Regents of the University of California v. Bakke*, where an unsuccessful White applicant to the University of California, Davis Medical School, sued the university for excluding him from consideration for one of the sixteen seats set aside for minority applicants. In *Bakke*, two sets of four justices each argued for and against an anti-classification approach to the government's use of race. This judicial fragmentation led to the rather narrow holding that UC Davis's particular admissions program was unlawful but that race may continue to be considered in other ways. Justice Powell's opinion has emerged over time as sowing the seeds for a colorblind approach to Equal Protection that encourages nonrecognition by concluding that strict scrutiny applied to all racial categorizations, regardless of whether the person is a member of a "discrete and insular minority." Powell's declaration that "racial and ethnic distinctions of any sort are inherently suspect and thus call for the most exacting judicial examination" strips the affirmative action debate of the very context that renders such programs socially necessary.[37] Thus, "in advocating the same standard in all cases, Powell effectively argued that for constitutional purposes preferential treatment and Jim Crow laws amounted to the same thing—the central claim of reactionary colorblindness."[38] This claim is premised upon a particular understanding of race: that it is a superficial, "skin deep," and merely descriptive characteristic that is inherently dubious for government consideration—regardless of whether such consideration is done to entrench existing racial privilege or remedy racial subordination. Race is sociologically flat; it is thought to only describe an individual's physical traits or group membership rather than confer any particular social benefits or burdens. The lack of conceptual depth accorded to understanding precisely what race is and how it impacts individuals' lives leads to a reductionist understanding that draws heavily upon commonsense perspectives that (1) the salience of race comes from its visually obvious character and (2) that blindness or nonrecognition, in terms of an inability or unwillingness to see race, necessarily leads to racial equality.[39]

Powell's language has had a resounding effect on Equal Protection jurisprudence beyond *Bakke*'s holding that race can continue to have limited consideration in university admissions. Powell did not side with the justices in *Bakke* that explicitly advocated colorblindness through forgoing constitutional deliberations and instead arguing that Title VI prevented such race-conscious university admissions. But Powell's opinion greased the wheels for subsequent successful claims of constitutional colorblindness, where the Fourteenth Amendment itself was read to bar race-conscious decision making. This is first seen *Richmond v. Croson*, which entailed a program that gave preferences for municipal contracts to minority-owned businesses in Richmond, Virginia. Drawing upon many of the same sentiments as Justice Powell expressed in *Bakke*, Justice O'Connor's majority opinion held this scheme to violate the Equal Protection clause, through a jurisprudential lens of colorblindness. Ian Haney-López articulates an important connection between Powell's dicta in *Bakke* and O'Connor's reasoning in *Croson:*

Like Powell, O'Connor used the version of ethnicity picturing whites as black to mandate strict scrutiny. Then, just as Powell did, in considering whether structural disadvantage justified affirmative action, O'Connor reverted to the version of ethnicity depicting all groups as the masters of their own destiny, none suffering particular disadvantage. Despite the heavy particularity of Virginia's history, *Croson* posited a veritable tug of war between various identically situated ethnic groups competing for the spoils of government largess. O'Connor wrapped her opinion in the moral legitimacy afforded by the "dream of a Nation of equal citizens in a society where race is irrelevant." But by drawing blacks as white, she in effect reasoned as if this end state even now existed: race was ostensibly already irrelevant to the life chances of minorities in America. In this context, not only was affirmative action unnecessary, but it threatened the American racial paradise by victimizing whites, making them the new minority. In its first instantiation as Equal Protection law, colorblindness drew heavily on the re-description of race constitutionally pioneered by Powell in *Bakke*, positing whites as black to justify heightened review, but blacks as white to deny the persistence of racial hierarchy and the necessity of racial reconstruction.[40]

This move to ethnicity is key to making colorblindness and its jurisprudence of nonrecognition a constitutional norm for understanding Equal Protection. The uptake and rearticulation of colorblind norms can be seen in the 1995 Supreme Court decision *Adarand Constructors v. Peña*, in which the Court considered the lawfulness of racial preferences in federal government subcontracting that are designed to benefit minorities. Primary contractors with the Central Federal Lands Highway Division (part of the Department of Transportation) would receive additional money if they subcontracted with small businesses owned or controlled by "socially and economically disadvantaged individuals," where the federal law explicitly stated that race was a presumptively qualifying characteristic.[41] Even though the racial classification used here was designed to benefit minorities (presumably to counteract the impact of past discrimination), the Court concluded that such preferences violate Equal Protection through reasoning that incorporated colorblind logic as a constitutional norm. By holding that strict scrutiny applies any time government uses *any* racial classification, the Court obfuscated the ongoing impact of racial discrimination as well as the contemporary existence of racial hierarchy. As Justice O'Connor stated in the majority opinion, "Whenever the government treats any person unequally because of his or her race, that person has suffered an injury that falls squarely within the language and spirit of the Constitution's guarantee of equal protection."[42] Drawing upon a visual metaphor in line with this colorblind application of Equal Protection, Justice Scalia stated in his concurrence that "under our Constitution there can be no such thing as either a creditor or debtor race. . . . *In the eyes of government, we are just one race here. It is American*"[43] (emphasis added). And, as if there were any doubt yet regarding the role of colorblindness in understanding the Equal Protection's boundaries, Justice Thomas powerfully concurred by stating, "I believe that there is a moral and constitutional equivalence between laws designed to subjugate a race and those that distribute benefits on the basis of race in order to foster some current notion of equality."[44] Thus, from this perspective, race consciousness by government actors—even to amend for past wrongs—is not only constitutionally impermissible, but transcends legal norms to also be immoral.

From this perspective of constitutional colorblindness that continues to this very day with Chief Justice Roberts's declaration in *Parents Involved* that "the best way to stop discrimination on the basis of race is to stop discriminating on the basis of race," the rather uncomfortable conclusion that Jim Crow is legally and morally equivalent to affirmative action somehow makes sense.[45] But it only does so through a particular understanding of race that is remarkably superficial—a commonsensical presumption that race only reflects visually obvious group differences that all people have that are of no significance beyond what we see and should not be recognized, even for remedial purposes. From *Bakke* to *Parents Involved*, we can see how the embedding of colorblindness into Equal Protection law encourages a jurisprudence that operates from a specific understanding of race—*"race" ipsa loquitur*, or that race is a simplistic physiological trait that speaks for itself and deserves no deeper sociological or historical contemplation, which ultimately conceals the continuing significance of racial subordination. *"Race" ipsa loquitur* makes certain jurisprudential "moves" in furtherance of constitutional colorblindness possible if not preferable when they might otherwise be seen as what they are: reductionist and ridiculous. For example, by reconceiving race as a series of ethnic groups in pluralistic competition where there is no subordinate or privileged group, *"race" ipsa loquitur* allows Equal Protection's moral sensibilities to shift from using law to remedy past injustices to using law to mandate nonrecognition of difference in the distribution of resources even when done to level a historically and sociologically uneven playing field. Thus, the assumption that race is visually obvious plays a subtle yet powerful role in maintaining racial hierarchy.

The Intent Doctrine

The intent doctrine is traditionally understood as emerging from the Supreme Court's 1976 decision in *Washington v. Davis* to require a demonstration of discriminatory purpose or "bad intent" to sustain claims that a facially neutral law or practice violates Equal Protection. This doctrine has made it extremely difficult for plaintiffs to successfully make claims of discrimination; demonstrating that a law or practice disproportionately impacts a particular group is not enough, and direct evidence of individuals' specific intent to discriminate is rare except in the most extraordinary cases.

Yet this narrative that *Washington v. Davis* marks the origins of the intent doctrine has recently come under scrutiny as not only inaccurate but inattentive to the critical role of colorblindness in giving rise to the doctrine's current incarnation as requiring a specific demonstration of "bad intent."[46] What is missing from the traditional story of the intent doctrine's origins is that the judicial examination of intent existed before *Washington v. Davis*, but in a different form, where social context was used to *infer* inappropriate motives rather than requiring direct evidence of malice.[47]

Washington v. Davis focused in large part on whether Test 21 (an examination used by the Washington, DC, police department for hiring purposes) impermissibly discriminated against African Americans since they were four times as likely to not achieve a passing score. The Court of Appeals, using a standard borrowed from Title VII analyses, held that Test 21 had an unconstitutionally disparate impact on Blacks that violated Equal Protection norms.[48] In reversing the Court of Appeals, the Supreme Court in *Davis* found that there was no discrimination in the administration of Test 21 and held that government action is not unconstitutional "solely because it has a racially disproportionate impact."[49] But what often gets lost in the standard narrative on *Washington v. Davis* and the emergence of the intent doctrine is that context still mattered for the *Davis* court in inferring whether or not an unconstitutional purpose existed. The *Davis* court stated in its opinion that "necessarily, an invidious discriminatory purpose may often be inferred from the totality of the relevant facts, including the fact, if it is true, that the law bears more heavily on one race than another. . . . Disproportionate impact is not irrelevant, but it is not the sole touchstone of an invidious racial discrimination forbidden by the Constitution."[50] Thus, as Ian Haney López notes, the Court "did not just extol contextual intent, [it] employed it—albeit to find no discrimination."[51]

From this standpoint, *Davis* did not usher in a jurisprudence fixated on individual malice that does not take seriously the ways in which social context can clue courts in to legal actors' intent. This turn toward individualized malice to the exclusion of any serious attention to social context in Equal Protection analysis has been shown to fully mature *after Davis*, through *Bakke*'s subsequent prism of constitutional colorblindness. Recall that Justice Powell's opinion in *Bakke* encouraged deemphasizing context in affirmative action cases in a manner that subjects all uses of race—remedial or discriminatory—to strict scrutiny and promoted an ethos of nonrecognition. While this position was not signed onto by the other justices in *Bakke*, it has become a formidable influence in Equal Protection analysis—particularly in transforming intent doctrine. The year following *Bakke*, the Court in *Pers. Adm'r of Mass. v. Feeney* relied heavily upon Powell's colorblind logic to assert—in a case that was ultimately about gender discrimination—that "a racial classification, regardless of purported motivation, is presumptively invalid and can be upheld only upon an extraordinary justification."[52] *Feeney* solidified the shift in how courts conceptualized the constitutional problem as law "seeing" or classifying individuals[53]; the context that mattered so much up through and past *Davis* was now reduced to an immediately suspect act of government taking notice of group-based traits, where the *Feeney* court asserted that "race is the paradigm."[54] But *Feeney* also reflects a reconfigured meaning of discriminatory purpose or intent: "Discriminatory purpose . . . implies more than intent as volition or intent as awareness of consequences. It implies that the decisionmaker . . . selected or reaffirmed a particular course of action at least in part 'because of,' not merely 'in spite of,' its adverse effects upon an *identifiable group*"[55] (emphasis added).

Therefore it was *Feeney* in 1979, not *Davis* in 1976, that reflects the coming of age of the modern intent doctrine. But what has been underappreciated until recently is the extent to which the shift in Equal Protection analysis from contextual inquiries to an acontextual emphasis on categorization and malice was mediated by the infusion of constitutional colorblindness as emphasized by Justice Powell's 1978 *Bakke* opinion. The intent doctrine as we currently know it is a product of colorblindness—in other words, fruit from the poisonous tree. What occurs is an increasingly decontextualized understanding of race and racism that moves it from being a contextual interaction between human difference and social structure to a reductionist approach that emphasizes visible traits—what the *Feeney* court terms as "adverse effects upon an identifiable group." The focus is on bad faith categorization, yet race itself remains undertheorized and conceptually reduced to something that is presumptively self-evident or obvious. In disaggregating race from context or social structure, the *Feeney* court through this post-*Bakke* turn toward constitutional colorblindness effectively embraces *"race" ipsa loquitur* as its theory of race. Race needs no contextual explanation or investigation. It simply speaks for itself.

Theory of Race Emanating from Equal Protection Doctrine

The doctrinal point that should be taken from this three-tiered analysis is that Equal Protection jurisprudence has evolved in a manner that reduces race to a series of discrete categories that exist outside of any broader social or political process and whose significance and salience are thought to come from mere observation. Race is thought to be a visually obvious characteristic of the body—what Alan Hyde calls a "naturalizing account of race . . . [whereby] race is an obvious fact that inheres in each body from birth."[56] Hyde uses naturalizing not in the sense of understanding the relative worth of groups, but in how the visual distinctions that are strongly associated with racial categories seem objective and real. Yet as demonstrated in the data presented in Part 1, what we see and the importance we give to racial differences are constituted by social practices. Thus, as Hyde notes, "race in American law is thus unthinkable without a body and an eye. . . . Law veils its own power . . . by pretending to find what it in fact makes itself."[57]

This critique suggests an important yet largely unarticulated trend. In relation to the inordinate attention paid to thinking through the difficulties and appropriate relationship between Equal Protection and judicial review, race has been conceptually reduced to its lowest common denominator: a set of discrete and visually obvious categories primarily known by phenotype and other visual cues. Thus, the reductionist theory of race driving Equal Protection law is that race speaks for itself; *race is what you see, and what you see is presumed to be self-evidently salient.* "Seeing" race is presumed to be a fact of life that is both exogenous to and unmediated by any broader social, legal, or political process. Moreover, the self-evident salience of this variable is thought to be the trigger giving rise to Equal Protection conversations.

By saying that Equal Protection doctrine has a reductionist theory of race, I do not mean to simply reassert that race is socially or legally constructed or that a broader process of racial formation creates the meanings that we associate with racial groups—points that have already been made. Instead, drawing upon the empirical findings in Part 1, I question the practice whereby visual distinctions between racial groups are thought to be self-evident boundaries of difference that serve as a conceptual predicate for Equal Protection conversations. Law's focus on visibility might privilege a certain way of thinking about race that historically has been intertwined with racial subordination, that is, that the self-evident visual salience of race reflects differences that are real, tangible, and obvious rather than being a function of social practices that, tied to subordination itself, produce the very salience of race thought to be obvious. The *"race" ipsa loquitur* trope in Equal Protection doctrine may very well limit discussions of what race is and, more importantly, might obscure the most effective way to use racial categorizations in a thoughtful, non-discriminatory manner.

Destabilizing *"Race" Ipsa Loquitur* in *Equal Protection Jurisprudence*

The empirical findings from Part 1 suggest that visual understandings of race are not dependent upon any need or ability to actually see the visual cues that define racial boundaries. Instead, they are produced by social practices that are so compelling that even blind people "see" and organize their lives around these visual cues. Sighted people are, in a sense, *blinded by sight;* their vision prevents them from appreciating the role of social practices in producing the salience of race. Blind people's inability to be misled by the seemingly self-evident nature of race brings the production of the visual salience of race into focus, which allows us to understand the significance of social practices to the perceptibility of group differences to race and beyond. Gerry, a blind respondent, nicely summarizes this concept:

> Race is very often not a mystery to blind people, which is in a sense kind of sad. I think that sometimes [sighted] people look at blind folks and they think [that] these people can show us the way to a kind of Star Trek race-blind society. And it would be great if we could do that. But we're just as much a victim

of racial prejudice, stereotypes, and misconceptions as anybody else. And the fact that we're not clued to it directly by vision doesn't, in my mind, change that a bit. I think that I suffer all of the unfortunate characteristics of my upbringing regarding race that my [sighted] brothers and sisters do.

Ginny echoes this sentiment: "I really don't think it's a matter of vision truthfully. . . . I was so amazed when this professor of mine had the premise [that blind people do not understand race]. . . . He said, 'Well then, you're not prejudiced at all, are you?' I thought [it's] so odd that he thinks that [it] is all about vision." Mason also corroborated this thought, noting that race is "very much a learned thinking and behavior that doesn't have much to do with what you can see or not."

This empirical study of blind people's understandings and experiences with race has important implications for Equal Protection in that it calls into question the *"race" ipsa loquitur* sensibility embedded in this jurisprudence and draws attention to how this misguided theory of race may warp important aspects of this area of law. For example, the attention paid to visibility in Equal Protection's scrutiny inquiry where race is treated as a trait whose salience and social significance come from its self-evident character trivializes Equal Protection by framing constitutionally impermissible discrimination as something that starts from the visual perception of seemingly obvious human differences. The empirical evidence suggests otherwise; the salience of race is produced by social practices rather than merely observed, which suggests that judicial review should pay less attention to visibility as an ocular experience and more attention to the social practices—such as embedded forms of privilege and subordination—that make certain human traits salient in the first place. Re-orienting the scrutiny inquiry to focus on these social practices as a constitutional problem of first concern opens up a jurisprudential discussion of how the discriminatory treatment of certain groups currently not considered to be a suspect class—such as homosexuals and poor people—may nevertheless merit more than mere rational-basis review due to the history of discrimination and current practices that produce their social salience (at times visible, and at times not) as targets for state-sponsored classifications that work against their group interest.[58] Such an approach would alter the Equal Protection inquiry to be sensitive to the social practices of homophobia and classism that repeatedly make homosexuals and poor people the subject of discriminatory state actions, leading to a more sociologically robust jurisprudence. This might engender a more coherent and consistent Equal Protection jurisprudence that places justice rather than deceptively self-evident categories of "visible" and "invisible" at the heart of the inquiry.

Using the empirical data from this study to disrupt constitutional color-blindness is also significant. Chapter 4 discussed the importance of disrupting the colorblind metaphor to the extent that it fosters a reductionist theory of race being simply what you see and blindness, or nonrecognition, as an appropriate check against discrimination. To the extent that colorblindness has become the primary filter through which the Court understands Equal Protection (which has led to troubling outcomes), disrupting this logic is of the utmost importance for re-envisioning this area of the law. By offering qualitative data showing the inaccuracies of the metaphor as an ideological tool and as a specific iteration of constitutional law, colorblindness can be exposed as incoherent and damaging to social relations and basic notions of justice.

By focusing on the social practices that produce individuals' ability to see the world in particular ways, this disruption draws attention to the need for alternative conceptions of society and human relationships that reflect reality. Reorienting the normative commitments to Equal Protection around constitutive social practices rather than *"race" ipsa loquitur* suggests that constitutional colorblindness as a jurisprudence of nonrecognition should be done away with. Taking social practices seriously as the stimulant of race becoming visually salient suggests a new understanding of race that might inform Equal Protection jurisprudence in a manner that highlights the roles of context and racial hierarchy in fulfilling Equal Protection's mandates.

The empirical evidence also substantially disrupts the intent doctrine. Much of the intent inquiry—theoretically, historically, and doctrinally connected with colorblindness—focuses on a particular reductionist understanding that disaggregates race from social context and hierarchy to recast it as a discrete trait that is purposefully targeted and presumptively self-evidently known. The intent doctrine replicates a discreteness regarding race and how it is apprehended as well as comprehended that is sociologically bankrupt; social practices, not merely discrete, acontextual racial markers of human difference, give rise to the visual salience of race that often leads to discriminatory actions and experiences. To the extent that the empirical findings draw attention to the role of social practices in producing the salience of race, the intent doctrine also needs to be substantially revisited in favor of an approach that emphasizes social practices, context, and racial hierarchy rather than embarking on the elusive quest of finding and punishing individual bad actors.

Taken together, putting the empirical findings regarding blind people's visual understandings of race in conversation with the *"race" ipsa loquitur* thread of reasoning embedded in Equal Protection's scrutiny inquiry, colorblindness, and intent doctrine suggests that this line of legal reasoning must be thoroughly eviscerated. The *"race" ipsa loquitur* sensibility reproduces a troubling typological conception of race and discrimination that overemphasizes what people look like to the detriment of having a more sophisticated understanding of the social practices that make certain groups visible targets of discrimination to begin with. By emphasizing the ways in which groups' visual salience is produced, not merely observed, I suggest a stronger engagement with the discriminatory social practices that constitute the coherency of certain groups' visibility—whether it be by race, class, religion, or any other characteristic central to individual or group identity. The point here is not that vision does not matter. Rather, the constitutionally relevant issue should be the social practices and outcomes that make race and other group traits salient lines of human difference.

Equal Protection's emphasis on visibility distorts discussions on the nature of race and, more importantly, may hinder judicial deliberations of the most effective way to use racial categorizations in a thoughtful, non-discriminatory manner. Focusing on visibility privileges a certain way of thinking about race that historically has been intertwined with racial subordination, that is, that race differences are real, tangible, and obvious rather than a product of social practices. This not only hurts other groups facing discrimination, but encourages a limited perspective on racial discrimination that harms racial minorities and impedes social justice. Without seriously considering how social practices constitute visual understandings of race, the legal emphasis on visual cues obscures the extent to which we are socialized to *think racially*, which can be at the crux of many discriminatory actions that may go without remedy due to the current scheme's emphasis on what litigants look like.

The point of putting the qualitative analysis in conversation with the legal doctrine is not to simply make sure law conforms to the empirical realities of social life on the ground, but to encourage more sophisticated and responsible conceptions of race by legal actors and legal scholars. It is time to begin a series of conversations about the future relationship between race and law, focusing in particular on what can be done to escape the reductionist theoretical quagmire that has defined race in American jurisprudence for the past four hundred years. Thinking empirically about Equal Protection is an important first step.

6 On Post-racialism

HOODED SWEATSHIRTS, OR "HOODIES," ARE OFTEN ASSOCIATED with trendy adolescents trying to make some type of fashion statement. However, the modern commercial hoodie has been around since the 1930s, when Champion manufactured the first hooded sweatshirt with the idea that it could help keep laborers warm as they worked in cold warehouses.[1] Since then, hoodies have found a broader appeal and have become a staple of the American wardrobe. But hoodies have become more of a political statement than mere clothing accessory since the February 26, 2012, shooting of Trayvon Martin in a gated community in Sanford, Florida.

Martin, a seventeen-year-old Black male, was wearing a hoodie while walking back to his father's girlfriend's house after buying snacks from a local 7-Eleven. George Zimmerman, a neighborhood watch captain, found his behavior—WWBWH, or walking while Black with hoodie—to be "really suspicious" according to a 911 call he made while watching Martin walk down the street.[2] Zimmerman, with some uncertainty, told the dispatcher that Martin "look[ed] Black." Yet he assuredly described him as wearing "a dark hoodie" that led him to believe that Martin was "up to no good."[3] The 911 dispatcher advised Zimmerman to stay in his car until officers arrived. Ignoring this instruction, Zimmerman followed Martin, left his car with a 9-millimeter handgun, and confronted the teenager. An altercation ensued, and Zimmerman fatally shot Martin.

This case was thrust into the national spotlight when several weeks passed before Sanford police arrested Zimmerman. The public outcry attributed the shooting and the delayed arrest to racism. Zimmerman defended his actions by saying that his use of force was justified under Florida's "stand your ground law," which has an expanded understanding of self-defense that does not require any attempt to retreat and permits the use of deadly force if the person believes it is necessary to prevent death or bodily harm.[4] Thus, both Zimmerman and the Sanford Police Department countered accusations of racism by suggesting that this case was primarily about whether Zimmerman reasonably feared for his safety. While a situation involving an unprovoked defendant pursuing a victim and initiating a confrontation may sound like a strange application of "standing your ground," it is not without precedent. In nearly one-third of two hundred "stand your ground" cases in Florida analyzed by the *Tampa Bay Times*, "defendants initiated the fight, shot an unarmed person or pursued their victim—and still went free."[5] Thus, the issue quickly became whether or not Zimmerman had reason to find Martin suspicious and a threat to his life or others—which brings us back to the hoodie.

To some, hoodies are a timeless and unequivocal sign of sinister behavior; many consider hiding one's face to be indicative of bad intentions. From this vantage point, the suspicious nature of wearing a hoodie may have reasonably led Zimmerman to fear for his life and others—at least enough to justify the shooting under Florida law. Geraldo Rivera made this point most forcefully when he said that the hoodie "is as much responsible for Trayvon Martin's death as George Zimmerman was."[6] Comments such as this both reflected and galvanized a certain sensibility that Martin somehow provoked the attack by dressing like someone who is a threat and therefore tragically triggered Zimmerman's perhaps overly aggressive yet nonetheless lawful act of standing his ground. Celebrities and politicians showed their support for Martin and against hoodie stereotypes by wearing hoodies in public—everyone from the Miami Heat basketball team to former Michigan governor Jennifer Granholm to CNN political commentator Roland Martin to Congressman Bobby Rush donning a hoodie on the floor of the House of Representatives (see Figures 16 and 17). This public display of support even led to a "million hoodie march" in New York City.

In the midst of this public discussion came a voice of clarity from a surprising place: the White House. During an unrelated public address in the Rose Garden, President Obama responded to a reporter's request to comment on the Trayvon Martin case by sympathizing with Martin's parents and noting in deeply personal terms that "when I think about this boy, I think about

FIGURE 16. Former Michigan governor Jennifer Granholm. AP Photo/
Current TV.

my own kids. . . . You know, if I had a son, *he'd look like Trayvon*"[7] (emphasis
added).

When I heard this, it immediately took me back to my days growing up
in a middle-class suburb of Cincinnati—a city where police officers killed
fifteen Black males over a six-year period, with the 2001 shooting of unarmed
Timothy Thomas generating four days of riots.[8] These protests were the
culmination of decades-long racial tensions in the city and its surrounding
neighborhoods, where relationships between Blacks and Whites—not to
mention between the police and minority communities—were nothing short
of dismal.[9] As a teenager, I was endlessly frustrated by what I then thought
to be the irrational rules created by my parents as I transitioned to adulthood. For example, they discouraged me from jogging in my neighborhood,
for fear that someone might question why a young Black male was running or
what criminal activity he was running from. When I turned sixteen, a family friend decided to move out of town and was looking to quickly sell his
car, a fairly nice low-end model Mercedes. He proposed selling it to us for
substantially below market value—presumably as a gift to me as I had just
received my driver's license. Of course, my sixteen-year-old self had visions
of pulling into my high school parking lot in a new ride that would elicit the
envy of my peers. I was crestfallen when my parents declined the offer. When

FIGURE 17. Congressman Bobby Rush wearing a hoodie on the floor of the House of Representatives. AP Photo/House Television.

I asked why, my father flatly said, "When people see a young Black male driving a Mercedes, they will think you are a drug dealer, and we don't want any trouble from the police." I ended up with a fifteen-year-old hand-me-down blue Datsun 210 that leaked oil and had rusted doors, holes in the seats, and manual windows. Needless to say, the kids at school were not impressed.

While my parents' actions seemed utterly paranoid at the time, I slowly began to realize that they were exercising a parenting technique used by many people raising males of color.[10] Unlike Rivera's "blame the victim" approach, it is common in communities of color to "blame the society" in making their young men aware of the unjust ways in which their actions and behaviors are viewed. This is the sensibility—the racial panopticon that envelops Black men and uses their socially produced hypervisibility as a means of social control— that President Obama tapped into when remarking on the Martin shooting. This brief but poignant statement was important in at least two regards. First, it brought clarity to what was then becoming an increasingly muddled public conversation on race. Hoodies' increasingly indeterminate meaning and Zimmerman's claim to a *Hispanic* ethnicity (not white racial identity) obscured the central role of race and racism in this incident. Zimmerman's supporters emphasized how the covering of one's face, not the race of the face itself, can lead to tragic mistakes that are nonetheless legally justified. They also claimed that this is not a simple case of White on Black prejudice since Zimmerman is biracial (his father is White and his mother is Latino), giving Zimmerman a claim to an ethnic identity that ostensibly rebutted accusations that he is a White racist.[11] But by highlighting how the visibility of race would expose his son, if he had one, to a similar fate, Obama put the issue of race squarely back into the public discourse. With great subtlety, he drew attention to the panoptic powers of visual surveillance and observation that are exerted upon Blacks and enforced by social practices such as neighborhood violence that the law excuses through mechanisms such as "standing your ground."[12] Through these comments, President Obama resituates the problem as not being about the dialectics of the hoodie or Zimmerman's racial background. Rather, it is important to pay closer attention to how society trains individuals to look upon and react to race and racial cues in a manner that produces the visibility of "looking suspicious" in ways that rationalize forms of violence that would otherwise be unjustifiable (a jury ultimately found Zimmerman not guilty). Thus, by emphasizing his personal connection to Martin's visibility and how the social practices surrounding seeing race both apart from and through markers such as the hoodie, the president draws attention to the fact that we still live in a world where someone can be incorrectly suspected of wrongdoing, killed, and have their killer go unpunished for no reason other than that *they look a certain way.*[13]

But this statement from the rose garden was also an interesting contrast to Obama's presidency and approach to governing. Since his introduction to the nation at the 2004 Democratic convention, Barack Obama has assiduously avoided even the appearance of being race conscious, or acknowledging the central role of race in subordinating people of color and privileging the White majority.[14] Randall Kennedy notes that "President Obama has consistently attempted to evade racial issues. If he cannot avoid them, he reframes them, minimizing the racial element. If forced to confront a racial issue squarely, he does so in a fashion calculated to assuage the anxieties of Whites. This is the Obama way.[15]

President Obama's public comments on race often have temporal limits, either focusing on how far the country has come since its roots in slavery and Jim Crow or congratulating Americans for reaching a historical moment of relative racial harmony when all individuals, regardless of race, simply want the same opportunities in life. Yet he has largely avoided discussion of the ways that past wrongs continue to shape present injustices that, without deeper consciousness of race in developing remedies, limit the feasibility of substantive equality. This avoidance of race consciousness has led President Obama to be heralded as the post-racial president—indeed, an icon of post-racialism itself. Much of Obama's political viability has been premised upon his campaign and governing strategy of minimizing race consciousness in favor of universalisms that American society has transcended the "old" race and no longer needs to make it central to public discourse. Where the civil rights movement was based upon the aspiration that "We Shall Overcome," Obama's post-racial strategy has effectively been a declaration that "We Have Overcome."

But by emphasizing that it was the way that Trayvon Martin looked—not simply because of any clothing—Obama made an interesting divergence away from his overall post-racial strategy that many consider was his ticket to the White House. Regardless of this isolated moment of clarity, post-racialism continues to ascend on Obama's coattails as a powerful ideology in American social and political discourse that deserves serious examination.

The Obama Way

In many ways, post-racialism is not an entirely new development. The notion that race consciousness is overly divisive and that social and political commonality should be pursued along other shared experiences dates back at the very least to old debates concerning race versus class consciousness in political mobilization. But Barack Obama's presence on the national political stage gave these debates an entirely new appeal and feasibility that allowed the public to re-experience anti-race consciousness anew. At the 2004 Democratic National Convention, then Senate candidate Obama ended his momentous speech as follows: "There's not a black America and white America and Latino American and Asian America; there's the United States of America. . . . We are one people, all of us pledging allegiance to the stars and stripes, all of us defending the United States of America."[16] These words marked what many argue to be the birth of a post-racial political strategy that would lead to Obama's election as president just a few years later. Journalists, pundits, and scholars have feverishly dissected this post-racial approach and its effect on public understandings of race. In short, it involved a "rhetorical tightrope [that] reassured Whites without seeming to abandon blacks" by focusing not on how race defines life opportunities, but by concentrating on the common things desired by everyone and how he, as president, can help all Americans

achieve them.[17] Even in moments such as the Revered Jeremiah Wright epi-
sode—in which Obama's relationship with someone who passionately advocated race consciousness and racial justice raised questions about the sincerity of his post-racialism—Obama eloquently rebuked race consciousness and
reasserted his political strategy of universalisms that transcended the particu-
larities of racial subordination and White racial privilege.[18]

Obama has stated publicly that he does not personally adhere to the claim
that his election signals the twilight of race and the beginnings of a post-racial
society.[19] This is inconsistent with his political rhetoric, where his own life
story and achievements are used to advance policies that eschew race consciousness in favor of race-neutral approaches that are inattentive to the particular challenges faced by racial minorities. Obama would hardly be the first
politician to demonstrate such inconsistencies between personal belief and
political rhetoric. But the consistent role of post-racialism in his approach
to governing has led some Black politicians to question President Obama's
overall commitment to racial justice. For example, members of the Congressional Black Caucus accused the Obama administration in June 2011 of failing
to address why Black unemployment is nearly double that of Whites. Caucus
chairman and Missouri representative Emanuel Cleaver said: "Can you imagine a situation where any other group of workers [were in the same position],
if 34 percent of White women were out there looking for work and couldn't
find it? You would see congressional hearings and community gatherings.
There would be rallies and protest marches. There is no way that this would
be allowed to stand."[20]

While perhaps politically savvy and expedient, post-racialism as a campaign strategy and theory of governance is problematic. This can be understood through at least three traits that characterize this approach. First,
post-racialism works from the premise that the long history of race relations—from slavery to Jim Crow and beyond—is now over; society has
evolved from these primitive forms of social relations characterized by racial
conflict, subordination, and privilege to arrive at a final destination of racial
equality where the state no longer needs to be conscious of race for remedial
purposes.[21] Post-racialism is in many ways self-congratulatory; it is society
celebrating itself for transcending the sins of previous generations to finally
achieve a state of racial equality where race no longer matters. Moreover, it
suggests that going forward, race will no longer play a role in how future societies organize themselves. Race, like other political systems that are no longer

viable such as fascism and communism, is thought to be dead and without any reasonable chance of ever being resuscitated. Post-racialism marks the end of race history, and therefore the end for the need for race-conscious law and public policy.[22]

Secondly, in proclaiming that the long and pitiful history of race is now at an endpoint, post-racialism finds all types of race consciousness—from Jim Crow forms of subordination to affirmative action types of remedies—to be equally reprehensible.[23] To the extent that post-racialism envisions a society that has transcended and overcome past societies' struggles and divisiveness—where the state conferred various privileges and burdens to racial groups—it does not differentiate between various forms of race-conscious governance. Post-racialism builds social consensus by endorsing a historical and moral time line that frames the "we have arrived" post-racialist moment through a specific evolutionary narrative in which society has progressed from the most brutal forms of racial oppression (slavery, Jim Crow), endured necessary forms of social and political resistance (civil rights movements), and atoned through an era of formal remedies for past wrongs (affirmative action) to have now reached the proverbial mountaintop where we have presumably worked through our issues so as to now be able to live in a society as one America. To tolerate race consciousness at this point—either to subordinate or remedy subordination—is seen as a step backward from this post-racialist moment and therefore de-evolutionary in terms of running against the proper progression of social relations.

Lastly, post-racialism posits that race is no longer a salient or meaningful characteristic of group difference that affects social relations. As part of the general narrative of transcendence that links each of these three characteristics, post-racialism describes the current society as one where race is no longer a barrier to one's life opportunities. Race is simply no longer salient; society either no longer sees it or pays attention to it in any signficant way. In his now famous "A More Perfect Union" speech, delivered in response to the questions surrounding his relationship with Rev. Jeremiah Wright, then presidential candidate Obama said:

> The profound mistake of Reverend Wright's sermons is not that he spoke about racism in our society. It's that he spoke as if our society was static; as if no progress has been made; as if this country—a country that has made it possible for one of his own members to run for the highest office in the land and build a coalition of white and black; Latino and Asian, rich and poor, young

and old—is still irrevocably bound to a tragic past. But what we know—what we have seen—is that America can change. That is the true genius of this nation. What we have already achieved gives us hope—the audacity to hope—for what we can and must achieve tomorrow.[24]

In suggesting a break from a race-conscious society that has evolved on its own terms, post-racialism attempts to produce the change that it says already exists. For example, in focusing on the fact that Obama was a viable presidential candidate at the time of this speech (and eventually won the election), the post-racialist strategy creates the state of social and political affairs that it claims already prevails to make its perspective valid if not inevitable—all through limiting the ongoing salience of race while racial (if not *racist*) opposition to Obama's very legitimacy continues throughout his presidency. The irony inherent in President Obama's post-racial approach is that his campaigns and presidency have been nothing but racial. From Representative Joe Wilson calling President Obama a liar during a speech to Congress to ongoing questions about his religion and place of birth to a sitting governor waving her finger in his face as if the Leader of the Free World was a misbehaving child, President Obama has endured indignities that simply would be unimaginable if he were White. This highlights the remarkable tension between President Obama's post-racial aspirations and his anything-but-post-racial treatment as commander in chief.

Post-racialism and Colorblindness
Is the post-racialism advanced and mainstreamed by Obama's campaign strategy and presidency merely colorblindness by a different name? Not quite. To be sure, post-racialism and colorblindness are similar in that they are both critical of race consciousness; both approaches shun the idea that society's racial past is determinative of present and future trajectories regarding race relations and instead pursue a politics of racial blindness. But, post-racialism and colorblindness can be distinguished in important ways that highlight the work that each does independently and how their convergence poses important challenges for law and society. The most important distinction to make is that while colorblindness offers a *normative* perspective on how race ought to be treated in law and public policy, post-racialism operates as a *descriptive* account of where society currently is.[25] This distinction is crucial. Advocates of colorblindness often argue that we are not yet at a post-racial state of equality precisely because of ongoing racial preferences for minorities and

continuing efforts to attribute existing racial disparities to racial discrimination. However, post-racialism's notion of racial transcendence suggests that we are already at this end of race history precisely because past conflicts and struggles have allowed society to evolve to a point where, for example, even a Black man can be president. Indeed, it is this very claim that American society has already "arrived," as a descriptive matter, at a post-racial state (i.e., beyond the typical polemics and divisiveness characterized by race consciousness) that allowed Barack Obama to introduce this post-racialist strategy to the American public.[26]

A second distinction is the role of context. While context is not relevant to colorblindness's normative assertions regarding how we ought to govern ourselves, context is crucial to the post-racialist project of crafting a compelling race narrative and temporality that banish race consciousness from the polity precisely because we have ostensibly worked through and gone beyond a troublesome race history. Context is fully acknowledged in post-racialist discourses to specifically exclude race consciousness from present and future race conversations. Anti-race consciousness is promoted as the evolutionary goal in post-racialist discourse, while the role of context and history in colorblindness discourses is largely sidestepped and undertheorized in favor of flat, acontextual claims that race consciousness is race consciousness is race consciousness; the Klansman and the affirmative action supporter suffer from the same folly of paying too much attention to race.

This leads to an interesting tension between the two approaches: the normative appeal of colorblindness is to create laws and policies that will produce the moment of racial transcendence that post-racialism suggests already exists. Yet both approaches nevertheless operate in a manner that denies the ongoing significance of racial subordination and White racial privilege. With colorblindness operating from the political right to delegitimize ongoing claims for race consciousness in law and public policy and post-racialism operating largely (in the current political moment) from the political left to celebrate the historic election of Barack Obama as an indicator that race struggle as race consciousness is over, modern efforts at racial justice are at a political and intellectual stalemate. Colorblindness and post-racialism—despite their origins in opposing political traditions—serve each other in important regards. By delegitimizing efforts at getting social, legal, and political attention paid to ongoing structural racism and racial hierarchy, they provide the intellectual and political momentum for the continued subordination of people of color.

Despite different political standpoints and historical contexts, colorblind-ness and post-racialism offer each other mutual support and coherence in giving rise to a synergistic effect that each individually could not effectively pursue in the absence of the other. This effect is the redemption of White-ness.[27] By the term Whiteness, I write in the tradition of Cheryl Harris and others who see the accumulated privileges of being White in a racially strati-fied society as a property value that improves Whites' life opportunities at the expense of racial minorities.[28] The purpose of *Brown v. Board of Education* and the civil rights movement was to check Whiteness as a social and political identity whose power came from the dual processes of privilege and subordi-nation. From this perspective, the diminution of a hyperinflated Whiteness that existed at the expense of racial minorities was an important aspect of the social, legal, and political commitment to racial equality throughout much of the late twentieth century—whether it was by the desegregation of schools, affirmative action in employment and education, or increasing minorities' access to resources such as home loans. These efforts diversified both public and private spheres in a manner that attempted to level the playing field by muting the privileges of Whiteness so as to offer opportunities to a broader section of the population.

In the face of widening racial disparities in the post–civil rights era in virtually every measurable social category across the life spectrum—from infant mortality to education to unemployment to incarceration to nurs-ing home care and end-of-life decision making—colorblindness and post-racialism operate individually and, most importantly, *in concert* to obscure and deny the existence of race hierarchies.[29] This synergistic relationship of normative colorblind appeals and post-racial descriptive accounts of racial transcendence reframe existing racial disparities as not the product of struc-tural racism but the natural state of things that can only be rectified through *individual* efforts. The synergistic effect is to resurrect old justifications for White racial dominance through new social and legal framings imbued with colorblind aspirations and post-racial descriptive transcendence, which ulti-mately hide the structural continuities between past and contemporary forms of White racial dominance. Individually, neither colorblindness nor post-racialism effectively achieves this rehabilitative aim. Colorblindness's norma-tive assertions can be exposed as out of touch without an evolutionary social narrative, and post-racialism on its own terms makes good campaign rhetoric but lacks a consistent theory for how one ought to govern. Together, however, the two approaches—unintentionally and without coordination—nevertheless cement a disdain for race consciousness and entrench an indifference to racial injustice that is devastating for any sensible project seeking to address persistent racial hierarchies that continue to shape the life outcomes of people of color. By effectively taking race out of law and society, colorblindness and post-racialism resurrect Whiteness as it was before race-conscious efforts challenged its legitimacy and restrained its power in the name of fairness and equality.

Resisting Whiteness's Redemption

Several blind respondents mentioned Barack Obama when describing their understanding of race, which highlights the impact that his candidacy and presidency have had on public perceptions—even for those who cannot engage with race in the same manner as sighted individuals. These respondents mentioned Obama as a way to discuss racial dynamics that often focus on visual distinctions. For example, blind White respondent Dale said that in defining race, "people focus, tremendously, on the color of the skin. So, for example, the person who is lighter skin. Politicians like [Colin] Powell and even someone like Barack Obama. You know people make distinctions. They try to make distinctions between the darker ones and the lighter ones. So, I think, here in America, color in the visual aspect becomes more pronounced than in other places." Blind White respondent Laura, who believed that Obama's voice sounded Black, was dismayed by some people's continued questioning of whether Obama was "Black enough" due to his privileged background and mixed-race heritage. She said: "You know, it just kills me, because like Barack Obama, you know he's Black by his voice, but the community has given him a lot of shit, because he's not dark enough. And, I'm like, 'Well, hell he sounds Black. What's your problem?' " Other blind respondents were not so sure that Obama sounded Black at all. For example, Jackson, a White male, said that Obama "talks more like [he's] White," leading him to conclude that "race is not only skin color but it's also a social thing."

Beyond issues of voice and visuality, President Obama's ascension as a public figure also impacted the way blind people understood and experienced race on a personal level . For example, Heidi, a blind White woman, recounted:

> It was only when Obama ran for president that I realized that my father is really a big asshole. . . . He was telling me about how inferior they are to us and that it would take another hundred years before they are evolved enough

to be running for president or be doing something like that. . . . He was saying this stuff, and I'm thinking the fact that he is saying this stuff says a whole lot about who has evolved.

But perhaps most striking was a statement by James, a blind White male, regarding President Obama as a post-racialist icon:

> So I think people who want to say there is no difference between the races, like [there's] a lot of people say[ing] Barack Obama is post-racial America. I don't buy it. I think America has advanced enough to the point that an African American like President Obama who gets well educated and does these things can advance to the highest of heights. I think we've come that far, but we certainly haven't come far enough to believe that we don't need to do more to make sure that African American schools are better, are on the same playing field, the same level of opportunity as White children. And so, I actually think there is a danger, a small danger that a lot of White people will see President Obama's victory as "we can close the door on that" because I think a lot of White people are very interested in saying, "We're not racist. We've solved all that. We don't have to do it anymore."
>
>   . . . The reality of it is it's a falsehood. I mean, I remember I did a presentation in [a large metropolitan city], and this really taught me a lot about being blind. The school [was] overwhelmingly African American kids. I was walking down the hallway, and I found a net, and I said to the teacher, "What is this net here for?" And she said, "Oh, that's to catch the bricks that sometimes fall off the ceiling." I remember thinking, "No wonder these kids can't learn." I mean, when I was in elementary school, . . . my biggest concern was when were they going to let us go to recess. I wasn't worrying about getting hit on the head with bricks and whether or not we would have enough food and whether we had books for everybody. And so, I mean personally, I believe that racial discrimination is alive and well in America. I think the downside is that we've made enough improvements so that the majority, the White people, are finding it less and less of an urge to solve the remaining problems.

The sensibility evoked here regarding the implausibility of post-racialism and its latent dangers is quite similar to blind respondents' rejection of color-blindness as an apt way to frame social relations. These interviews with blind people allow us to see how the "post" rhetoric operates like the "blind" metaphor in producing a vision of society that reduces race to its lowest common denominator—visually obvious traits that define group membership—that can either be normatively ignored or ostensibly transcended in an effort to claim that society's racial struggles are over.[30] In doing this, colorblind post-racialism creates the conditions for reaffirming typological thinking about race that leads to a form of essentialism that feeds Whiteness's reemergence and new forms of racial hierarchy.[31] The separate but interconnected and synergistic relationship between colorblindness and post-racialism recreates the same type of typological thinking at the heart of previous eras of racial subordination—from scientific racism to the eugenics movement to Jim Crow—by simultaneously describing status quo racial inequalities as a natural byproduct of group relations that descriptively cannot be altered and normatively should not be. These ideas converge to give legitimacy to the approach that society should be blind to any social and legal conditions that may produce racial disparities not only because it is the moral thing to do, but because we have already, in fact, transcended race. The fallout from this twin approach is that inequalities that characterize persistent racial hierarchy are thought to be caused by racial minorities' inherent limitations and, conversely, Whites' racial superiority. Through this reemergence of typological thinking, colorblind post-racialism redeems Whiteness and places it back in the cherished social position that it occupied before the civil rights movement.

But blind people are able to see through this socio-legal charade, and their perspective helps us appreciate the extent to which social practices produce the salience and visibility of race in a manner that resists the typological thinking giving rise to the fantasies of colorblind post-racialism. To be sure, if blind people see and pay attention to race in a manner not unlike sighted individuals, claims of post-racialism and colorblindness are exposed as premature expressions that only serve to conceal and further entrench racial subordination. Blind people's experiences reveal the socially productive nature of seeing race, which suggests that much more work needs to be done before society can claim to have transcended what its blind constituents still see. Blind people's perspective on race provides an empirical basis from which to resist these efforts at redeeming Whiteness by bringing attention back to the social practices that produce the visibility of race, which are linked to the very same social practices of decontextualizing race that are connected to the broader subordination of people of color. It is precisely blind people's lack of vision that can enable the rest of society to see the folly of their ways and the damaging effects of these redemptive efforts.

Epilogue

Rebooting Race

O N A RECENT TRIP BACK HOME TO THE SAN FRANCISCO BAY AREA
from a conference, I found myself in the middle of an epic
airline mix-up. In short, the plane that I was supposed to be on had
mechanical problems, which meant that another plane had to be used.
Unfortunately, the new plane had an entirely different seating layout. Each
passenger had to be issued a new boarding pass and seat assignment in less
than an hour—and not necessarily in accordance with their previously
selected preferences.

As you can imagine, this led to chaos. I ended up being the last person
issued a ticket to board the plane. In the midst of this confusion, people
essentially ignored their new seating assignments. A gentleman flying with
two young children was sitting in my newly assigned seat. He asked me to
take his seat on the other side of the plane so that he could stay with them.
"No problem," I said. When I arrived at my new seat, a gentleman who did
not want to be separated from his wife had already taken it. He offered me his
assigned seat—which was in first class. Jackpot.

I had heard of these mysterious stories where coach flyers end up in first
class but had never had the experience myself. This was my first time on the
other side of the curtain; with a six-hour flight ahead of me, I was quite grateful. I initially felt like an imposter, but then I decided to just go with it and
enjoy the amenities. Sadly, my sense is that first class today is essentially what
coach was fifteen years ago: a warm meal and decent leg room. After fiddling

around with the on-demand entertainment system, I decided to settle in and watch a movie. On a whim, I turned on *In Time*.

In Time stars Justin Timberlake as Will Salas, a young man living in a not-too-distant future in which time is literally money; currency is no longer measured in dollars and cents, but in hours and minutes. In this future world, people are genetically engineered to stop aging at age twenty-five, at which point they live only one more year unless they earn more time through work or other legal or illegal activities—just like money. Each person has a glowing digital clock embedded in their forearm that counts down the time they have until their demise. Unless they earn more time. This keeps the poor engaged in an all-consuming hustle to stay alive. As Salas narrates in the opening scene, "Time is now the currency. We earn it and spend it. The rich can live forever. And the rest of us? I just want to wake up with more time on my hand than hours in the day."[1]

In Time was written, directed, and produced by Andrew Niccol—a talented filmmaker with a knack for using genetic technologies to explore and rethink the human condition, as he did in his previous film *GATTACA*. Salas ends up saving the life of a troubled man by the name of Henry Hamilton, who is 105 years old and has a century remaining—an extraordinary amount of wealth. Like most people living their lives day to day, Salas never stops to think about the social structures that lead him, his friends, and family to scrape by to keep enough minutes on their clocks to stay alive. Survival is of the utmost importance, not thinking about whether their situation is just, fair, or even necessary. *The system feels natural.* The film's main villain, Philippe Weis (played by Vincent Kartheiser, who brings the same sense of unrelenting privilege to this character as he does to Peter Campbell in *Mad Men*), notes that using time as currency is no different from what has occurred in previous societies: "Of course, some think what we have is unfair. . . . But, hasn't evolution always been unfair? It's always been survival of the fittest. This is merely Darwinian capitalism—natural selection."[2] But Hamilton gives Salas a bit of insight:

> For a few to be immortal, many must die. . . . Everyone can't live forever. Where would we put them? . . . Why do you think taxes and prices go up the same day in the ghetto? The cost of living keeps rising to make sure that people keep dying. How else could there be men with a million years while most live day-to-day? But the truth is that there's more than enough. No one has to die before their time.[3]

Before Hamilton ultimately commits suicide, he transfers his century to Salas while he sleeps. Excited that he will finally be able to give his mother a better life, Salas goes to pick her up after her shift. But she runs out of time and dies after repaying a loan and not having enough fare for the bus ride home. Salas decides to use his newfound time to infiltrate high society to make the wealthy pay for setting up a system that led to his mother's untimely death.

At this point, *In Time* essentially becomes a futuristic Robin Hood movie. But it resonated with me for many reasons—particularly as I viewed the film while straddling class lines at thirty-five thousand feet. What is intriguing about this film is its ability to get the audience to rethink that which seems so transparently ordinary, obvious, and natural—money as currency—and how its unnecessarily uneven distribution leads to pain, suffering, and premature death. Volumes of studies on the social determinants of health have shown the strong correlation between wealth and health outcomes.[4] A stronger commitment to reducing poverty and improving access to resources such as high-quality education would undoubtedly improve and save lives. Yet we, as a society, routinely ignore this evidence in favor of an unthinking assumption that the current distribution of wealth and resources reflects a natural social order and that outcomes such as premature death are a sad yet unavoidable reality. But by simply telling a story that substitutes one currency for another—time for money—*In Time* is able to disrupt this series of assumptions and offer a critique of capital that gives the viewing audience a certain amount of pause. Viewers slowly realize that they are not simply watching some commentary on a futuristic society, but rather a critique of the here and now that only resonates because using time as currency is just as arbitrary as money; in both cases, its disproportionate accumulation and distribution lead the masses to experience unspeakable suffering.

While it is certainly a coincidence that *In Time* opened in theaters around the same time that the Occupy Wall Street movement began, this film represents the consciousness raising that can potentially come out of disrupting everyday assumptions concerning the social order. It is this type of disruption and attempt at raising our collective consciousness to reimagine society that I have tried to replicate with this book. My hope is to create an intellectual and political space for rethinking our core assumptions about race so as to understand that every aspect of our racial experiences—not simply the meanings attached to human bodies *but the very ability to see racial difference itself*—is produced by social practices entwined with larger projects of racial subordination. The visual obviousness with which we experience the salience of race—like the obviousness in which we experience money and its misdistribution as a politically neutral form of currency—is part of an unthinking and seemingly transparent social hierarchy used to privilege certain groups at the expense of others. It is only through disruptive moments in which we radically critique the premise of the system itself that we can rethink human relations in furtherance of social justice. In this book, this "rethinking" is done by exploring the racial experiences and understandings of blind people, who are able to disrupt sighted people's assumptions that race is salient because it is visually obvious so as to give insight into a world that the sighted simply cannot see *precisely because of their vision.* The way we currently frame the relationship between vision and justice—particularly with regard to race and discrimination—is sociologically thin in that it bears little resemblance to the secondary nature of vision in how race becomes salient. The primary problem is that the standard approach to race—the assumption that it speaks for itself, or what I have termed *"race" ipsa loquitur*—treats the visual salience of race as a phenomenon anterior to the social practices that make human bodies visible in certain ways. Treating the salience of race as self-evident obscures these practices, which diminishes a deeper understanding of the way race *becomes* rather than simply *is* visible. Sighted people are therefore *blinded by their sight;* vision itself seduces them to treat immediately perceptible human differences as visually obvious distinctions in a manner that masks the social practices that make these distinctions visible.

Like an old computer that has become sluggish, unresponsive to one's needs, and unproductive, existing race discussions have become similarly dull and not useful. It is past time to reboot race, in terms of developing new approaches to thinking about, examining, and remedying the enduring problem of substantive inequalities across the life spectrum in light of formal equality by law. The modern tendency is to tilt toward colorblind post-racialism as a lens to view contemporary race problems, but these approaches only aggravate and retrench the problem when what is needed is a complete reboot of the conversation. This book offers a model for rebooting by encouraging greater synergy between Critical Race Theory and empirical methods. These two approaches have not engaged each other's claims and methodologies as substantively as they could. This limits Critical Race Theory's insights by not leveraging empirical data to support its claims, while empirical approaches may not reach their full theoretical potential.[5] In building a constitutive theory of race through empirically investigating blind people's understandings, this book highlights the benefits of joining these two fields to yield insights on race and law that might otherwise go unexplored. In order to successfully face the remarkable social and legal challenges ahead regarding race, it is no longer adequate for race scholarship to be either theoretically sophisticated or empirically robust; it must do both. And it must do both well. This path can be best forged by research that is simultaneously attentive to these fields' theoretical and empirical dimensions.

The key finding from this research—that blind people have a visual understanding of race—has significant implications for each field. For Critical Race Theory, it suggests that it is time to expand its critique beyond first-generation constructionist accounts to pursue second-generation constitutive analyses that embrace empirical methods to flesh out the broader implications of the micromechanics of race, that is, how individual human interactions reflect, (re)produce, and embed structures of racial dominance. And for empirical scholars, these research findings draw attention to how the surface level treatment of race as a coherent and stable variable perpetuates a theoretically impoverished basis from which to collect, analyze, and report data.

But the empirical findings from this book suggest more than an opportunity for synergistic scholarship between Critical Race Theory and empirical methods. They also have profound implications for law and society. Blending Critical Race Theory and empirical methods enables innovative critiques of law and policy that disrupt existing discourses of race to encourage racial justice. Embracing a constitutive theory of race and the empirical findings pertaining to blind people's visual understanding of race raise profound questions regarding Equal Protection jurisprudence in addition to normative theories of colorblindness and descriptive accounts that we have entered a post-racial society. By theoretically situating and empirically destabilizing the underlying assumption behind these legal, policy, and political trends that facilitate a *"race" ipsa loquitur* mentality, I have tried to draw attention to the injustices perpetuated by the status quo so as to provide a conceptual and evidence-based foothold from which to rethink and reboot our commitments to social justice.

Last but not least, it is my hope that this book will stimulate a broader public re-engagement with race. Think about it: how twisted must American race relations be when blind individuals—folks who cannot see the very racial distinctions that mediate human interactions—nevertheless "see" race and organize much of their daily lives around it? This finding provides a diagnosis that despite important achievements, American race relations are in many ways sicker than we ever imagined. Radical transformations are needed to even begin a sensible and coherent conversation about the entrenched nature of race and racism in society. It is my hope that this book and future race scholarship in this vein can encourage a new generation of public conversations on race that can lead us to a future of true equality and human liberation.

Appendix A: Critical Race Theory— Background and Critiques

The Development of Critical Race Theory

Background: Critical Legal Studies

Critical Race Theory can be most accurately understood as an outgrowth of the Critical Legal Studies movement—a group that emerged in the 1970s to introduce legal academia to some of the reflections and recalibrations society endured during the prior decade. Critical Legal Studies can be juxtaposed to the then-prevailing orthodoxy prevalent throughout legal academia and the practice of law. Here, law was thought to be an internally coherent set of rules whereby objective and consistent decisions could be rendered through rigorous application of value-neutral principles.[1]

Critical Legal Studies (CLS) itself has been described as an outgrowth of the Law and Society Association. A key breaking point was the increasing disenchantment CLS founders had with what they perceived to be the association's undue emphasis on empiricism. Allan Hutchinson and Patrick Monahan write:

> The [Critical Legal Studies] movement was formally founded in 1977 by a small group of scholars who had become dissatisfied with the intellectual mood and direction of the Law and Society Association. These scholars took the view that the Association had become too closely identified with the "empirico-behaviorist" wing of social science and the road to jurisprudential enlightenment lay down a less data oriented, more theoretical path. The lifeblood of the CLS movement was to be philosophy, not science.[2]

This tension was also evident from the perspective of law and society scholars. For example, in their review of critical traditions within law and society research, Susan Silbey and Austin Sarat write: "If [law and society] takes as our subject the constitutive effect of law, we cannot be content with literary theory applied to legal doctrine. We must instead study families, schools, work places, social movements, and yes, even professional associations to present a broad picture in which law may seem at first glance virtually invisible."[3] Today, the Law and Society Association includes many scholars who do not identify strongly (or much at all) as empiricists. But particularly at the time of these debates, much of the tension between Critical Legal Studies and law and society was not only methodological—philosophy versus science— but also normative in terms of differing perspectives on what *ought* to be the role of legal scholars. Critical Legal Studies strongly identifies as a *political* movement—an ideological position that often is in tension with the data-driven, value-free objectivism of the social sciences.[4] The implications of this tension for the development of Critical Race Theory will be further discussed later in this appendix.

Critical Legal Studies is far from the first scholarly movement to question classical legal thought. Legal realists of the early twentieth century raised many of the same questions a half-century before Critical Legal Studies would take off as a sustained legal critique.[5] These scholars rejected legal orthodoxy, or the idea that law could be an objective science, and instead argued that law is constituted by all of the imperfections, foibles, and subjectivities present in other human interactions. As such, the realists "called into question three related ideals cherished by most Americans: the notion that, in the United States, the people (not unelected judges) select the rules by which they are governed; the conviction that the institution of judicial review reinforces rather than undermines representative democracy; and the faith that ours is a government of laws, not of men."[6]

In reviving this thread of thought, Critical Legal Studies added a new spin to the critique of legal orthodoxy that, in the context of then-burgeoning social upheavals such as the civil rights movement, gave it a new significance. While Critical Legal Studies may be somewhat difficult to pin down, its scholars share at least three broad commitments. The first is a critique of legal formalism and objectivism, or "the idea that there is an autonomous and neutral mode of 'legal' reasoning and rationality through which legal specialists apply doctrine in concrete cases to reach results that are independent of the specialists' ethical ideals and political purposes."[7] The argument put forth by Critical Legal Studies is that law is indeterminate:

> Legal rules and arguments fail to compel or justify definite answers in legal disputes. CLS advances several sophisticated arguments in support of the indeterminacy thesis. An internal critique takes the rules and arguments making up orthodox legal doctrine as premises and shows them to be inconsistent, incomplete, and ambiguous—and therefore indeterminate. An external critique, in contrast, stands outside the conventions of ordinary legal analysis and establishes indeterminacy by appealing to language, philosophy, or history. For example, CLS has used modern linguistic theory and deconstructive techniques to show that the nature of language renders law indeterminate, and has also focused on the role of social forces and power relations as the actual determinants of legal outcomes.[8]

Second, Critical Legal Studies sees traditional liberal legalisms—notably, the concept of the rule of law—as playing a critical role in masking the indeterminacy of law and legitimizing the social order as natural, normal, and right. At the heart of this is what Critical Legal Studies sees as a series of contradictions that liberalism attempts to smooth over: between individual autonomy and communal forces, public versus private spheres of activity, free will versus determinism, and so on.[9] Critical Legal Studies argues that with each set of contradictions, "the legal system (unconsciously) privileges one pole of each dichotomy, presumptively making it govern. What results is a legal order that is not neutral, but 'remarkably right wing,' hierarchical, and morally objectionable."[10] In order to neutralize this perception, the rule of law functions to make these contradictions seem not so contradictory—in part by creating on the fly rules of entitlement that take the edge off of fundamental incongruencies in the social order. This is where an important theme of Critical Legal Studies comes into play: its critique of rights. Critical legal theorists take a pessimistic view of rights in a liberal democracy, noting that "in constructing elaborate schemes of legal rights and entitlements which are intended to permit individuals to interact with others without being obliterated by them, mainstream legal theorists simply justify the prevailing conditions of social life and erect formidable barriers to social change."[11] In short, rights just don't matter all that much. Or, at the very least, they matter much less than lawyers think they do.[12] We will return to this point and its role in the formation of Critical Race Theory later in this section.

Lastly, Critical Legal Studies focuses on the effect such indeterminacy, and its masking, has on consciousness in terms of how individuals experience the social world. Instead of experiencing society as if its ordering is natural or the way it has to be, Critical Legal Studies is interested in demonstrating how social and legal realities are relative and historically contingent. Nature does not determine social and legal outcomes. Rather, these outcomes stem from embedded class hierarchies and group antagonisms predicated on injustice and inequalities that repeat themselves across generations. Therefore, in focusing on how law shapes a consciousness that sees social relations as unproblematic,

> the distinctive feature of the CLS movement is its desire to shatter the limiting conceptions of the possibilities of human association and of the social transformation embodied in liberal legal thought. The CLSers' enterprise is to complete the modern rebellion against the view that social arrangements are natural or inevitable. They want to expose society as the vulgar and contingent product of interrupted fighting. The central strategy is to suggest that social order exists only because, at some arbitrary point, the struggle between individuals was halted and truce lines were drawn up. These truce lines define the structure of a society's politics and production. Although these truce lines initially are simply the product of an uneasy deal between combatants, eventually they stabilize and become fixed. A sense of stability is generated by the insistence that the truce lines represent more than the residue of interrupted fighting: Strength becomes right, obedience becomes duty, and the *ad hoc* nature of hierarchal division in society is obscured. Inspired by a vision of the contingent nature of all social worlds, the CLS project is to identify the role played by law and legal reasoning in the process through which social structures acquire the appearance of inevitability.[13]

Thus, a key goal of Critical Legal Studies is to expose the false reality shaped by legal consciousness to demonstrate alternate possibilities for social ordering.

The Emergence of Critical Race Theory

Minority scholars committed to racial justice and their allies found Critical Legal Studies attractive. As a group that was interested in questioning legal practices that produce inequality and systemically disfavor those at the bottom of the social hierarchy, Critical Legal Studies provided a community that was remarkably sympathetic to minority scholars' commitment to reforming law and deconstructing race and class hierarchies. Critical Legal Studies' emphasis on the *institutional* character of such oppression—especially the role of law—made CLS a natural home for the burgeoning post–civil rights critique of law developing in the 1980s.

Mari Matsuda describes the appeal of Critical Legal Studies to minority scholars in both descriptive and normative terms. Matsuda notes that Critical Legal Studies was "attractive to minority scholars because its central descriptive message—that legal ideals are manipulable and that law serves to legitimate existing misdistributions of wealth and power—rings true for anyone who has experienced life in non-White America. Frederick Douglass realized this truth about law before Oliver Wendell Holmes ever picked up a pen."[14] Viewed from the standpoint of historically marginalized racial minorities, many of the claims made by Critical Legal Studies were less than radical, yet nonetheless appreciated. Thus, Matsuda notes: "CLS is a legitimation process for outsiders" in that this long-standing yet mostly ignored minority perspective on law was finally gaining traction in mainstream legal conversations.[15]

But the attraction minority scholars had toward Critical Legal Studies also had a strong normative component in that "the willingness at least to consider the utopian prospect and the passionate criticism of existing conditions of racism and poverty attracts non-White readers to CLS. Moreover, an elevated understanding of the traditional legal concepts of neutral principles and rights helps protect victims of oppression from unsophisticated rights-thinking that can be a seductive trap for those at the bottom."[16] This normative commitment to racial justice reflects what Monica Bell terms the obligation thesis within modern race scholarship. Bell notes that for these scholars, "scholarship is not just about producing interesting ideas. It is often also about producing societal benefit."[17] Thus, CLS's commitment to leveraging legal academia as a catalyst for social change was yet another important draw.

While several minority scholars participated in Critical Legal Studies meetings, conferences, and discussions in the late 1980s, serious tensions quickly developed that eventually led to the emergence of a more particularized movement of scholarship critical of the relationship between race, racism, and law. At least three issues led these minority scholars to break from Critical Legal Studies to form a separate group that came to be known as Critical Race Theory. First, minority scholars participating in Critical Legal Studies felt that "CLS scholars had not, by and large, developed and incorporated a critique of racial power into their analysis[;] their practices, politics, and theories regarding race tended to be unsatisfying and sometimes indistinguishable from those of the dominant institutions they were otherwise contesting."[18] Key to this sentiment was the notion that legal consciousness does not act alone in providing boundaries that legitimate status quo arrangements that restrict imagining alternative arrangements for human interaction. Critical Race Theorists asserted that racial power, as a similar consciousness-shaping activity that makes racial hierarchies and subordination seem normal, also plays a central role in understanding modern society. Crenshaw et al. note that "as race moved from the margins to the center of discourse within Critical Legal Studies—or, as some would say, Critical Legal Studies took the race turn—institutional and theoretical disjunctures between Critical Legal Studies and the emerging scholarship on race eventually manifested themselves as central themes within Critical Race Theory."[19] Thus, this notion of the centrality of racial power—that racism does not reflect aberrant, isolated, or episodic events but is rather a systemic aspect of modern social life—became the theory of race within Critical Race Theory that set it apart from Critical Legal Studies.

A second but related disjuncture between Critical Race Theory and Critical Legal Studies is their understanding of law. Crenshaw et al. explain that, although Critical Legal Studies attempted to move away from instrumentalists' accounts of race and law that viewed legal outcomes adverse to minorities as a reflection of social preferences *external* to law, minority scholars were more strongly committed to understanding *how law constructs and produces racial meaning*.[20] The authors continue by noting that in Critical Legal Studies, the "prevailing theorizations of race and law seemed to represent law as an instrumental reflection of racial interests in much the same way that vulgar Marxists saw the legal arena as reflecting class interests."[21] But the minority scholars that eventually formed Critical Race Theory wanted to look deeper at law, beyond the notion that it simply reflects social preferences. For Critical Race Theory, law constructs race and racism rather than merely reflecting broader structural or class divisions as superstructure:

> We began to think of our project as uncovering how law was a constitutive element of race itself: in other words, how law constructed race. Racial power, in our view, was not simply—or even primarily—a product of biased decision-making on the part of judges, but instead, the sum total of the pervasive ways in which law shapes and is shaped by "race relations" across the social plane. Laws produced racial power not simply through narrowing the scope

of, say, of anti-discrimination remedies, nor through racially biased decision-making, but instead, through myriad legal rules, many of them having nothing to do with rules against discrimination, that continued to reproduce the structures and practices of racial domination.[22]

Lastly, and most likely the proverbial nail in the coffin for many minority scholars' decision to formally break away from Critical Legal Studies, was the CLS argument that rights are not useful and may indeed inhibit progress toward a more equitable society. The argument generally proceeds along these lines: rights are unstable in that they are subject to interpretation and thus can change according to interpreters' values or politics; claiming a right produces no certain outcomes; rights talk mediates and thus obscures the authentic human relations that should be focused upon; and rights inhibit progress in that their indeterminacy allows elite interests to use them to prevent social change.[23] Indeed, leading Critical Legal Studies scholar Mark Tushnet goes so far as to argue that "it is not just that rights talk does not do much good. In the contemporary United States, it is positively harmful."[24]

For many minority scholars, this heated discussion over the utility of rights represented fundamental differences between the social visions embraced by Critical Legal Studies and those of the racial minorities that would come to create Critical Race Theory.[25] Richard Delgado argues: "The CLS critique of rights and rules is the most problematic aspect of the CLS program, and provides few answers for minority scholars and lawyers."[26] For Delgado and many others, the Critical Legal Studies argument reflects a profound misunderstanding of the crucial role rights have played in the protection of minority communities. Despite their indeterminacy, these communities' oppressive histories and realties give rights a special meaning in that rights "give pause to those who would otherwise oppress us" while also "serv[ing] as a rallying point [to] bring us closer together."[27] Many minority scholars shared the sentiment that Martin Luther King Jr. expressed years before this rights debate commenced: "It may be true that the law cannot make a man love me, but it can keep him from lynching me, and . . . that's pretty important."[28] From the perspective of minority scholars, the inability of Critical Legal Studies to grasp the importance of rights to racial minorities in the context of their remarkable histories demonstrated a distinct lack of sensitivity.[29]

At the same time that minority scholars within Critical Legal Studies were becoming increasingly dissatisfied, scholars and lawyers of color elsewhere were becoming frustrated with diminished returns from traditional civil rights approaches to racial justice. Marches, sit-ins, new litigation strategies, and other types of traditional reform measures simply failed to produce sustainable returns in terms of improving the lives of racial minorities. Indeed, many felt that by the late 1970s, a retrenchment toward pre-*Brown* race relations was being ushered in. Crenshaw et al. note that "by the late seventies, traditional civil rights lawyers found themselves fighting, and losing, reargued attacks on the limited victories they had only just achieved in the prior decade, particularly with respect to affirmative action and legal requirements for the kinds of evidence required to prove illicit discrimination."[30]

In some ways, this experience legitimates the Critical Legal Studies perspective that rights, civil or otherwise, are indeterminate, subject to interpretation, and can be used by elites to inhibit social justice. Yet the emerging critical race analysis of the civil rights movement, led by Derrick Bell, did not see this frustration as a product of indeterminacy, but rather as a function of racial power. Here is where Bell developed the interest convergence dilemma that has been profoundly influential on critical race scholarship: racial minorities' progress will only occur when their intersts align with the interests of elites.[31]

Bell's pessimism toward the current and future status of race relations certainly differs from the utopia put forth by the Critical Legal Studies movement that many Critical Race Theorists formally participated in. And not all Critical Race Theorists share Bell's radical view. But what these two threads of thought represent—one critical of leftist movements within legal academia, the other critical of anti-discrimination legalisms—is a shared effort to "reexamine the terms by which race and racism have been negotiated in American consciousness, and to recover and revitalize the radical tradition of race consciousness among African-Americans and other peoples of color—a tradition that was discarded when integration, assimilation, and the ideal of colorblindness became the official norms of racial enlightenment."[32]

Critical Race Theory's Defining Characteristics

It would not be entirely accurate to frame Critical Race Theory as a race-specific version of Critical Legal Studies. While heavily influenced by CLS, the preceding discussion describing the dissatisfaction felt by many minority scholars within CLS should not lead one to view Critical Race Theory as an identical movement that merely replaced the CLS focus on class hierarchy with a corresponding race analysis. Rather Critical Race Theory has an affirmative scholarly agenda that goes beyond deconstructing the perceived shortcomings of Critical Legal Studies, bringing entirely new critiques of the law and demanding different levels of accountability. While a number of different threads of scholarship have come to influence the development of Critical Race Theory, no one set of characteristics can accurately describe this diverse scholarship.[33] Nevertheless, at least three commitments can be accurately portrayed as the field's most known traits: the social and legal construction of race, intersectional and anti-essentialist understandings of identity, and storytelling as a method of legal analysis.

The Social and Legal Construction of Race

First, while Critical Race Theory did not unilaterally conceive the idea that race is a social construction, it brought the concept to legal scholarship to develop a specific conversation about the ways in which law constructs and maintains racial meanings and hierarchies.[34] By this, it is meant that (1) race is not a biologically determined variable; law assists in creating these labels and the significance that we attach to human bodies, and (2) the process by which racial categories and meanings are created is not simply a social practice that happens anterior to law, but is deeply influenced by legal developments. This contribution has been crucial to Critical Race Theory's core effort at "challeng[ing] the ways in which race and racial power are constructed and represented in American legal culture and, more generally, in American society as a whole."[35] Much of the bridgework to bring this insight to law was done by Ian Haney López, first with his 1994 article *The Social Construction of Race: Some Observations on Illusion, Fabrication, and Choice,* in which he

> emphasize[s] the role of law in reifying racial identities. By embalming in the form of legal presumptions and evidentiary burdens the prejudices society attached to vestiges of African ancestry, . . . law serves not only to reflect but to solidify social prejudice, making law a prime instrument in the construction and reinforcement of racial subordination. Judges and legislators, in their role as arbiters and violent creators of the social order, continue to concentrate and magnify the power of race in the field of law. Race suffuses all bodies of law, not only obvious ones like civil rights, immigration law, and federal Indian law, but also property law, contracts law, criminal law, federal courts,

family law, and even "the purest of corporate law questions within the most unquestionably Anglo scholarly paradigm." I assert that no body of law exists untainted by the powerful astringent of race in our society.[36]

Haney-López develops this argument further in his book *White by Law: The Legal Construction of Race,* in which he provides an extended discussion of the various ways in which law gives legitimacy and coherence to social categories of race.

Other Critical Race Theorists have further examined the ways in which law produces racial meaning and disparate outcomes among minority groups. For example, Charles Lawrence's *The Id, the Ego, and Equal Protection* draws upon psychoanalytic theory to argue that the fixation on discriminatory intent in Equal Protection law fails to take account of unconscious bias— non-intentional discriminatory behavior that nonetheless affects minorities. By providing Equal Protection remedies only where intent can be established, many discriminatory experiences go without a remedy.[37] In a similar vein, Richard Thompson Ford has written lucidly on how the persistence of racial segregation is not a product of purely private choices and market transactions, but rather an outcome stemming from legal and policy decisions that racialize certain spaces in a manner that reifies the underlying social meanings of race.[38]

This scholarship on how law *subordinates* through the creation and maintenance of racial categories has led to a corresponding set of work that examines how law *privileges*. Talking about race has usually been synonymous with talking about racial minorities and their discriminatory experiences, but a growing number of critical race scholars are examining Whiteness as a racial category that gives access to certain opportunities that are diametrically opposed to the burdens imposed upon minorities. One of the more significant pieces from this literature is Barbara Flagg's work on racial transparency. Flagg writes:

> The most striking characteristic of whites' consciousness of whiteness is that most of the time we don't have any. I call this the transparency phenomenon: the tendency of whites not to think about whiteness, or about norms, behaviors, experiences, or perspectives that are white-specific. Transparency often is the mechanism through which white decision makers who disavow white supremacy impose white norms on blacks. Transparency operates to require black assimilation even when pluralism is the articulated goal; it affords

substantial advantages to whites over blacks even when the decision makers intend to effect substantive racial justice.[39]

Here, Flagg connects this transparency phenomenon to the aforementioned intent requirement in Equal Protection law. Flagg argues that the privileging effect of transparency is to render certain norms and perspectives concerning what counts as discrimination as the universal experience and therefore the definitive legal rule. As a result, Flagg argues that the experiences and perspectives of one group are privileged over another; the birth of the intent standard out of particular racial experiences is rendered invisible precisely through the language of law.[40]

Cheryl Harris goes a bit further in describing the contours of race and privilege in relation to its social and legal construction by describing Whiteness as a property interest—both literally and figuratively. As a matter of real and tangible property interests, Harris argues that "the set of assumptions, privileges, and benefits that accompany the status of being White have become a valuable asset that Whites sought to protect. . . . Whites have come to expect and rely on these benefits, and over time these expectations have been affirmed, legitimated, and protected by the law."[41] This is how Harris explains the phenomenon of racial passing whereby non-Whites who "looked" White enough "to pass" leveraged these blurred racial lines to partake in the privileges and benefits of being White—a set of circumstances that conferred significant value.[42] While the literal property interest in Whiteness was largely confined to the times of slavery and Jim Crow, Harris argues that a property interest continues in modern times "in that relative White privilege was legitimated as the status quo."[43] That is, by dismantling overt forms of state-sponsored and private discrimination without addressing the gross inequities such practices embedded in society, the resulting privileges continue today as new forms of property interests that are obscured by the perception that the playing field is level.[44] Harris argues that law plays a significant role in morphing past illegitimate property interests into the appearance of neutrality—a significant aspect of the legal construction of race—and argues for a new commitment to affirmative action to address past and present inequalities.

The central theme that ties together these and other theses on the legal construction of race is that the racial meanings and disparate racial outcomes that we encounter in society do not reflect the natural abilities of groups, but are rather a product of intricate social and legal choices that privilege certain groups and disadvantage others. Therefore, race is not something that is only contested in social or cultural realms, but is deeply implicated by legal, policy, and other institutional forces.

Intersectionality and Anti-essentialism

Another major contribution made by Critical Race Theory has been its scholarship on intersectionality and anti-essentialism. Intersectionality is a term that has been used in social science circles, but has been most closely connected to Kimberlé Crenshaw's legal scholarship to reflect "the need to account for multiple grounds of identity when considering how the social world is constructed."[45] Crenshaw and other intersectional writers have argued that identities cannot be reduced to their constitutive parts; the experiences of Black women cannot be understood as the sum of the experiences of Blacks and women in society. Intersectionality puts forth the idea that we must understand how the convergence of multiple identities produces unique experiences that must be recognized and accounted for—especially when law is involved.[46]

Dorothy Roberts offers profound insights into the intersectional experiences of poor Black women in her article examining the criminal prosecution of drug dependent women who become pregnant and have children. Roberts argues that such prosecutions are not simply adverse to women or Blacks in general; non-Black and middle-class pregnant women are rarely screened for drug use, and men's drug use during pregnancy is viewed as irrelevant to the gestational health of the fetus. Rather, Roberts argues that such policies have a *specific* effect on Black women in that "they are the least likely to obtain adequate prenatal care, the most vulnerable to government monitoring, and the least able to conform to the White, middle-class standard of motherhood. They are therefore the primary targets of government control."[47] Hence, Roberts argues that it is not women or Blacks in general who are potentially having their privacy violated by surreptitious drug testing minutes after giving birth, but poor Black women in particular. This practice draws attention to specific experiences that can occur at the intersection of converging identities and how law often targets them.

Kimberlé Crenshaw describes the importance of incorporating an intersectional analysis in employment cases and other aspects of anti-discrimination law and policy:

[There is] a common political and theoretical approach to discrimination which operates to marginalize Black women. Unable to grasp the importance of Black women's intersectional experiences, not only courts, but feminist and civil rights thinkers as well have treated Black women in ways that deny both the unique compoundedness of their situation and the centrality of their experiences to the larger classes of women and Blacks. Black women are regarded either as too much like women or Blacks and the compounded nature of their experience is so absorbed into the collective experiences of either group or as too different, in which case Black women's Blackness or femaleness sometimes has placed their needs and perspectives at the margin.[48]

As she describes further in this article, the failure of law to conceptualize the intersectional experiences of Black women has prevented them from receiving relief for discriminatory experiences because their claims did not fit neatly within pre-existing anti-discrimination statutes that offer relief for discrimination experienced on the basis of race *or* sex, not their intersection. Therefore, many of the unique discriminatory experiences that Black women might find themselves in—such as an employer prohibiting certain hairstyles in the workplace—go without a remedy.[49]

Other writers have extended these contributions on intersectionality to offer alternative ways to think about the convergence of multiple identities that provide a bit more flexibility in how we understand the experiences of individual subjects. These authors suggest that intersectionality "fixes" subjects at a particular epistemological location in a manner that may unduly limit our understanding of how subordination works.[50] For example, Peter Kwon offers a theory of cosynthesis to "go beyond static and autonomous notions of categories that stand alone or next to or within others . . . to recognize the mutual dependence of such categories and hence the importance of dealing with all modes of oppression simultaneously rather than artificially favoring one over another—or, as intersectionality forces us to do, opening up a third space [that] reifies a new set of borders."[51] Darren Hutchinson offers a similar post-intersectional theory of "multidimensionality" that is developed to focus on the systemic and overlapping character of identity-based oppression in a manner that suggests that these categories—race, gender, class, sexuality, and others—do not merely overlap, but are "inextricably and forever intertwined."[52] My own work in this field has suggested a theory of interactionality that builds upon intersectional analyses and draws upon qualitative and quantitative social science methodologies. As such, interactionality works from sociological contributions concerning symbolic interactionism and interaction effects to "examine not only identity construction and its significance when subjects experience discrimination along two separate identity axes, but also *the construction of subordination*: the iterative process between identity and social context that helps explain the nature, continuities, and discontinuities between individual discrimination and group stratification."[53] The attempt here is to distinguish intersectionality as a theory of identity (not a theory of subordination, as it is often taken for) and to develop interactionality as a step toward a proper way to assess the relationship between subordination along multiple categories of identity.

At the same time of these intersectional and post-intersectional developments, a separate but related anti-essentialist critique has developed among Critical Race Theorists that is a more direct challenge to traditional feminist writings that often make the essentialist assumption "that one authentic female or minority voice exists[;] much of feminist legal theory presumes that White middle class women's experiences can speak for all women."[54] Moreover, anti-essentialism highlights the extent to which "much of the jurisprudence on race has unconsciously presumed that Black males' experience holds true for Black women and all minorities. [Anti-essentialism] calls for a deeper understanding of the lives of women of color based on the multiple nature of their identities."[55]

Angela Harris's contributions to this field of anti-essentialism have been profound, as she issued what many people continue to regard as one of the most serious challenges to feminist legal scholarship. In *Race and Essentialism in Feminist Legal Theory*, Harris applauds the contributions of feminist scholars such as Catherine MacKinnon, yet argues:

> [These scholars rely] on what I call gender essentialism—the notion that a unitary, "essential" women's experience can be isolated and described independently of race, class, sexual orientation, and other realties of experience. The result of this tendency toward gender essentialism is not only that some voices are silenced in order to privilege others . . . but that the voices that are silenced turn out to be the same voices silenced by the mainstream legal voice of "We the People"—among them, the voices of black women.[56]

Trina Grillo and Stephanie Wildman draw upon these anti-essentialist sentiments to discuss the problems inherent in analogizing the experience of racism with that of sexism. They note that although the analogy is often undertaken by women not subject to racial discrimination, such analogies leave "the significance of race marginalized and obscured, and the different role that race plays in the lives of people of color and whites [is] overlooked."[57] From the authors' perspective, this leads to essentialist presumptions about each experience, which allow "people with little experience in thinking about racism, but who had a hard-won understanding of the allegedly analogous oppression, [to] assume that they comprehended the experience of people of color and thus had standing to speak on their behalf."[58]

Intersectionality and anti-essentialism overlap significantly. It is difficult to find any hard and fast distinctions between the two, except perhaps the fact that intersectionality entails a more affirmative engagement with how multiple identities converge, while anti-essentialism has largely been conceived as an intervention against mainstream feminist and civil rights discourse in resisting "one size fits all" identity politics. Taken together, this critical race scholarship reflects a commitment to resist thinking about identity categories in separate, autonomous, or essential terms in order to highlight the extent to which converging identities create multiple social experiences that deserve recognition.

Storytelling

Critical Race Theory has also been distinguished by its methodological contribution of telling stories—those that are fictitious, drawn from personal experiences, or otherwise—as a way to make broader claims about the nature of race and racism in contemporary society. Derrick Bell has described the underlying logic behind using personal or fictitious stories in scholarly settings as a way to communicate "views to those who hold very different views on the emotionally charged subject of race. People enjoy stories and will often suspend their beliefs, listen to the story, and then compare their views, not with mine, but with those expressed in the story.[59] Alex Johnson has further described the usefulness of storytelling in that it highlights the distinctive voice of minority scholars, "which rejects narrow evidentiary concepts of relevance and credibility."[60] The strongest version of this argument is that the utility of a story does not depend on its accuracy, but rather on its ability to convey a particular perspective that traditionally has been obscured by dominant discourses such as law.

Perhaps this distinctive approach is part of the reason Critical Race Theory has been called "voice scholarship";[61] it not only attempts to "create new oppositionist accounts of race," but draws heavily upon the voices and experiences typically excluded from what many consider to be proper legal discourse to provide these perspectives.[62] A review of the Critical Race Theory canon reveals the use of many types of stories to discuss the relationship between race and law. Probably the most well-known story is Derrick Bell's *The Space Traders*. Bell tries to convey what he perceives to be the persistent advancement of other groups' interest at the expense of Blacks by describing a situation in which aliens promise to give wealth and technological advances to the United States in exchange for all of its Black people.[63] Bell's rather pessimistic ending to the story has the United States accepting the Space Traders' offer, with millions of "Black people [leaving] the New World as their forebears had arrived," in large ships, this time headed toward outer space.[64]

Patricia Williams begins her critique of the Critical Legal Studies argument that rights are not useful with a phrase that is uncommon among law review pages: "Once Upon a Time."[65] Williams uses this mythical fairy tale (titled "The Brass Ring and the Deep Blue Sea") about priests, a celestial city, and their pursuit of godliness at the expense of mortals in need of basic help as a way to describe the lack of reflection among Critical Legal Studies scholars in discarding the utility of rights at the very moment that rights represented one of the few opportunities for vulnerable people to improve their lives.

Fictional accounts are not the only type of stories used by Critical Race Theorists to convey their perspectives. Sometimes an author's life experience or those from family or friends is used as a starting point to engage in a legal analysis of a particular topic. For example, the aforementioned piece by Cheryl Harris on the property interests in Whiteness begins with a description of her grandmother's experience as a Black woman who could "pass" as White during the early twentieth century and could thus avail herself of employment opportunities that women readily perceived as Black were categorically denied. Harris notes her grandmother was "not merely passing, but *tres*passing"—availing herself of the property interests in Whiteness to partake in its privileges.[66] This story is used to further a key sentiment in Critical Race Theory: that "legal scholarship about race in America can never be written from a distance of detachment or with an attitude of objectivity."[67] By embracing storytelling as a critical methodology, Critical Race Theory draws attention to the subjectivity in law that is always already there.

Russell Robinson published an article arguing "that outsiders and insiders tend to perceive allegations of discrimination through fundamentally different psychological frameworks."[68] The underlying premise is that there is a disjunction between the way in which Whites and Blacks understand the same acts of discrimination, with "many whites expect[ing] evidence of discrimination to be explicit, and assum[ing] that people are colorblind when such evidence is lacking, [while] many blacks perceive bias to be prevalent and primarily implicit."[69] Robinson introduces this concept with a personal story on what he perceives to be an example of discrimination and the different reactions his White and Black colleagues had in interpreting the situation. He notes that his White colleagues were more likely to describe his experience as one person being unfriendly to him, while his Black colleagues interpreted his experience as part of a broader discriminatory pattern that Black men in academia often have. As such, Robinson's personal narrative is used to ground and give insight into what he sees as a broader psychological phenomenon that has significant legal implications.

Critical Race Theory and Its Critics

Critical Race Theory has been criticized for several different reasons. Daniel Farber and Suzanna Sherry describe Critical Race Theory as "extremist" and "radical multiculturalism" whereby "the very nature of social constructionism poses serious risks to our intellectual community."[70] For example, Farber and Sherry suggest that the critique of mainstream assessments of merit by members of traditionally underrepresented groups may adversely affect members of other minority groups (such as Asian Americans) that succeed under the current system. Similarly, Randall Kennedy suggests that the very foundations of Critical Race Theory — that minority scholars offer a perspective and voice on race that is marginalized in the mainstream legal academy—may misrepresent the value of such contributions in a manner that may ultimately "be used against the cause of racial justice."[71] Kennedy argues:

> This eager yearning to perceive and celebrate moral and intellectual differences between racial groups is part of a more general tendency. One sees it in the extraordinary extent to which certain feminist theorists have successfully entrenched the concept of "women's voice," even in the face of compelling (although largely ignored) empirical and theoretical challenges. One also sees it in the work of certain educators who conclude, on the basis of transparently flimsy evidence, that there exists a "black learning style" that distinguishes black children from the children of other racial groups. Left unchallenged, this tendency will seep into the culture at large and reinforce beliefs about "natural" divisions that have, for too long, constricted our imaginations.[72]

From Kennedy's perspective, such race-specific critiques used in service of demonstrating the social construction of race may, in the end, ironically serve to show that there are natural or inherent differences between races.

But it is this notion of storytelling as a scholarly method that seems to be one of the more controversial and contested aspects of Critical Race Theory. For example, although scholars in law and literature and other fields have used stories to make broader points about the nature of law, Farber and Sherry distinguish (and problematize) the use of stories among Critical Race Theorists in that (1) they "view narratives as central to scholarship while deemphasizing conventional analytic methods"; (2) they assert the particular value of stories from women and minorities—voices "from the bottom"; and lastly, (3) they are "less concerned than conventional scholars about whether stories are either typical or descriptively accurate, and they place more emphasis on the aesthetic and emotional dimensions of narration."[73] Concerned that this method may be (mis)taken as proper legal scholarship, Farber and Sherry implore Critical Race Theorists to "ensure that their stories are accurate and typical, to articulate the legal relevance of the stories, and to include an analytic dimension in their work."[74]

Other scholars have been more blunt in their assessment of the value of storytelling to legal scholarship. Jeffrey Rosen described this featured method of Critical Race Theory on the pages of the *New Republic* as "*reductio ad absurdum* . . . with its celebration of subjectivity over objectivity, of emotion over truth, . . . the scholarly romanticizing of black conspiracy theories."[75] Despite the rather heated nature of these critiques, Critical Race Theory continues to embrace these distinctive features and encourages further scholarship along these lines.

Taking the Visual Turn in Critical Race Theory

Critical Race Theory and Vision

The preceding sections have discussed the particular conditions leading to the establishment of Critical Race Theory and the contributions the field has made to thinking about the relationship between race, racism, and the law. For the purposes of this book, the contribution of most significance is the scholarship demonstrating the social and legal construction of race. This work highlights the extent to which social categories of race do not reflect any inherent or natural differences between groups. This constructionist view "rejects the most widely accepted understanding of race, which [can be termed] biological race, . . . [which holds that] there exist natural, physical, divisions among humans that are hereditary, reflected in morphology, and roughly but correctly captured by terms like Black, White, and Asian."[76] A constructionist view recognizes that "social meanings connect our faces to our souls."[77] This means that the seemingly obvious connections made between a person's appearance and their predispositions or abilities stem from social convention, not nature.

While this has been a substantial contribution and has set forth a number of challenges for how we think about race, a fruitful direction for this work is to go beyond yet complement *descriptive* accounts of how race is constructed to engage a *constitutive* examination of how and why societal notions of race have largely come to be oriented around particular visible differences in skin color and other visual cues. The constructionist account has largely focused its critique on how visual cues and bodily markings become a proxy for various social meanings that, taken together, help construct the notion of race. While Critical Race Theory has largely limited its critique to the idea that the visual cues that have come to define racial groups do not reflect any inherent abilities or disabilities, it has not examined the social process by which notions of race have come to focus on visual cues that are thought to be self-evidently known. This has a tendency to treat race as primarily a phenomenon that revolves around a set of attributes that are presumed to be visually obvious. But, by not paying attention to how visual cues come to be socially salient to individuals, Critical Race Theorists may inadvertently reify the notion that these visual distinctions between groups (skin color, facial features, etc.) are self-evident boundaries of difference rather than a product of a constitutive process that produces this presumed obviousness.

A number of Critical Race Theorists have gone beyond general conversations on race to discuss the particular significance of various visual cues such as skin tone or hair texture. Yet they have not theorized or problematized the constituted nature of these visual cues (beyond making broad historical parallels) in terms of how iterative social processes give rise to visual understandings of race. For example, Trina Jones offers an illuminating analysis on how colorism, or *within*-group discrimination based on gradations in skin tone (e.g., light- versus dark-skinned Blacks), is a common experience in many people's lives yet largely goes without remedy under current anti-discrimination schemes that focus on prejudice occurring *between* racial groups. Jones

starts from the premise that "both race and skin color are social constructions; their importance comes from the salience that we give them."[78] She
goes on to provide a sophisticated distinction between racism and colorism:

> Racial categorization does not rest solely upon skin color. Multiple factors are
> and have been used to indicate race. One should not confuse, however, the
> indicator (e.g. skin color or ancestry) with the thing that it is indicating (e.g.
> race). Skin color is one device for assigning people to a racial category. Race is
> the social meaning attributed to that category. It is a set of beliefs or assump-
> tions about individuals falling within a particular racial group. . . . Thus, with
> colorism, it is the social meaning afforded to one's color that determines one's
> status. With racism, it is the social meaning afforded one's race that deter-
> mines one's status.[79]

While Jones provides a rich historical context for the development of these
various social meanings, her depiction of the significance of the visual cues
that structure the meanings of race and color remains descriptive and does
not reach the constitutive. That is to say, it is one thing to describe the inner
workings of a social system based on meanings that attach to visual cues. It
is quite another to provide details on day-to-day social interactions whereby
constructed racial boundaries take on an air of visual obviousness. How is it
that race and color come to stand out as visually significant phenomenon?
While important, the explanatory mechanism provided by Jones—past and
present practices of race mixing in the United States—does not sufficiently
account for the robust yet subtle process in which individuals are socialized
to have radically different responses to individuals based on the perception of
slight gradations in skin tone.[80]

Taunya Banks provides a similar discussion of law and colorism in her
article *Colorism: A Darker Shade of Pale.* Banks's article is distinguishable
in that she examines the peculiar response to colorism by some courts. She
argues that while some courts have been amenable to claims of skin tone discrimination brought by White ethnics or Latinos whereby "courts sometimes
view ethnicity or color as a proxy for race," they have been less likely to sustain such claims when the plaintiff is Black.[81] This leads Banks to argue that
"U.S. courts rigidly adhere to the commonly accepted notion that a person
with any known African ancestry is raced as Black" without recognizing the
subtle privileges and burdens that are associated with slight variations in skin
tone.[82] Banks notes that these cases "demonstrate the extent to which courts

recognize, explicitly or implicitly, the fluidity of race when determining who is white and who is nonwhite, but not black."[83] While an insightful commentary on the response of some courts to skin tone variation and how they interpret the meaning and social significance of these visual cues, Banks's analysis largely describes these phenomena without engaging the social conditions and practices that give rise to visual understandings of race.

Paulette Caldwell broadens this conversation on race and visual cues by discussing the legal significance of hair as an intersectional critique of the relationship between race and gender in employment discrimination cases. Caldwell provides an extended critique of *Rogers v. American Airlines*, a case upholding an employer's right to prohibit women from wearing their hair in braids.[84] The plaintiff in the case argued that she was not simply being discriminated against as a woman or as a Black person, but specifically as a Black woman—an argument that the court was not amenable to. The court in *Rogers* distinguishes between natural and artificial hairstyles in applying Title VII:

> Plaintiff may be correct that an employer's policy prohibiting the "Afro/bush" style might offend Title VII and section 1981. But if so, this chiefly would be because banning a natural hairstyle would implicate the policies underlying the prohibition of discrimination on the basis of immutable characteristics. In any event, an all-braided hairstyle is a different matter. It is not the product of natural hair growth but of artifice. An all-braided hair style is an "easily changed characteristic," and, even if socioculturally associated with a particular race or nationality, is not an impermissible basis for distinctions in the application of employment practices by an employer.[85]

Caldwell criticizes this distinction between natural and cultural aspects of race: "Wherever they exist in the world, black women braid their hair. They have done so in the United States for more than four centuries. African in origin, the practice of braiding is as American—black American—as sweet potato pie."[86] Caldwell engages in a thoughtful analysis of the shared mutable and immutable characteristics of hair and its importance to Black women as a mode of self-expression in a society where standards of beauty often conflict with their attributes. Indeed, she goes as far as to state that "one may argue that hair texture, rather than skin color, determines racial classification."[87] Despite the care with which Caldwell examines the role of hair in racial identity and racial identification, this distinction is taken as a visually obvious characteristic. That is, there is little discussion beyond historical parallels to demonstrate how hair as a visual or physical cue comes to be understood as an obvious and distinguishing race characteristic.

Taken together, these articles demonstrate how Critical Race Theory has a deep appreciation of how the meanings that attach to visual differences are constructed, yet this appreciation lends itself to a *descriptive* analysis rather than a *constitutive* one. A constitutive approach can begin to examine the social interactions that, of all of the visual markings that distinguish people, make particular visual distinctions seem like obvious boundaries of difference. This book takes this approach to challenge the idea that racial distinctions are visually obvious by empirically examining the social processes that give rise to visual understandings of race. This is distinguishable from previous Critical Race Theory contributions that look at the social conditions that give rise to certain meanings that attach to race and how the privileges and limitations embedded in these meanings come to be understood as a product of nature rather than society. Within this conception, the visual cues to which these meanings attach are thought not only to be visually obvious, but a precondition to the concept of race itself.

This book's contribution is to work from and extend the assertion put forth by Critical Race Theorists that race is a social construction to have a more particular understanding of the social interactions that give racial boundaries a strong sense of visual obviousness. This will help us understand how what we see as race is constituted by broader social practices. This investigation is separate from but related to previous engagements with race not reflecting biological differences. I am not examining how meanings attach to various racial bodies. Rather, I am inquiring into the importance of vision and visual cues—which have come to define race for most people—to the concept of race itself. How important is being able to see to individuals' racial consciousness? To what extent is "seeing race" *not* an objective or neutral engagement with observing human variation, but rather a process mediated by social practices? And how might these social practices produce the visual obviousness which we ascribe to presumptively objective racial boundaries?

Appendix B: Further Considerations on Methods and Research Design

IN TERMS OF THE METHODOLOGICAL APPROACH USED TO GATHER data for this book, qualitative research methods offer a remarkable set of social scientific tools to measure respondents' beliefs, feelings, and experiences. While many methods are available (e.g., surveys, questionnaires, ethnography, and participant observation), several characteristics make interviews the most suitable approach for this project.[1] This method is good for research topics that are largely explanatory and examine individuals' perspectives or attitudes. Interview methods are also useful for gathering information about a person's knowledge, values, and preferences. This approach can get at the meanings that people ascribe to social phenomena as well as how certain experiences shape their understanding of the world. Interviews also give people an opportunity to reflect on their thoughts without feeling overly committed by writing them down. This gives data collectors the opportunity to clarify unclear questions and respond to other concerns. Lastly, this approach is useful when there is a need to gather highly personal data.

Each of these advantages is crucial for a research project that explores blind people's understanding of race. Hilary Arksey and Peter Knight highlight the main reason interviews are most useful for this project: "Interviewing is a powerful way of helping people to make explicit things that have hitherto been implicit—to articulate their tacit perceptions, feelings, and understandings."[2] There is a strong implicit association between race and visual cues such as skin color, hair texture, and body type, and interviews offer the best opportunity to probe respondents' thoughts and feelings on a topic that most have not thought about.

Another consideration for choosing interviews as the main research method is the disability of most of the respondents. It would have been impractical for the blind respondents, as well as for the researcher, to use a written questionnaire. Since they would not have been able to visually read a questionnaire form, either the questions would have had to be transcribed into Braille or each respondent would have had to enlist the assistance of a sighted person to read the questions and write answers. Given the sensitive nature of this research topic, bringing in a third party could have raised issues regarding confidentiality or limited the openness with which respondents would have answered such questions.

In terms of the type of interview to use, there are generally three different categories: structured, nonstructured, and semi-structured.[3] Structured interviews ask the same questions more or less word-for-word in order to collect the same information from each respondent. Questions are asked the same way and there is minimal interaction between interviewer and respondent so as to not have an influence on the answers. Nonstructured interviews, on the other hand, do not work from a standardized interview schedule and focus instead on the classes of information sought, giving the interviewer freedom to tailor questions for each respondent in a manner that best gets at the desired information. Although these first two approaches have their benefits, there is a third that embraces the most advantageous characteristics of both: semi-structured interviews. This approach allows the interviewer to work from a prepared list of questions that allows responses to be compared, but also gives the interviewer the freedom to ask additional questions to clarify a respondent's answer, to follow up on an interesting answer, or to engage in a brief back-and-forth that leads to fruitful data collection. Since this project seeks to be able to meaningfully compare respondents' answers yet might require substantial probing and clarification to get beyond commonsensical understandings of race, semi-structured interviews are most appropriate. As a result, data collection for this project was based on a series of semi-structured interviews with sighted and totally blind adults of various ages, racial backgrounds, and residences.

Interview Schedule

The interview schedule was the same for both sighted and blind respondents, but was designed with enough flexibility to permit follow-up questions as

needed in order to have the clearest possible understanding of the interviewees' responses. Certain questions such as "Did you lose your sight at a specific
time?" were asked only of blind respondents, while others such as "Do you
think race is an issue for blind people?" were asked only of those who are
sighted. Nevertheless, the vast majority of questions were asked of both sets
of respondents.

The interview schedule contained six main sets of questions: background,
race as a concept, race and self-identification, race and identifying others,
race and social interactions, and concluding questions. Background questions
focused on gaining more information about respondents, such as age and city
of residence. The importance of the background questions was simply to collect demographic data and to "warm up" respondents, getting them used to
talking about themselves to a stranger. The first substantive set of questions
focused on race as a concept, where respondents were asked a few general
questions about race (e.g., "How do you define race? What is it?") to get them
thinking abstractly about the subject before jumping into the more personal
topics found in the third set of questions concerning race and self-identification. Here, the focus was on respondents' own racial identity, why they identify that way, and what they think their racial identity means socially. Next,
in the fourth section on race and identifying others, the focus shifted to how
respondents identify others and what racial categories mean. The fifth set of
questions on race and social interaction were designed to give respondents an
opportunity to talk about their past and present social interactions and how
race played a part, such as in their high school friendships or among family
members. The last set of questions was designed to give the respondent an
opportunity to reflect on what they said, to add any other thoughts about
race that the interview did not cover, and to obtain their thoughts on race and
blindness. With regard to this last objective, blind respondents were asked
whether they thought race is an issue in the blind community and if they have
known someone to be blind and show racial prejudice. Sighted respondents
were asked whether they think race could be an issue for blind people, which
was a way to get them to think about the importance of vision in understanding race.

Since race is a topic that can elicit strong personal opinions and may lead
some people to recall past experiences, respondents frequently went off on
tangents beyond the scope of the initial questions asked. This was not only
permitted but encouraged; these extemporaneous statements often provided

rich insights into the personal experiences and social situations that shaped respondents' understanding of race and, moreover, how visual cues associated with race became important to their daily lives.

Selecting Respondents

Robert Weiss notes that "there are two distinct categories of potential respondents: people who are uniquely able to be informative because they are expert in an area or were privileged witnesses to an event; and people who, taken together, display what happens within a population affected by a situation or event."[4] The former, known as a panel study, is not appropriate for this project. It would be difficult for experts knowledgeable about the blind community, such as representatives from the large consumer organizations that represent blind individuals (e.g., the American Council of the Blind or the National Federation of the Blind), to speak meaningfully about the relationship between race and blindness among blind people. Indeed, some of the respondents were active members of one or both of these groups and their membership did not necessarily yield any fruitful insights regarding the racial perceptions of blind people simply because it was not a particularly common topic of conversation in these organizations. As a result, respondents for this study were selected through the other method, sampling, in which the goal is to interview a group of people "who together can adequately represent the experiences of a larger group."[5]

Of the numerous ways to sample a population, snowball sampling was the most feasible method for identifying qualifying respondents. This method entails an interviewer speaking to anyone in the desired group rather than relying upon probability sampling or choosing specific people because of their experiences. Given that I am a sighted person without significant connections to disabled or blind communities, the biggest hurdle I faced was gaining access to an unfamiliar group and earning their trust. I started by asking sighted friends and colleagues if they knew any blind or visually impaired persons. I was introduced to three people who were friends of friends and interviewed them, asking each respondent at the end of the interview to introduce me to as many of their blind or visually impaired friends as possible. While the project focuses on people who have been totally blind since birth, I spoke to any and all visually impaired persons (including those who were partially sighted or lost their sight later in life) at the beginning of the project for three reasons: to earn trust within the community, to learn as much about the experiences of all visually impaired persons as possible, and to acquire more contacts that could eventually lead to qualifying respondents that have been totally blind since birth. Data from individuals who had partial sight or who lost their vision later in life were not included in the findings reported in this book. Their visual capabilities mooted any unique insight they could provide regarding the relationship between race and vision as they either could see or have seen the visual cues associated with race. As a result, these "mini-interviews" or discussions did not go through all of the standard questions on the interview schedule and were only used to help me gain a broader perspective within the community.

Conceptually, it was important for this project to focus on those who have been totally blind since birth, as opposed to those who are partially sighted or lost their vision as an adult, since the hypothesis driving this research was that visual conceptions of race are so institutionalized that they exist independent of the ability to see. Partially sighted individuals can often see the visual cues associated with race and individuals who lose their sight later in life often have memories of what these visual cues look like that shape their understanding of race after they lose their sight. The best way to get any sense of the social influences leading to visual understandings of race is to talk to individuals who have not visually engaged with the cues and physical characteristics that come to define race, such as skin color and facial features.

The Internet was an unplanned yet crucial tool for finding respondents. One of my first few respondents suggested posting my research topic and a request for interviews on an e-mail distribution list dedicated to blind people discussing issues related to their community. Once this respondent posted this information on two or three such lists, the number of interview opportunities increased substantially. Not only did I suddenly have many people to speak with, but they were individuals from every region of the United States. This significantly diversified respondents' perspectives and experiences, allowing the data to become incredibly rich while being more representative than the initial sampling structure.

The use of the Internet as a recruitment tool may raise legitimate concerns about selection bias. Since not all people use or have access to the Internet, this method may appear to run the risk of yielding the same type of respondents over and over again, e.g., younger adults or professionals who are more accustomed to online communication or have more access to it. Similarly, this approach may seem to be biased toward individuals wealthy enough to be able to afford a computer and online connection. Yet the demographics of my respondents suggest that this is not the case; recruiting people through the Internet yielded individuals of diverse ages, economic means, educational backgrounds, geographic regions, and political persuasions. Indeed, a strong argument can be made that this approach decreased the chance of selection bias rather than increasing it, as Internet access is becoming more common among a broader range of Americans.[6] While "a sample that is not chosen randomly cannot be claimed to be representative even if some of its demographic characteristics match those of the country as a whole," the data set certainly benefited from this expansion, allowing it to be more robust than it might otherwise be.[7]

For this project, 161 interviews were conducted with blind respondents, with 106 qualifying as totally blind since birth. Althought the 55 non-qualifying interviews with people who were partially sighted or became totally blind later in life were not included in the results, these non-qualifying interviews were essential to not only finding qualifying respondents but also deepening my understanding of the blind community and its relationship with race. Since there are many more individuals who are partially sighted or who became blind later in life, building enough trust to have non-qualifying respondents refer me to qualifying individuals was a key component of finding the interviewees whose experiences are the crux of this empirical research.

In qualitative research, it is often useful to incorporate a smaller number of comparison cases made of individuals who are *not* part of the group that is primarily under study. Typically, comparison cases are used to ensure that the "phenomena associate[d] with the situation . . . are in fact more frequent there than among people who are not in the situation."[8] For this project, interviews with sighted individuals helped to empirically ground part of the project's motivating hypothesis—that sighted people primarily think visually about race—in order to draw similarities to the experiences of the main group under study, i.e., blind individuals. The comparison group helped determine whether or not blind people's understandings of race are different from sighted people's. This comparison, and the use of sighted people in particular, allowed me to unearth a thoroughly unexamined and unchallenged assumption throughout society: that race is primarily visually significant and therefore has a diminished or nonexistent importance for blind people. Thus, this comparative research design allowed the experiences of blind people to clarify the social process through which race becomes visually salient for all individuals, sighted or blind.

Sighted respondents were recruited and interviewed through convenience sampling. In order to have a truly lay perspective on race, I was careful to make sure that I did not only interview people connected with a university or my peers. I self-consciously tried to balance the median ages of the two groups so that they were comparable. The median age for blind respondents is 44.5 years and 47.08 years for sighted respondents. When selecting sighted respondents, I was also concerned with making sure that the proportion of White and non-White sighted respondents roughly approximated the proportion of White versus non-White blind respondents. In my final sample, 83.9 percent of the blind respondents identified as White and 16 percent identified as non-White, compared to 68 percent of the sighted respondents identifying as White and 32 percent identifying as non-White.

The main qualifying criteria for the blind respondents was that they had to have been totally blind since birth or shortly thereafter; they could have no visual memory of seeing anything. As noted in Table 1 in Chapter 2, 34.1 percent of the blind respondents (fifty-five people) did not qualify either because they became blind later in life and thus had some memory of the visual appearances of different races or were not totally blind and could see visual distinctions under certain conditions, such as up close or under the right light. While a subsequent study based on these respondents' racial perspectives might be interesting, data from these respondents were excluded for the purposes of this project since the main objective was to flesh out the understanding of race among people who have never had any direct perception of the visual cues that society uses to define racial boundaries.

Interviewer Bias

The interviews were primarily conducted by telephone for three reasons. First, as previously mentioned, limiting the sample to people who live in one area may skew the responses. Talking to blind people in thirty-four different states covering each region enriched and diversified the data. Secondly, many blind people do not live entirely independent lives; talking by phone was the most accessible means for their participation in that it provided the least disruption and most comfort. Third, conducting all of the interviews by phone meant that sighted respondents could not see the interviewer, which reduced the chance that their visual perception of the interviewer's race would introduce bias. If any bias was transmitted over the phone by the perception of having a racialized voice or surname, such bias would likely be uniform across blind and sighted respondents, making the data more comparable than if the bias was skewed by only having the blind group not have information about the interviewers' race while the comparison sighted group would. There may be certain advantages to conducting interviews face-to-face, such as being able to have an unmediated human connection with the respondent. But for the purposes of this study, this advantage is far outweighed by having a larger sample, greater diversity among the respondents, and an interviewing process that is more accessible to respondents with disabilities.

Asking Hard Questions

Race is a difficult topic to discuss among friends and family, let alone strangers. The first and most important aspect of conducting these interviews was to build trust with the respondents. Trust building began with reading the informed consent document to each person and emphasizing that everything they said was entirely confidential and would be reported anonymously. With regard to the race-specific questions, I found it was useful to constantly reaffirm to respondents that there were no right or wrong answers and that their honest thoughts and opinions were most useful. Some respondents voiced a hesitancy to talk candidly about experiences such as having a prejudiced parent or when they as individuals said or did something racially insensitive. Respondents were assured that this research was not designed to judge anyone, but rather to have a better understanding of people's experiences. Most respondents were incredibly generous with their time and talked openly about their personal experiences, suggesting minimal interviewer bias.

Being Sensitive to Disability

It is important to note that the snowball sample method used to find qualifying respondents, along with the smallness of the blind community, suggests that this project presents an unusually high possibility that respondents might be identifiable if their statements are not stripped of as many identifying characteristics as possible. For this reason, all respondents—as well as any names that respondents mentioned in their interview—were given pseudonyms to conceal individuals' identities.

While many "softer" terms are frequently used to describe individuals who do not have vision (e.g., visual impairment, visual disability), I use the term *blind* since that is how the overwhelming majority of blind respondents described themselves. One of the first questions posed to each respondent was how they prefer to describe their condition. Almost each blind respondent either had no preference and referred to themselves as blind or explicitly preferred the term *blind*. This may reflect some type of consensus within parts of the blind community—particularly those who are totally without sight. Heidi put it this way:

> You know *blind* is fine with me. I'm not really caught up in that political correctness nonsense. I mean you just tell it like it is. You know what I mean? So I just tell things as they are. I mean to me, I presume a person [who] is visually impaired to be a person who has impaired vision, that he's not totally blind. It's there. But it's impaired. So a person with impaired vision, I would imagine to be someone who has some vision, who maybe is seeing objects. I would say visually impaired is being partial sight. But I'm totally blind. All the blind organizations that I know of in the twenty-first century, all use the word *blind* in their title.
>
> I don't know why sighted people get off on this political correctness. . . . It's the sighted folks that get off on this nonsense. Blind folks couldn't care less about all this political gibberish that they're doing. It comes across rather hypocritical to me. They use all these nicey-nice terms. But yet they don't care to hire us [for jobs]. . . . So just a lot of political crazy talk. In other words, duplicity.

Coding

Interviews were conducted by myself and trained research assistants. Roughly eighty hours of interviews were conducted, each averaging thirty-six minutes. Each telephone interview was recorded with the respondent's consent, transcribed by a third party, and imported into qualitative research software for coding by one research assistant. Coding qualitative data entails using labels ("codes") to refer to specific text passages that contain useful information. Several codes were used to parse and find commonalities between the interview data, such as "sighted think race unimportant to blind," and "color-blindness." The coding yielded over eleven hundred pages of data, which form the basis of the empirical findings in this book.

In conclusion, this research design was motivated by the main theoretical question pursued by this project: how do blind people understand race? This question was investigated by examining blind people's understanding of and experiences with race. Since I was interested in providing an empirical basis from which to theoretically explore the role of vision in racial consciousness, a semi-structured interview schedule with open-ended questions was essential to broadly exploring an issue that has not been examined before. By having a diverse sample of blind respondents and a good comparison sample of sighted individuals, this research raises questions about the presumed obviousness and objectivity of the visual cues associated with race to clarify the social process through which race becomes visually salient for all people.

Notes

Preface

1. "Frederick K. C. Price Announces Semi-Retirement; Hands Leadership of Church to Son," BCNN1.com, November 26, 2008, http://www.blackchristiannews .com/news/2008/11/frederick-kc-price-announces-semi-retirement-hands-leader-ship-of-church-to-son.html (last viewed June 14, 2010).

2. It is important to note that Dr. Price is not without controversy. Like many televangelists, some have questioned the remarkable wealth that he has personally accumulated through his ministry. And his recent support of Proposition 8—a California initiative to ban same-sex marriage—raises significant questions regarding his commitment to civil and human rights for all members of society. *See* "Frederick K.C. Price and Others Endorsing YES on Prop 8," Christian Web News, October 23, 2008 (last visited June 17, 2010).

3. Dr. Frederick K. C. Price, *Living By Faith: A Lifestyle*, www.ccconnects.net/ weekly/42.html (Last accessed June 18, 2010). Other commentators have different interpretations, with much of the debate centering around the proper translation of the passage into English. Price relies upon an interpretation of this passage based on the King James version of the Bible. Writing a commentary based upon the New International Version (NIV) of the Bible, Baker notes: "The word 'live,' more literally translated 'walk,' for [the speaker] Paul normally has moral connotations, as in living 'decently' (Rom 13:13), acting 'in love' (Rom 14:15), not incorporating 'deception' (2 Cor 4:2), not behaving 'by the standards of the world' (2 Cor. 10:2). That this is so in 5:7 becomes clearer when Paul talks about "pleasing him" in 5:9 and being judged by "things done while in the body" in 5:10. The NIV's translation of the word 'sight' (*eidos*) is disputable. No other biblical rendition of the word in this way can be substantiated, and even outside the biblical literature the more

prominent meaning of *eidos* is 'form' or 'shape.' . . . The fact that this verse is so often quoted out of context as a general Christian principle makes a translation like 'For we live by faith and not by form' sound wrong even though it should be preferred." William R. Baker, 2 *Corinthians* (The College Press NIV Commentary), College Press, 214–215 (1999).

4. David L. Lipe, *Faith and Knowledge,* Apologetics Press, http://www.apologetics press.org/rr/reprints/Faith-and-Knowledge.pdf.

Introduction

1. Throughout this book, I will use variations of the word *salient* to reference the visually striking nature of race and the impression it makes on the visual senses.

2. *Res ipsa loquitur* is a Latin phrase often used in tort law that means "the thing speaks for itself." I use the term *"race" ipsa loquitur* to signify the phenomenon that race is conceptualized as speaking for itself in terms of being visually obvious. This is different from other usages of the term. *See, e.g.*, Jody Armour, *Race Ipsa Loquitur: Of Reasonable Racists, Intelligent Bayesians, and Involuntary Negrophobes,* 46 STAN. L. REV. 781 (1994) (discussing "the legal implications of the disturbing notion that, given the perception that blacks are more prone to commit violent acts than nonblacks, it is rational for criminal defendants claiming self-defense to consider race in assessing the risk of violence posed by a supposed assailant" [781]).

3. The view of race "still popular today [is] that there exist natural, physical divisions among humans that are hereditary, reflected in morphology, and roughly but correctly captured by terms like Black, White, and Asian." Ian Haney López, *The Social Construction of Race: Some Observations on Illusion, Fabrication, and Choice,* 29 HARV. C.R.-C.L. L. REV. 1, 6 (1994). Morphology is the "size, shape, and structure of an organism or one of its parts," e.g., visually observable attributes. *The American Heritage Science Dictionary.* Houghton Mifflin Company. 09 Jul. 2008. <Dictionary. com http://dictionary.reference. com/browse/morphology>.

4. Reva Siegel notes that colorblindness is a "rhetorical system [that] is used to characterize the social practices that enforce and perpetuate the differential status of racial groups." Reva B. Siegel, *Discrimination in the Eyes of the Law: How "Color Blindness" Discourse Disrupts and Rationalizes Social Stratification,* 88 CAL. L. REV. 77, 89 (2000).

5. *See, e.g.*, Noel Ignatiev, *How the Irish Became White* (1996); Matthew Frye Jacobsen, *Whiteness of a Different Color: European Immigrants and the Alchemy of Race* (1999); Laura Gómez, *Manifest Destinies: The Making of the Mexican American Race* (2008).

6. For previous discussions on the merits of blending Critical Race Theory and empirical methods, see Osagie K. Obasogie, *Race in Law and Society: A Critique,* in RACE, LAW, AND SOCIETY 445 (Ian Haney López, ed. 2006); Laura Gómez, *A Tale of Two Genres: On the Real and Ideal Links Between Law and Society and Critical Race Theory,* in BLACKWELL COMPANION TO LAW AND SOCIETY (edited by Austin Sarat. Wiley-Blackwell,

2004); Laura Gómez, *Looking for Race in All the Wrong Places*, 46 Law & Society Review 221 (2012).

Chapter 1

1. Susan D. Moeller, *Pictures of the Enemy: Fifty Years of Images of Japan in the American Press, 1941–1992*, 19 Journal of American Culture 29, 31 (2004).

2. *Parcells Apologized for Making Ethnic Remark*, ESPN.com, June 9, 2004, http://sports.espn.go.com/nfl/news/story?id=1817592.

3. The first paragraph of the *Life* magazine article noted, "In the first discharge of emotions touched off by the Japanese assaults on their nation, U.S. citizens have been demonstrating a distressing ignorance on the delicate question of how to tell a Chinese from a Jap. Innocent victims in cities all over the country are many of the 75,000 U.S. Chinese, whose homeland is our staunch ally. So serious were the consequences threatened, that the Chinese consulates last week prepared to tag their nationals with identification buttons. To dispel some of this confusion, LIFE here adduces a rule-of-thumb from the anthropometric conformations that distinguish friendly Chinese from enemy alien Japs." *How to Tell the Japs from the Chinese*, 11 Life Magazine 81, December 22, 1941.

4. Justice Black noted in the majority opinion upholding the constitutionality of the Civilian Exclusion Order 34: "It is said that we are dealing here with the case of imprisonment of a citizen in a concentration camp solely because of his ancestry, without evidence or inquiry concerning his loyalty and good disposition towards the United States. Our task would be simple, our duty clear, were this a case involving the imprisonment of a loyal citizen in a concentration camp because of racial prejudice. Regardless of the true nature of the assembly and relocation centers—and we deem it unjustifiable to call them concentration camps, with all the ugly connotations that term implies—we are dealing specifically with nothing but an exclusion order. To cast this case into outlines of racial prejudice, without reference to the real military dangers which were presented, merely confuses the issue. Korematsu was not excluded from the Military Area because of hostility to him or his race. He was excluded because we are at war with the Japanese Empire, because the properly constituted military authorities feared an invasion of our West Coast and felt constrained to take proper security measures, because they decided that the military urgency of the situation demanded that all citizens of Japanese ancestry be segregated from the West Coast temporarily, and, finally, because Congress, reposing its confidence in this time of war in our military leaders—as inevitably it must—determined that they should have the power to do just this. There was evidence of disloyalty on the part of some, the military authorities considered that the need for action was great, and time was short. We cannot—by availing ourselves of the calm perspective of hindsight—now say that, at that time, these actions were unjustified." *Korematsu v. United States*, 323 U.S. 214, 223–224 (1944).

5. *How to Tell the Japs from the Chinese*, 11 Life Magazine 81, December 22, 1941.

6. *How to Tell the Japs from the Chinese*, 11 LIFE MAGAZINE 81, December 22, 1941.

7. *How to Tell the Japs from the Chinese*, 11 LIFE MAGAZINE 81–82, December 22, 1941.

8. *How to Tell the Japs from the Chinese*, 11 LIFE MAGAZINE 82, December 22, 1941.

9. *How to Tell the Japs from the Chinese*, 11 LIFE MAGAZINE 82, December 22, 1941.

10. John Dower writes that "so common was [the belief that Japanese were sub-human] that a popular American scientific magazine could publish a short entry in 1945 entitled 'Why Americans Hate Japs More than Nazis' without first demonstrating that this was the case. No one questioned such an observation. And although the explanation offered may have been simplistic (the Japanese were more hated because of their greater outward physical differences), the very manner in which the magazine phrased the problem was suggestive in unintended ways. In addition to using the conventionally pejorative 'Japs' for Japanese, the article followed the telltale phrasing of the war years by speaking not of the Germans and the Japanese, but of the Nazis and the Japanese. . . . The implications of perceiving the enemy as 'Nazis' on the one hand and 'Japs' on the other were enormous, for this left space for the recognition of the 'good German,' but scant comparable place for 'good' Japanese. Magazines like *Time* hammered this home even further by frequently referring to 'the Jap' rather than 'Japs,' thereby denying the enemy even the merest semblance of pluralism." John W. Dower, *War Without Mercy: Race and Power in the Pacific War*, 78–79 (1986).

11. Dower states that "the closest counterparts to good Germans and bad Germans which [media outlets] seemed able to muster for Asia were good nationalities (the Chinese, the Filipinos) and bad (the Japanese). That this distinction between the enemy in Asia and the enemy in Europe derived less from the events of the war than from deep-seated racial bias was reflected in the opening months of 1942, when the U.S. Government incarcerated Japanese-Americans en masse, while taking no comparable action against residents of German or Italian origin. Indeed, U.S. citizens of Japanese extraction were treated with greater suspicion and severity than German or Italian aliens—despite the fact that the German-American Bund (with an estimated membership of twenty thousand) had agitated on behalf of Hitler in the United States prior to the outbreak of war, and despite the fact that there never was, at Pearl Harbor or later, any evidence or organized subversion among the Japanese community." John W. Dower, *War Without Mercy: Race and Power in the Pacific War*, 79 (1986).

12. Omi and Winant state in their highly influential book *Racial Formation in the United States* that "we have now reached the point of fairly general agreement that race is not a biological given but rather a socially constructed way of differentiating human beings." This reflected their view of racial formation, defined as "the socio-historical process by which racial categories are created, inhabited, transformed, and destroyed." Michael Omi and Howard Winant, *Racial Formation in the United States: From the 1960s to the 1990s*, 65, 55 (1994).

13. Morton amassed a data set consisting of over six hundred skulls, mostly from Native Americans, to show "that a ranking of races could be established objectively by physical characteristics of the brain, particularly by size." Stephen Jay Gould, *The Mismeasure of Man*, 83 (1996). Gould's argument that Morton fudged his measurements

to fulfill White supremacist ideologies has recently been reexamined. According to the authors, "Morton did not manipulate data to support his preconceptions." Jason E. Lewis et al., *The Mismeasure of Science: Stephen Jay Gould versus Samuel George Morton on Skulls and Bias*, 9 PLOS BIOLOGY 1 (2011). Upon reviewing this article, the editors of *Nature* concluded that, taken at face value, the authors' "critique leaves the majority of Gould's work unscathed" and noted the article's limitations in that the authors "couldn't measure all of [Morton's] skulls, [meaning that] they do not know whether the average cranial capacities that Morton reported represent his sample accurately." The *Nature* editors also stated that although Lewis et al. accuse Gould of being driven by certain commitments in his reassessment of Morton's data, "Lewis and his colleagues have their own motivations." Editorial, *Mismeasure for Mismeasure*, 474 NATURE 419 (June 23, 2011).

14. Stephen Jay Gould, *The Mismeasure of Man*, 83 (1996).

15. "The great genius of *On the Origins of Species* was its application of a simple, plausible theory to a problem that people in many disciplines had been trying to solve. In fact, the simplicity of Darwin's model must have embarrassed some of his predecessors who had not thought of it first. The theory of natural selection in biology required only the production of numerous organisms and an environment so impoverished that it could accommodate only a few of them. The organisms thrown into this predicament were forced to compete, with the result that only a small number survived and reproduced. The theory relied on but three essential ingredients: scarcity, variation, and inheritance. It needed nothing else, and the variation could be absolutely random." Herbert Hovenkamp, *Evolutionary Models in Jurisprudence*, 64 TEXAS L. REV. 645, 651 (1985).

16. Stephen Jay Gould, *The Mismeasure of Man*, 105 (1996).

17. Stephen Jay Gould, *The Mismeasure of Man*, 105 (1996).

18. Thomas Gossett, *Race: The History of an Idea in America*, 69 (1963). Gould corroborates this sentiment by noting that the second half of the nineteenth century was distinguished by "the allure of numbers, the faith that rigorous measurement could guarantee irrefutable precision, and might mark the transition between subjective speculation and a true science as worthy as Newtonian physics. Evolution and quantification formed an unholy alliance. . . . Anthropologists had presented numbers before Darwin, but the crudity of Morton's analysis belies any claim to rigor. By the end of Darwin's century, standardized procedures and a developing body of statistical knowledge had generated a deluge of more trustworthy numerical data." Stephen Jay Gould, *The Mismeasure of Man*, 106 (1996).

19. Ariela Gross, *Litigating Whiteness: Trials of Racial Determination in the Nineteenth-Century South*, 108 YALE L. J. 109, 177 (1998).

20. Ariela Gross, *Litigating Whiteness: Trials of Racial Determination in the Nineteenth-Century South*, 108 YALE L. J. 109, 177 (1998).

21. Lee D. Baker, *From Savage to Negro: Anthropology and the Construction of Race, 1896–1954*, 27 (1998).

22. "Regarding society as an organism, we may say that it is impossible artificially to use up social vitality for the more active performance of one function without diminishing the activity with which other functions are performed. So long as society

is let alone, its various organs will go on developing in due subordination to each other." Herbert Spencer, *Social Statics or the Conditions Essential to Human Happiness*, 426 (2005)

23. Thomas F. Gossett, *Race: The History of an Idea in America*, 145 (1963).

24. Spencer wrote: "How races differ in respect of the more or less involved structures of their minds, will best be understood on recalling the unlikeness between the juvenile mind and the adult mind among ourselves. In the child we see absorption in special facts. Generalities even of a low order are scarcely recognized, and there is no recognition of high generalities. We see interest in individuals, in personal adventures, in domestic affairs, but no interest in political or social matters. We see vanity about clothes and small achievements, but little sense of justice: witness the forcible appropriation of one another's toys. While there have come into play many of the simpler mental powers, there has not yet been reached that complication of mind which results from the addition of powers evolved out of these simpler ones. Kindred differences of complexity exist between the minds of lower and higher races; and *comparisons should be made to ascertain their kinds and amounts*. Here, too, there may be a subdivision of the inquiries. (a) What is the *relation between mental complexity and mental mass*? Do not the two habitually vary together? (b) What is the relation to the social state, as more or less complex? that is to say—Do not mental complexity and social complexity act and react on each other?" Herbert Spencer, *The Comparative Psychology of Man*, JOURNAL OF THE ANTHROPOLOGICAL INSTITUTE OF GREAT BRITAIN AND IRELAND, 301, 303–304 (1876).

25. Garland Allen notes that "while eugenicists were interested in all aspects of human heredity, they were particularly concerned with social and personality traits such as intelligence, 'feeble- mindedness,' criminality, alcoholism, pauperism and mental disorders such as schizophrenia and manic depressive insanity. Most eugenicists believed that such traits were to a large degree, if not exclusively, genetically determined. The perception was widespread that these conditions were increasing at a rapid rate in modern industrial society, and that since 'low-grade' individuals with these traits were having more children than 'high-grade' individuals, eventually good traits would be swamped by bad and society would deteriorate. The answer, according to eugenicists, was to control reproduction by scientific means in order to increase the number of children born to high-grade, and reduce the number of children born to low-grade individuals and families." Garland E. Allen, *Eugenics and Modern Biology: Critiques of Eugenics*, 1910–1945, 75 ANNALS OF HUMAN GENETICS 314 (2011).

26. Philip R. Reilly, *Involuntary Sterilization in the United States: A Surgical Solution*, 62 THE QUARTERLY REVIEW OF BIOLOGY 153, 161 (1987).

27. For an up close examination of forced sterilizations in North Carolina that continued until 1974, see the *Winston-Salem Journal*'s award-winning special report "Against Their Will," http://againsttheirwill.journalnow.com/.

28. UNESCO, *The Race Question*, 33 (1950).

29. *New York Times*, July 18, 1950.

30. Peter Berger and Thomas Luckman, *The Social Construction of Reality: A Treatise in the Sociology of Knowledge,* 19–20 (1967).

31. "Talking about gender for most people is the equivalent of fish talking about water. Gender is so much the routine ground of everyday activities that questioning its taken-for-granted assumptions and presumptions is like thinking about whether the sun will come up. Gender is so pervasive that in our society we assume it is bred into our genes. Most people find it hard to believe that gender is constantly created and re-created out of human interaction, out of social life, and is the texture and order of that social life. Yet gender, like culture, is a human production that depends on everyone constantly 'doing gender.' " Judith Lorber, *"Night to His Day": The Social Construction of Gender,* in RACE, CLASS, AND GENDER IN THE UNITED STATES: AN INTEGRATED STUDY (Paula S. Rothenberg, ed.), 54 (1998).

32. *See generally* Bart W. Miles and Scott K. Okamoto, *The Social Construction of Deviant Behavior in Homeless and Runaway Youth: Implications for Practice,* 25 JOURNAL OF CHILD ADOLESCENT SOCIAL WORK 425 (2008).

33. "Most population geneticists concur that the bulk of genetic variation (90 to 95 percent) occurs within, not among, continental populations. The central observations remain: variation is continuous and discordant with race, systematic variation according to continent is very limited, and there is no evidence that the units of interest for medical genetics correspond to what we call races." Richard S. Cooper, Jay S. Kaufman, and Ryk Ward, *Race and Genetics,* 348 NEW ENGLAND JOURNAL OF MEDICINE 1166, 1167 (2003).

34. *See* Nancy E. Adler and Katherine Newman, *Socioeconomic Disparities in Health: Pathways and Politics,* 21 HEALTH AFFAIRS 60 (2002)

35. Statements 11 and 12 in the first UNESCO Statement on Race concluded: "So far as temperament is concerned, there is no definite evidence that there exist inborn differences between human groups. There is evidence that whatever group differences of the kind there might be are greatly overridden by the individual differences, and by the differences springing from environmental factors"; and "As for personality and character, these may be considered raceless. In every human group a rich variety of personality and character types will be found, and there is no reason for believing that any human group is richer than any other in these respects." UNESCO, *Statement on Race,* 32 (1950).

36. UNESCO, *Statement on Race,* 35 (1950).

37. *See* Ann Morning, *The Nature of Race: How Scientists Think and Teach About Human Difference* (2011).

38. "First, investigators studying the population genetics of indigenous groups from around the world have constructed ancestral tree diagrams showing branching relationships among the various indigenous groups. Despite differences in the types of markers used, these studies have been consistent in showing that the human population has major branches corresponding to the major racial groups, with sub branches within each racial group associated with indigenous groups. Second, analysis of genetic clusters has been applied to persons of diverse ancestry, with a focus

on genotypes at multiple genetic loci. These analyses have also consistently resulted in the delineation of major genetic clusters that are associated with racial categories. The primary difference between the results of these studies and the categories used by the U.S. Census is that South, Central, and West Asians cluster with Europeans and are separate from East Asians. Third, studies have examined the distribution of differences among racial groups in the frequency of alleles (genetic variants) at both microsatellite and single-nucleotide–polymorphism (SNP) markers, demonstrating a median difference in allele frequency of 15 to 20 percent, with 10 percent of markers showing a difference of 40 percent or more. Thus, for an allele with a frequency of 20 percent or greater in one racial group, the odds are in favor of seeing the same variant in another racial group. However, variants with a frequency below that level are more likely to be race-specific. This race-specificity of variants is particularly common among Africans, who display greater genetic variability than other racial groups and have a larger number of low-frequency alleles. These results indicate that the frequency of variant alleles underlying disease or normal phenotypes can vary substantially among racial groups, leading to differences in the frequency of the phenotypes themselves. Such differences in frequency are also found among ethnic groups, but these differences are typically not as great. Furthermore, self-defined ancestry is very highly correlated with genetically defined clusters." Esteban Gonzalez Burchard et al., *The Importance of Race and Ethnic Background in Biomedical Research and Clinical Practice*, 348 NEW ENGLAND JOURNAL OF MEDICINE 1170, 1172 (2003).

39. Regarding asthma, see Ed Edelson, *Do Blacks Have a Genetic Weakness to Asthma*, WASHINGTON POST, September 30, 2007, http://www.washingtonpost.com/wpdyn/content/article/2007/09/30/AR2007093000569.html; regarding kidney disease, see "Genes Linked to High Kidney Disease Rates in Blacks: Study," AFP, July 15, 2010, http://www.google.com/hostednews/afp/article/ALeqM5i6OozT4Ow5-hGb_YfHTL9lzYc8_w.

40. Ian Hacking, *The Social Construction of What?* 35 (1999).

41. Hacking writes that with social constructionism, "we hear that things are not what they seem, . . . involv[ing] iconoclastic questioning of varnished reality, of what the general run of people take for real. Surprise, surprise! All constructions dwell in the dichotomy between appearance and reality set up by Plato, and given a definitive form by Kant. Although social constructionists bask in the sun they call post-modernism, they are really very old-fashioned." Ian Hacking, *The Social Construction of What?* 48–49 (1999).

42. Ian Hacking, *The Social Construction of What?* 39 (1999).

43. Hacking acknowledges that with regard to the issue of redundancy, "the emphasis made with the word 'social' becomes useful when we turn to inanimate objects, phenomena, or facts that are usually thought of as part of nature, existing independent of human society" (39–40). Arguably, this is precisely what social constructionists—especially those working in the fields of race and gender—are trying to do: flesh out the relationships and practices between races and genders that are thought to be natural to expose the social forces that produce them. Philosopher Sally Haslanger further makes this point by noting that Hacking "tends to ignore or

dismiss the kind of project I've been calling the 'debunking' project in which constructionists argue that there is a theoretically important social kind of category that has not been adequately acknowledged, or not been adequately acknowledged to be social. Debunking constructionists may seem to be offering radical and implausible 'analyses' of our ordinary concept. . . . Debunkers sometimes surprise us, however, in suggesting that what we thought were natural terms are in fact social terms." Sally Haslanger, *Social Construction: The "Debunking" Project*, in SOCIALIZING METAPHYSICS: THE NATURE OF SOCIAL REALITY (Frederick F. Schmitt, ed.) 322 (2003).

44. Michael Omi and Howard Winant, *Racial Formation in the United States: From the 1960s to the 1990s*, 55 (1994).

45. *New Oxford American Dictionary* (2nd ed.) (electronic).

46. *See generally* Theodore W. Allen, *The Invention of the White Race: Racial Oppression and Social Control* (1994), and Theodore W. Allen, *The Invention of the White Race: The Origin of Racial Oppression in Anglo-America* (1997).

47. *See* Matthew Frye Jacobson, *Whiteness of a Different Color: European Immigrants and the Alchemy of Race* (1998); Noel Ignatiev, *How the Irish Became White* (1996); and Karen Brodkin, *How Jews Became White Folks and What That Says About Race in America* (1999).

48. David R. Roediger, *Working Toward Whiteness: How America's Immigrants Became White*, 9–10 (2005).

49. Roediger openly questions the work of other historians of Whiteness: "The elegance and drama of [Matthew Frye] Jacobsen's account comes at some cost. In order to generate a neater narrative of movement toward whiteness, Jacobsen assumes at times that the key sites of racial transformation are legal and intellectual. To summarize the triumph of the myth of a common 'Caucasian-ness' in those venues represents a formidable task but avoids the welter of further problems raised when we think of whitening as a process in social history in which countless quotidian activities informed popular and expert understandings of race of new immigrants, as a well as new immigrant understandings of race. Those problems introduce messiness to the plot of how new immigrants became fully white." David R. Roediger, *Working Toward Whiteness: How America's Immigrants Became White*, 8 (2005).

50. For additional essays on the social construction of Whiteness, see *Displacing Whiteness: Essays in Social and Cultural Criticism* (Ruth Frankenberg, ed.) (1997), and *Critical White Studies: Looking Behind the Mirror* (Richard Delgado and Jean Stefanic, eds.) (1997).

51. John Levi Martin and King-To Yeung, *The Use of the Conceptual Category of Race in American Sociology, 1973–99*, 18 SOCIOLOGICAL FORUM 521, 522 (December 2003). *See also* Tomás Almaguer and Moon-Kie Jung, *The Enduring Ambiguities of Race in the United States*, in SOCIOLOGY FOR THE TWENTY–FIRST CENTURY (Janet L. Abu-Lughod, ed.) (1999).

52. *See* Jack Niemonen, *The Race Relations Problematic in American Sociology*, 28 THE AMERICAN SOCIOLOGIST 15 (1997). *See also* Douglas Hartman, Paul Croll, and

Katja Guenther, *The Race Relations "Problematic" in American Sociology: Revisiting Niemonen's Case Study and Critique*, 34 THE AMERICAN SOCIOLOGIST 20 (Fall 2003).

53. Frankenberg notes: "My argument . . . is that race shapes white women's lives. In the same way that both men's and women's lives are shaped by their gender, and that both heterosexual and lesbian women's experiences in the world are marked by their sexuality, white people and people of color live racially structured lives. . . . If race shapes white women's lives, the cumulative name that I have given to that shape is 'whiteness.' Whiteness . . . has a set of linked dimensions. First, whiteness is a location of structural advantage, or race privilege. Second, it is a 'standpoint,' a place from which white people look at ourselves, at others, and at society. Third, 'whiteness' refers to a set of cultural practices that are usually unmarked and unnamed. The book seeks to begin exploring, mapping, and examining the terrain of whiteness." Ruth Frankenberg, *White Women, Race Matters: The Social Construction of Whiteness*, 1 (1994). Mary Waters, *Ethnic Options: Choosing Identities in America* (1990), looks at "the meaning or lack of meaning of ethnicity to people in the last stages of assimilation—people for whom ethnicity is an option rather than an ascribed characteristic" (12).

54. *See infra* for a specific discussion on social psychology and cognition with regards to race and blindness.

55. Matthew O. Hunt, Pamela Braboy Jackson, Brian Powell, and Lala Carr Steelman, *Color-Blind: The Treatment of Race and Ethnicity in Social Psychology*, 63 SOCIAL PSYCHOLOGY QUARTERLY 352, 360–361 (2000).

56. Matthew O. Hunt, Pamela Braboy Jackson, Brian Powell, and Lala Carr Steelman, *Color-Blind: The Treatment of Race and Ethnicity in Social Psychology*, 63 SOCIAL PSYCHOLOGY QUARTERLY 352, 353 (2000).

57. *See generally* Douglas Massey and Nancy Denton, *American Apartheid: Segregation and the Making of the Underclass* (1993); William Julius Wilson, *When Work Disappears: The World of the New Urban Poor* (1996); Melvin L. Oliver and Thomas M. Shapiro, *Black Wealth, White Wealth: A New Perspective on Racial Inequality* (1997).

58. In an influential 1945 essay on stratification, Davis and Moore write: "The main functional necessity explaining the universal presence of stratification is precisely the requirement faced by any society of placing and motivating individuals in the social structure. As a functioning mechanism a society must somehow distribute its members in social positions and induce them to perform the duties of these positions. It must thus concern itself with motivation at two different levels: to instill in the proper individuals the desire to fill certain positions, and, once in these positions, the desire to perform the duties attached to them." Kingsley Davis and Wilbert E. Moore, *Some Principles of Stratification*, 10 AMERICAN SOCIOLOGICAL REVIEW 242 (1945).

59. For a critical response to Davis and Moore, see Melvin M. Tumin, *Some Principles of Stratification: A Critical Analysis*, 18 AMERICAN SOCIOLOGICAL REVIEW 387 (1953); In their powerful response to the influential book *The Bell Curve,* which tries to naturalize certain racial disparities in, most notably, educational achievement, Claude Fischer et al. write: "We note that any debate over inequality can rest only in part on the weight of the social science evidence. It must also rest on our moral commitments.

The explicit commitments Americans have made for over two hundred years—despite our frequent failures to live up to them—include a political dedication to equality." Claude Fischer et al., *Inequality by Design: Cracking the Bell Curve Myth*, 216 (1996).

60. *See* Katherine M. Haskins and H. Edward Ransford, *The Relationship Between Weight and Career Payoffs Among Women*, 14 SOCIOLOGICAL FORUM 295 (1999); Matthew Mulford, John Orbell, Catherine Shatto, and Jean Stockard, *Physical Attractiveness, Opportunity, and Success in Everyday Exchange*, 103 AMERICAN JOURNAL OF SOCIOLOGY 1565 (1998); Susan Averett and Sanders Korenman, *The Economic Reality of the Beauty Myth*, 31 JOURNAL OF HUMAN RESOURCES 304 (1996).

61. *See* Douglas Massey and Nancy Denton, *American Apartheid: Segregation and the Making of the Underclass* (1993). William Julius Wilson writes: "Blacks were denied access to valued and scarce resources through various ingenious schemes of racial exploitation, discrimination, and segregation, schemes that were reinforced by elaborate ideologies of racism. But the situation has changed. . . . Many of the traditional barriers have crumbled under the weight of the political, social, and economic changes of the civil rights era. . . . Now the life chances of individual blacks have more to do with their economic class position than with their day-to-day encounters with whites." William Julius Wilson, *The Declining Significance of Race: Blacks and Changing American Institutions*, 1 (1980). Despite Wilson's provocative argument, it is difficult to deny that, as Haney López notes, "human fate still rides upon ancestry and appearance. The characteristics of our hair, complexion, and facial features still influence whether we are figuratively free or enslaved." Ian Haney López, *The Social Construction of Race: Some Observations on Illusion, Fabrication, and Choice*, 29 HARV. C.R.-C.L. L. REV. 1 (1994).

62. *See generally* Verna M. Keith and Cedric Herring, *Skin Tone and Stratification in the Black Community*, 97 AMERICAN JOURNAL OF SOCIOLOGY 760 (1991); and Keith B. Maddox and Stephanie A. Gray, *Cognitive Representations of Black Americans: Reexploring the Role of Skin Tone*, 28 PERSONALITY AND SOCIAL PSYCHOLOGY BULLETIN 250 (2002).

63. An example of this can be seen in economist Joni Hersch's research on skin tone and market outcomes. She finds "that skin color and height affect wages among new lawful immigrants to the U.S. controlling for education, English language proficiency, occupation in source country, family background, ethnicity, race, and country of birth. Immigrants with the lightest skin color earn on average 17 percent more than comparable immigrants with the darkest skin color." Joni Hersch, *Profiling the New Immigrant Worker: The Effects of Skin Color and Height*, 26 JOURNAL OF LABOR ECONOMICS 345 (2008). *See also* Joni Hersch, *Skin Tone Effects among African Americans: Perceptions and Reality*, 96 AMERICAN ECONOMIC REVIEW PAPERS AND PROCEEDINGS 251 (2006).

64. Law & Society scholar Richard Abel writes: "When asked what I study, I usually respond gnomically: everything about law except the rules. This may be oxymoronic, but it is also accurate. Lawyers seek to understand rules—ascertain, criticize, change, organize, apply, and manipulate them. Social scientists examine everything

else: institutional structures, processes, behavior, personnel, and culture." Richard Abel, *What We Talk About When We Talk About Law*, in The Law & Society Reader (Richard L. Abel, ed.) 1 (1995).

65. Osagie K. Obasogie, *Race in Law and Society: A Critique*, in Race, Law, and Society (Ian Haney López, ed., 2006).

66. *See generally* Laura Gómez, *A Tale of Two Genres: On the Real and Ideal Link Between Law and Society and Critical Race Theory*, in Blackwell Companion to Law and Society (Austin Sarat, ed.) (2004).

67. Colin Barnes, Geof Mercer, and Tom Shakespeare, *Exploring Disability: A Sociological Introduction*, 3 (1999).

68. Beth Omansky Gordon and Karen E. Rosenblum, *Bringing Disability into the Sociological Frame: A Comparison of Disability with Race, Sex, and Sexual Orientation Statuses*, 16 Disability & Society 5, 15 (2001).

69. For a history of disability rights activism, see Doris Zames Fleischer and Frieda Zames, *The Disability Rights Movement: From Charity to Confrontation* (2000).

70. Aldon D. Morris wrote in the *Annual Review of Sociology* that "scholars of social movements have increasingly come to recognize the pivotal role that the civil rights movement has played in generating movements in America and abroad. A consensus is emerging that the civil rights movement was the catalyst behind the wave of social movements that crystallized in the United States beginning in the middle of the 1960s and continuing to the present. . . . This body of literature has shown that movements as diverse as the student movements, the women's movement, the farm workers movement, the Native American movement, the gay and lesbian movement, the environmental movement, and the disability rights movement all drew important lessons and inspiration from the civil rights movement. It was the civil rights movement that provided the model and impetus for social movements that exploded on the American scene." Aldon D. Morris, *A Retrospective on the Civil Rights Movement: Political and Intellectual Landmarks*, 25 Annual Review of Sociology 517, 527 (1999).

71. Lennard Davis notes: "Disability is not an object—a woman with a cane—but a social process that intimately involves everyone who has a body and lives in the world of the senses. Just as the conceptualization of race, class, and gender shapes the lives of those who are not black, poor, or female, so the concept of disability regulates the bodies of those who are 'normal.' In fact, the very concept of normalcy by which most people (by definition) shape their existence is in fact tied inexorably to the concept of disability, or rather, the concept of disability is a function of a concept of normalcy. Normalcy and disability are part of the same system." Lennard J. Davis, *Enforcing Normalcy: Disability, Deafness, and the Body*, 2 (1995).

72. Deborah Stienstra, *The Intersection of Disability and Race/Ethnicity /Official Language/Religion*, 3 (unpublished manuscript on file with author) (March 8, 2002). For an example of this emphasis on service provision, see generally *Diversity and Visual Impairment: The Influence of Race, Gender, Religion, and Ethnicity on the Individual* (Madeline Millan and Jane N. Erin, eds.) (2001).

73. Martin Jay and Teresa Brennan, *Vision in Context: Historical and Contemporary Perspectives on Sight*, 3 (1996). In the field of history, *see, e.g.*, Martin Jay, *Downcast Eyes: The Denigration of Vision in Twentieth-Century French Thought* (1994); and Martin Jay and Teresa Brennan, *Vision in Context: Historical and Contemporary Perspectives on Sight* (1996). Regarding philosophy, *see, e.g.*, David Michael Levin, *Modernity and the Hegemony of Vision* (1993); and Alva Noe and Evan Thompson, *Vision and Mind: Selected Readings in the Philosophy of Perception* (2002). And in the field of art history, *see, e.g.*, Jonathan Crary, *Techniques of the Observer: On Vision and Modernity in the 19th Century* (1992); and Jonathan Crary, Suspensions of Perception: Attention, Spectacle, and Modern Culture (2001).

74. Regarding gender, see Helga Geyer-Ryan, *Imaginary Identity: Space, Gender, Nation*, in VISION IN CONTEXT (Martin Jay and Theresa Brennan, eds.) (1996). Regarding sexuality, see Jacqueline Rose, *Sexuality in the Field of Vision* (1986).

75. Martin Jay and Teresa Brennan, *Vision in Context: Historical and Contemporary Perspectives on Sight*, 3 (1996).

76. Donna Haraway, *The Promises of Monsters: Reproductive Politics for Inappropriate/d Others*, unpublished manuscript cited in Joan W. Scott, *The Evidence of Experience*, 17 CRITICAL INQUIRY 773, 777 (1991).

77. Joan W. Scott, *The Evidence of Experience*, 17 CRITICAL INQUIRY 773, 777 (1991).

78. Crary notes that his book studies "an earlier reorganization of vision in the first half of the nineteenth century, sketching out some of the events and forces, especially in the 1820s and 1830s, that produced a new kind of observer and that were crucial preconditions for the ongoing abstraction of vision. Although the immediate cultural repercussions of this reorganization were less dramatic, they were nonetheless profound. Problems of vision then, as now, were fundamentally questions about the body and the operation of social power. Much of this book will examine how, beginning early in the nineteenth century, a new set of relations between the body on one hand and forms of institutional and discursive power on the other redefined the status of an observing subject." Jonathan Crary, *Techniques of the Observer: On Vision and Modernity in the Nineteenth Century*, 3 (1994).

79. Jonathan Crary, *Techniques of the Observer: On Vision and Modernity in the Nineteenth Century*, 6 (1994).

80. Jonathan Crary, *Suspensions of Perception: Attention, Spectacle, and Modern Culture*, 4 (1999).

81. Patricia Johnston, *Seeing High and Low: Representing Social Conflict in American Visual Culture* (Patricia Johnston, ed.), 1 (2006).

82. Kymberly N. Pinder, Introduction, in *Race-ing Art History: Critical Readings in Race and Art History* (Kymberly N. Pinder, ed.), 1 (2002).

83. Pinder explicitly frames this effort in constructionist terms: "Even though the last decade of the twentieth century was filled with events that have brought issues of race and ethnicity to our front pages and dinner tables, the last century and a half have seen the globally influential effects of the Civil War in the U.S., the colonization of Africa, Asia, and South America, and more recently, the civil disturbances in Los

Angeles and the genocidal conflicts in places like Serbia and Rwanda. All of these events have proven the centrality of ethnicity in class warfare and nationalistic struggles in recent memory. These realities and the critical (and not so critical) discourse in academia and the media generated by them have confirmed that both *race and ethnicity are more social and political constructs than the result of any biological factors"* (emphasis added). Kymberly N. Pinder, Introduction, in *Race-ing Art History: Critical Readings in Race and Art History* (Kymberly N. Pinder, ed.), 17 (2002).

84. Martin A. Berger: *Sight Unseen: Whiteness and American Visual Culture* 1 (2005).

85. Some historical scholarship on race and racial formation is a notable exception to this trend. *See, e.g,* Laura Gómez, *Manifest Destinies: The Making of the Mexican American Race* (2007); and Mara Loveman and Jeronimo Muniz, *How Puerto Rico Became White: Boundary Dynamics and Intercensus Racial Reclassification,* 72 AMERICAN SOCIOLOGICAL REVIEW 915 (2007).

86. *See, e.g.,* Michael Omi and Howard Winant, *Racial Formation in the United States: From the 1960s to the 1990s* (1994); Ian Haney Lopez, *White by Law: The Legal Construction of Race* (1996); and Cheryl Harris, *Whiteness as Property,* 106 HARV. L. REV. 1707 (1992).

Chapter 2

1. "Computer vision is a sub science of artificial intelligence. One of the key components of computer vision is the concept referred to as object recognition. Object recognition is the way that a computer system goes about identifying objects within images. It is an intense transformation of an image. These transformations result in finding the edges of the image. Once these edges are found, objects can be created and combined through complicated mathematics. The complex objects that have been created can determine if the created object model is similar to the goal object model. In the end, computer vision comes down to a hierarchy of processes: gradients and grayscales, edge detection, mathematical approaches, and advanced hybrids." Logan Keenan and Derek Sellnau, *Computer Vision Through Object Recognition—A Survey of Methods, Applications, and Technologies,* http://faculty.cns.uni .edu/~schafer/courses/previous/161/Fall2010/proceedings/papers/paperH.pdf.

2. *See HP Computers Are Racist,* http://www.youtube.com/watch?v= t4DT3tQqgRM.

3. Joz Wang, *Racist Camera! No I Did Not Blink . . . I'm Just Asian!* May 13, 2009, http:// www.jozjozjoz.com/2009/05/13/racist-camera-no-i-did-not-blink-im-just-asian/.

4. Brandon Sinclair, *Kinect Has Problems Recognizing Dark-Sinned Users?* GAMESPOT, November 3, 2010, http://www.gamespot.com/news/6283514.html?tag=latesthead lines;title;2.

5. Dawn Kawamoto, *Microsoft Kinect Heats Race Debate: Does Face Recognition Software Discriminate?* DAILY FINANCE, November 4, 2010, http://www.dailyfinance .com/2010/11/04/microsoft-kinect-game-heats-facial-recognition-race-debate/.

6. Mike Swift, *Blacks, Latinos, and Women Lose Ground at Silicon Valley Tech Companies*, SAN JOSE MERCURY NEWS, February 13, 2010, http://www.mercurynews.com/top-stories/ci_14383730?nclick_check=1.

7. In discussing the relationship between empiricism and Critical Legal Studies (CLS, the group from which minority scholars spun off of to create Critical Race Theory), David Trubek notes: "Part of the dispute within and about CLS involves what appear to be questions of method. Some dissenters question whether Critical Scholarship can produce valid knowledge about law in society because the method Critical scholars employ stresses the study of appellate cases and other indicia of legal doctrine, but overlooks 'empirical' evidence of the social 'impact' of law or the behavior of legal actors. On the other hand, people within the CLS movement sometimes attack research that focuses on attitudes, behavior, and impact as a form of 'social science mystification' that hides the true nature of social relations and the real importance of law in society. Participants in this debate seem to be arguing about method, and particularly about the value of 'empiricism' in legal studies." David Trubek, *Where the Action Is: Critical Legal Studies and Empiricism*, 36 STAN. L. REV. 575, 576 (1984).

8. One example is the growing literature on implicit bias jointly authored by social psychologists and individuals sympathetic to Critical Race Theory. *See, e.g.*, Kristin A. Lane, Jerry Kang, and Mahzarin R. Banaji, *Implicit Social Cognition and Law*, 3 ANN. REV. LAW. SOC. SCI. 427 (2007); and Anthony Greenwald and Linda Hamilton Krieger, *Implicit Bias: Scientific Foundations*, 94 CAL. L. REV. 945 (2006).

9. Laura Gómez notes that empirical scholars such as those working in the field of law and society "have not engaged the claims put forward by critical race scholars over the past 15 years or so. And even when they do so, they have not taken the literature as seriously as they might." Gómez suggests that the hesitancy on the part of these social scientists may stem from the fact that many "conceive of race as a readily measurable, dichotomous (black/white) variable that affects the law at various points[,] . . . a concept that is relatively easy to map. But race is complicated, and the relationship between race and law is messy." Gómez is not arguing that Critical Race Theory and Critical Legal Studies have had no impact on the social sciences, but only that there is a greater opportunity for these perspectives to theoretically orient empirical research investigating the relationship between law and society. Laura Gómez, *A Tale of Two Genres: On the Real and Ideal Links Between Law and Society and Critical Race Theory*, in THE BLACKWELL COMPANION TO LAW AND SOCIETY (Austin Sarat, ed.), 454 (2004).

10. *See, e.g.*, Tukufu Zuberi and Eduardo Bonilla-Silva, *White Logic, White Methods: Race and Methodology* (2008); and Tukufu Zuberi, *Thicker Than Blood: An Essay on How Racial Statistics Lie* (2001).

11. David Trubek asserts that "the real problem [that Critical Legal Studies has with empirical approaches] is that the behaviorists' methods accept the world as it seems to be, both to the observer and the observed. For the Critical scholar, this world is a dream, and the task of scholarship is not simply to understand the dream, but also to awaken the dreamers." David Trubek, *Where the Action Is: Critical Legal Studies*

and Empiricism, 36 STAN. L. REV. 575, 618 (1984). This sentiment might shed some light on the perspective of Critical Race Theorists toward empirical work.

12. Crenshaw et al. note that Critical Race Theory and Critical Legal Studies continue to have a relationship that has been described as a "coalition . . . [whereby they are] aligned in radical left opposition to mainstream legal discourse." Kimberle Crenshaw et al., *Introduction*, in CRITICAL RACE THEORY: THE KEY WRITINGS THAT FORMED THE MOVEMENT, xxvi–xxvii (1995).

13. *See generally* Mari Matsuda, *Looking to the Bottom: Critical Legal Studies and Reparations*, 22 Harv. C.R.-C. L.R. 323 (1987).

14. *See generally* Daniel Farber and Suzanna Sherry, *Telling Stories Out of School: An Essay on Legal Narratives*, 45 Stan. L. Rev. 807, 808 (1993).

15. Michael McCann, *Causal Versus Constitutive Explanations (or, On the Difficulty of Being so Positive)*, 21 LAW & SOC. INQ. 457, 463 (1996).

16. Susan Silbey, *Legal Culture and Legal Consciousness*, in INTERNATIONAL ENCYCLOPEDIA OF SOCIAL AND BEHAVIORAL SCIENCES (N. J. Smelser and P.B. Baltes, eds.), 8627 (2001).

17. On civil rights remedies, see Kristin Bumiller, *The Civil Rights Society: The Social Construction of Victims* (1992); on the everyday deployment of law, see Patricia Ewick and Susan Silbey, *The Common Place of Law: Stories from Everyday Life* (1998); and on advancement of causes, see Michael McCann, *Rights at Work: Pay Equity Reform and the Politics of Legal Mobilization*, 1994.

18. All respondents' names have been replaced with pseudonyms to preserve anonymity. It is common in qualitative research to report interview data using quasi-quantitative terms (e.g., most, many, few, etc.) instead of absolute counts or proportions. The overquantification of social and interpersonal dynamics can obscure the very richness that is brought to life by qualitative methods and unduly limit the nuance needed to report and interpret responses. As such, I follow in this methodological tradition. *See* Robert S. Weiss, *Learning from Strangers: The Art and Method of Qualitative Interview Studies* (1994). *See, e.g.*, Mary C. Waters, *Ethnic Options: Choosing Identities in America* (1990); Patricia Ewick and Susan Silbey, *The Common Place of Law* (1998); and Kristin Bumiller, *The Civil Rights Society: The Social Construction of Victims* (1988).

19. Ian Haney López, *Racism on Trial: The Chicano Fight for Justice*, 6 (2003)

20. Haney López notes: "All racial ideas can be explicitly debated and contested. But they rarely are. Instead, ideas regarding racial characteristics, categories, and properties usually remain in the background, a body of knowledge so widely shared and so frequently depended upon that most people treat racial beliefs as timeless truths. It is not just their ubiquity, though, that makes racial ideas seem like common sense. In addition, U.S. race ideology asserts that race is a part of nature, a feature of the physical world that exists outside of culture and beyond control. Race's property as a supposed natural fact combines with the prevalence of racial ideas and practices to ensure that most people take race for granted." Ian Haney López, *Racism on Trial: The Chicano Fight for Justice*, 119 (2003).

21. "The most striking characteristic of whites' consciousness of whiteness is that most of the time we don't have any. I call this the *transparency* phenomenon: the tendency of whites not to think about whiteness, or about norms, behaviors, experiences, or perspectives that are white-specific. Transparency often is the mechanism through which white decision makers who disavow white supremacy impose white norms on blacks. Transparency operates to require assimilation even when pluralism is the articulated goal; it affords substantial advantages to whites over blacks even when decision makers intend to effect substantive racial justice." Barbara J. Flagg, *"Was Blind, But Now I See": White Race Consciousness and the Requirement of Discriminatory Intent*, 91 MICH. L. REV. 953, 957 (1993).

22. Edward Sampson notes that "making one group out of some items and distinguishing them from items they categorize as different is a basic—some would argue *the* basic—process of human cognition. . . . Categorization is not only a fundamental cognitive process, but also the basis for stereotyping and prejudice. Edward E. Sampson, *Dealing with Differences: An Introduction to the Social Psychology of Prejudice*, 110 (1999).

23. *See generally* Ann Morning, *The Nature of Race: How Scientist Think and Teach About Human Difference* (2011).

Chapter 3

1. Demian Bulwa, Wyatt Buchanan, and Matthew Yi, *Behind Murder Charge Against ex-BART Officer*, SAN FRANCISCO CHRONICLE, January 15, 2009, http://www.sfgate.com/default/article/Behind-murder-charge-against-ex-BART-officer-3254683.php.

2. Darren Ravel, *LeBron's Q Score Takes a Huge Hit*, CNBC, September 14, 2010, http://www.cnbc.com/id/39170785/LeBron_s_Q_Score_Takes_Huge_Hit.

3. *LeBron James' 'Decision' draws nearly 10 million viewers*, USA Today, July 11, 2010, http://www.usatoday.com/sports/basketball/nba/heat/2010-07-11-lebron-decision-tv-viewers_N.htm.

4. *See* Shelby Steele, *Obama's Post-Racial Promise*, LOS ANGELES TIMES, November 5, 2008, http://www.latimes.com/news/opinion/opinionla/la-oe-steele5-2008nov05,0,6049031.story.

5. Jonathan Markovitz, *Racial Spectacles: Explorations in Media, Race, and Justice*, 3 (2011).

6. Markovitz argues that "racial spectacles are not merely part of the imagery of contemporary life, nor simply a part of a conversation. Instead, they matter materially because they work to shape popular understandings of the social world that can affect how people lead their daily lives. . . . Since they are ever changing and always open to challenge, racial spectacles present opportunities to contest commonsense understandings of powerful institutions and social structures, and they frequently allow for the emergence of critical voices into popular discourse.

They are, consequently, important sites of struggle for social change." Jonathan Markovitz , *Racial Spectacles: Explorations in Media, Race, and Justice*, 3 (2011).

7. Jonathan Markovitz , *Racial Spectacles: Explorations in Media, Race, and Justice*, 5 (2011).

8. KPI-TV survey, http://www.surveyusa.com/client/PollPrint.aspx?g= 36dcd0c0-900d-495e-83d2-c07c48060506&d=0.

9. Demian Bulwa, *Mehserle Fans, Foes Face Off in Walnut Creek*, SAN FRANCISCO CHRONICLE, July 20, 2010, http://articles.sfgate.com/2010-07-20/ bay-area/21989992_1_shooting-of-oscar-grant-bart-police-johannes-mehserle.

10. *Pardon the Interruption*, ESPN, September 30, 2010.

11. *See* Laura Anthony, *Judge Allows Criminal History Detail in BART Trial*, ABC7 News, May 7, 2010, http://abclocal.go.com/kgo/story?section=news/local/ east_bay&id=7428841. Mehserle's partner the evening of the shooting, Officer John Woffinden, testified at a preliminary hearing that the scene was hectic and the most frightening of his career. *See* Demian Bulwa, *Partner: Mehserle Was Shaken But Said Nothing*, SAN FRANCISCO CHRONICLE, May 21, 2009, http://www.sfgate.com/cgi-bin/article.cgi?f=/c/a/2009/05/20/BASC17O58B.DTL.

12. Dan Gilbert, *Open Letter to Fans from Cavaliers Majority Owner Dan Gilbert*, July 8, 2010, http://www.nba.com/cavaliers/news/gilbert_letter_100708.html.

13. *Rev. Jesse L. Jackson Sr. Reacts to Dan Gilbert's Open Letter*, Rainbow Push Coalition, July 11, 2010, http://www.rainbowpush.org/news/single/ rev._jesse_l._jackson_sr._reacts_to_dan_gilberts_open_letter.

14. *See generally* Russell Robinson, *Perceptual Segregation*, 108 COLUM. L. REV. 1093 (2008).

15. *See generally* Leon F. Litwack, *Trouble in Mind: Black Southerners in the Age of Jim Crow* (1998).

16. Barbara Bader, *Sambo, Babaji, and Sam*, 72 THE HORN BOOK MAGAZINE 536 (1996), quoted in David Pilgrim, *The Picaninny Caricature, Jim Crow Museum of Racist Memorabilia*, http://www.ferris.edu/news/jimcrow/picaninny/, (visited May 4, 2008).

Chapter 4

1. Glen Anthony Harris and Robert Brent Toplin, *Guess Who's Coming to Dinner: A Clash of Interpretations Regarding Stanley Kramer's Film on the Subject of Interracial Marriage*, 40 THE JOURNAL OF POPULAR CULTURE 700 (2007).

2. *Guess Who's Coming to Dinner*, Columbia Pictures, 1967.

3. Chris Rock, *Bigger and Blacker*, HBO, 1999.

4. Michael I. Norton and Samuel R. Sommers, *Whites See Racism as a Zero-Sum Game That They Are Now Losing*, 6 PERSPECTIVES ON PSYCHOLOGICAL SCIENCE 215, 216 (2011).

5. Pew Research Center, *Twenty to One: Wealth Gaps Rise to Record Highs Between Whites, Blacks, and Hispanics* (2011), http://pewsocialtrends.org/files/2011/07/SDT-Wealth-Report_7-26-11_FINAL.pdf.

6. Michael I. Norton and Samuel R. Sommers, *Whites See Racism as a Zero-Sum Game That They Are Now Losing*, 6 PERSPECTIVES ON PSYCHOLOGICAL SCIENCE 215, 216 (2011).

7. *See, e.g.*, Lydia Chavez, *The Color Bind: California's Campaign to End Affirmative Action* (1998).

8. Other thoughtful discussions of colorblindness include Eduardo Bonilla-Silva, *Racism Without Racists: Color-Blind Racism and the Persistence of Racial Inequality in the United States* (2003); and Michael K. Brown et al., *Whitewashing Race: The Myth of a Color-Blind Society* (2005).

9. For a extended description of the role of race as ethnicity in the evolution of colorblindness, see generally Ian Haney López, *A Nation of Minorities: Race, Ethnicity, and Reactionary Colorblindness*, 59 STAN. L. REV. 985 (2007).

10. *Adarand Constructors v. Peña*, 515 U.S. 200, 240 (1995).

11. *See, e.g.*, Eduardo Bonilla-Silva, *Racism Without Racists: Colorblind Racism and the Persistence of Racial Inequality in the United States* (2003); Lani Guinier and Gerald Torres, *The Miner's Canary: Enlisting Race, Resisting Power, Transforming Democracy* (2003); Ian Hancy López, *A Nation of Minorities: Race, Ethnicity, and Reactionary Colorblindness*, 59 STAN. L. REV. 985 (2007); and Reva Siegel, *Discrimination in the Eyes of the Law: How Colorblindness Discourse Disrupts and Rationalizes Social Stratification*, 88 CAL. L. REV. 77 (2000).

12. Andrew Kull, author of *The Color-Blind Constitution*, writes: "Wendell Phillips had demanded in 1864 that the federal government 'ignore difference between white and black, be blind to color.' Theodore Tilton, editor of the religious weekly *The Independent*, wrote at the same period in praise of impartial suffrage: 'Give the ballot to the negro on the same terms as to the white man. Why not? Is justice blind, as poets say? Then let her see no distinction of color.' " Andrew Kull, *The Color-Blind Constitution*, 119 (1992).

13. *Plessy v. Ferguson*, 163 U.S. 537, 559 (1896).

14. Andrew Kull, *The Color-Blind Constitution*, 130 (1992).

15. Andrew Kull, *The Color-Blind Constitution*, 119 (1992).

16. *Plessy v. Ferguson*, 163 U.S. 537, 559 (1896).

17. Andrew Kull, *The Color-Blind Constitution*, 121 (1992).

18. Ian Haney López writes: "The debate in *Plessy* over the state's use of race did not turn on affirmative action, as it does now—indeed, the Congress which drafted the Fourteenth Amendment also enacted numerous laws specifically benefiting blacks. Rather, the central question concerned where to place limits on the state's participation in fostering the separation of racial groups understood—by all members of the Court— to be unequal by nature (hence Harlan's comfortable endorsement of white superiority). Harlan and the majority agreed on the basic premise that the state could enforce racial separation in the social but not in the civic or political arenas; they differed on where to draw the line between those spheres. For Harlan, the segregated train cars at issue in *Plessy* implicated the capacity of blacks to participate as full citizens in civil life, whereas the majority saw such segregation only as a regulation of social relations sanctioned by

long usage and custom." Ian Haney López, *A Nation of Minorities: Race, Ethnicity, and Reactionary Colorblindness*, 59 STAN. L. REV. 985, 993 (2007).

19. Ian Haney López, *A Nation of Minorities: Race, Ethnicity, and Reactionary Colorblindness*, 59 STAN. L. REV. 985, 993 (2007).

20. Julie Novkov writes that the term *colorblindness* "went relatively unrecognized [after *Plessy*] until . . . the NAACP picked up the concept and included it in their brief before the Court in *Brown v. Board of Education*, along with several other arguments. The Court declined the invitation to rest their ruling on this basis, however, instead going with a context-sensitive analysis of the message sent by segregation, in effect echoing and augmenting Harlan's analysis in his *Plessy* dissent. Kull and Siegel note scattered uses of colorblind principles to ground various elements of the judicial campaign to dismantle Jim Crow in the 1960s. But the major public debates over the use of colorblindness in the legal community took place next around the US Supreme Court's affirmative action jurisprudence beginning with *Bakke* in the late 1970s. By the time of its use in these cases, it had emerged as a doctrinal principle largely raised to counter affirmative actions plans, and advocates for state-level referenda and initiatives against affirmative action have used it in this way as well. This history . . . suggests that the critical transformation of colorblindness to conservative ideology took place in the early 1970s." Julie Novkov, *Toward a Legal Genealogy of Color Blindness*, Midwest Political Science Association (unpublished paper), 4–5 (2007), http://works .bepress.com/julie_novkov/3.

21. For detailed accounts of the social, legal, and political forces leading to the rise of colorblindness in the second half of the twentieth century, *see, e.g.*, Julie Nokov, *Towards a Legal Genealogy of Colorblindness*, Midwest Political Science Association (unpublished paper) (2007), http://works.bepress.com/julie_novkov/3/; Reva B. Siegel, *Equality Talk: Anti-subordination and Anti-classification Values in Constitutional Struggles Over Brown*, 117 HARV. L. REV. 1470 (2003). and Ian Haney López, *A Nation of Minorities: Race, Ethnicity, and Reactionary Colorblindness*, 59 STAN. L. REV. 985 (2007).

22. Reva Siegel argues: "My work illustrates how struggles over group inequality can transform the rules and reasons by which social stratification is enforced and justified. This dynamic, which I call 'preservation through transformation,' suggests why the debate between antidiscrimination and anti-subordination principles transpired during the 1970s. As civil rights advocates challenged the conventional practices and rationales supporting race and gender inequality, they precipitated a shift in the rule structure and justificatory rhetoric of these status regimes." Reva Siegel, *Discrimination in the Eyes of the Law: How Colorblindness Discourse Disrupts and Rationalizes Social Stratification*, 88 CAL. L. REV. 77, 111 (2000).

23. Lera Boroditsky, Lauren A. Schmidt, and Webb Phillips, *Sex, Syntax, and Semantics*, in LANGUAGE IN MIND: ADVANCES IN THE STUDY OF LANGUAGE AND COGNITION (Genter and Goldin-Meadon, eds.) 61, 70 (2003).

24. Lera Boroditsky, Lauren A. Schmidt, and Webb Phillips, *Sex, Syntax, and Semantics*, in LANGUAGE IN MIND: ADVANCES IN THE STUDY OF LANGUAGE AND COGNITION (Genter and Goldin-Meadon, eds.) 61, 70 (2003).

25. George Lakoff, *The Contemporary Theory of Metaphor*, in METAPHOR AND THOUGHT (2nd ed.) (Andrew Ortony, ed.,) 204 (1992).

26. George Lakoff and Mark Johnson, *Metaphors We Live By*, 5 (2003).

27. *See generally* Diana Ponterotto, *The Cohesive Role of Cognitive Metaphor in Discourse and Conversation*, in METAPHOR AND METONYMY AT THE CROSSROADS: A COGNITIVE PERSPECTIVE (Antonio Barcelona, ed.) 2000.

28. "Metaphor has been shown to serve a number of important cognitive functions, including that of making new conceptual domains accessible through metaphorical 'scaffolds' imported from better known domains, such as in the case of metaphors in science, and providing a coherent framework or schema for understanding such everyday topics as time, arguments, and emotions. In addition, schemas derived from conceptual metaphors are capable of forming connections between elements within a text representation, suggesting that metaphor may play an important role in text comprehension. The most interesting things that we learn about metaphor may turn out to be not the mechanisms through which metaphors are understood but, rather, the things that metaphors allow us to do." David W. Allbritton, *When Metaphors Function as Schemas: Some Cognitive Effects of Conceptual Metaphors*, 10 METAPHOR AND SYMBOLIC ACTIVITY 33, 43 (1995).

29. Gwenda Schmidt et al., *Beyond Laterality: A Critical Assessment of Research on the Neural Basis of Metaphor*, 16 JOURNAL OF THE INTERNATIONAL NEUROPSYCHOLOGICAL SOCIETY 1 (2010).

30. Ellen Winner and Howard Gardner, *The Comprehension of Metaphor in Brain Damaged Patients*, 100 BRAIN 717, 724–725 (1977). These findings were replicated in 1999. *See* Catherine Mackenzie et al., *The Communication Effects of Right Brain Damage On the Very Old and the Not So Old*, 12 JOURNAL OF NEUROLINGUISTICS 79 (1999).

31. Regarding difficulty in understanding nonliteral language: "The results suggest a qualitative difference in the manner in which LHD [left-hemisphere-damaged] and RHD [right-hemisphere-damaged] patients process certain aspects of word meaning. Relative to LHD patients, RHD patients do not appreciate metaphoric meaning fully even at the single word level. . . . The selective deficit of RHD patients suggests a role for the intact right hemisphere in the identification and evaluation of metaphoric meanings." Hiram H. Brownell et al., *Appreciation of Metaphoric Alternative Word Meanings by Left and Right Brain-Damaged Patients*, 28 NEUROPSYCHOLOGIA 375, 380 (1990). Regarding difficulty understanding humor: "Brain-damaged patients differ from normal controls in their level of understanding and their subjective reactions to humorous displays. Each of the subject groups with brain injury scored significantly below the normal controls, thereby signaling a decreased sensitivity to humorous elements. In their apparent enjoyment of these displays, patients with left hemisphere lesions varied somewhat less among themselves than did normal controls; patients with right hemisphere lesions exhibited extremely different types of reactions to the cartoons." Howard Gardner et al., *Comprehension and Appreciation of Humorous Material Following Brain Damage*, 98 BRAIN 399, 408 (1975).

32. *See generally* Heath A. Demaree et al., *Brain Lateralization of Emotional Processing: Historical Roots and a Future of Incorporating Dominance.* 4 BEHAVIORAL AND COGNITIVE NEUROSCIENCE REVIEWS 3 (2005).

33. "Although as a group the patients performed significantly below normals on the figurative language subtests discussed here, [right-brain-damaged] individuals performed like normals on the Verbal Metaphor subtest, suggesting selective LH [left hemisphere] contribution to understanding salient language." Rachel Giora et al., *Differential Effects of Right and Left Hemisphere Damage on Understanding Sarcasm and Metaphor,*" 15 METAPHOR AND SYMBOL 63, 77 (2000).

34. "No significant differences in laterality across literal and metaphoric stimuli were found in the regions of interest under investigation. Relative to carefully matched literal control sentences, no significant differences in laterality were found in the superior temporal gyrus, the middle temporal gyrus, the inferior temporal gyrus, the triangular and the opercular part of the inferior frontal gyrus, the precuneus, the temporal pole, and the hippocampus." Alexander M. Rapp et al., *Laterality in Metaphor Processing: Lack of Evidence from Functional Magnetic Resonance Imaging for the Right Hemisphere Theory,* 100 BRAIN and Language 142, 144 (2007).

35. Ponterotto uses this term to describe the epistemological shift in recent scientific research on metaphors, in which they are no longer understood as a mere play on words but as playing "a central role in the interpretation and expression of human experience." She then states: "The question now arises as to why metaphor functions so efficiently as a cognitive pivot. . . . I would like to suggest however that it works because it is 1. rapid 2. concise and 3. vivid. . . . On the one hand, cognitive metaphor, brief, concise, and vivid, functions as a pivot which holds everything in place; on the other hand, the cognitive metaphor network, *multiple, open-ended, and flexible* permits constant reelaboration. Cognitive metaphor therefore guarantees both stability and dynamicity in discourse processes. As a specific discursive form, conversation is a fleeting encounter of multiple perspectives, a fast negotiation of competing goals, a rapid matching of complex positions. Conversation is after all a subtle meeting of minds. Often it is cognitive metaphor which guarantees the cohesion/coherence necessary for successful communication." Diana Ponterotto, *The Cohesive Role of Cognitive Metaphor in Discourse and Conversation,* in METAPHOR AND METONYMY AT THE CROSSROADS: A COGNITIVE PERSPECTIVE (Antonio Barcelona, ed.) 283, 294, 297 (2000).

36. Brief by Albion Tourgée, quoted in Brook Thomas, *Plessy v. Ferguson and the Literary Imagination,* 3 LAW, TEXT, CULTURE 33, 49 (1996).

37. This usage is particularly interesting given that the blindness metaphor is typically used in disparaging rather than empowering terms. *See generally* Naomi Scor, *Blindness as Metaphor,* 11 DIFFERENCES 76 (1999).

38. *See, e.g.* Michael K. Brown et al., *Whitewashing Race: The Myth of a Color-Blind Society* (2003); Ian Haney Lopez, *"A Nation of Minorities": Race, Ethnicity, and Reactionary Colorblindness,* 59 STAN. L. REV. 985 (2007); and Eduardo Bonilla-Silva, *Racism Without Racists: Color-Blind Racism and the Persistence of Racial Inequality in the United States* (2003).

39. While much of the taboos surrounding blindness in human history have been demonstrably unfavorable and were used to justify horrifically brutal practices, "not all of the fallacies and fables about blindness are negative. There are also positive images interwoven in its mystique. Chief among these is the belief that bounteous nature compensates blind people in a variety of ways: through desirable traits of character (spirituality, patience, cheerfulness); through virtuosity of accomplishment (musical talent, prophetic gifts, razor sharp memory); or through superhuman command of non-visual senses." Frances Koestler, *The Unseen Minority: A Social History of Blindness in the United States*, 4 (1976).

40. Bernard J. Hibbitts, *Making Sense of Metaphors: Visuality, Aurality, and the Reconfiguration of American Legal Discourse*, 16 CARDOZO L. REV. 229, 230–231 (1995).

41. Judith Resnik and Dennis Curtis, *Representing Justice: Invention, Controversy, and Rights in City States and Democratic Courtrooms* 8 (2011).

42. Resnik and Curtis note: "Before the sixteenth century, images of Justice were shown with their eyes open. During the Medieval and Renaissance periods, blindfolds had a deeply derisive symbolism that was readily appreciated and reinscribed. By the seventeenth century, closed or covered eyes for Justice were uncommon but not unknown." Resnik and Curtis explain that this shift occurs as a result of various social and technological developments during this period of transition: "As Earthly justice came to the fore and the instances of its application proliferated in the growing urban centers, so did a preoccupation with the quality of knowledge and the caliber of those who made judgements. Eyes could play tricks and, as science had begun to demonstrate, new optical instruments could enhance sight. The camera obscura gained currency in the sixteenth century, followed around 1600 by the invention of the telescope and microscope and by interest in the idea of probability. Moreover, in addition to being inadvertently misled, judges could be looking for bribes. Ripa put a blindfold on one Justice 'so she can not see anything that might be used by judges in a way that is against reason.' Descartes wrote of the desirability of escaping the confusion of the senses. Lutheran theology could also be cited as supporting the need to affix a blindfold to Justice, for truth was to come from inner light." Resnik and Curtis then note: "By the eighteenth century, the blindfold on Justice had shed its connections to the blindness of Synogoga failing to see the light of Christianity, to jesters made buffoons because they could not see, and to the condemned blindfolded before execution. Instead, when placed on Justice, the blindfold was turned into a symbol of law's commitment to rationality and even-handedness. The depiction of a Justice whose vision was obscured came to represent something sought after—a needed neutrality, inner wisdom, a lack of distraction, or incorruptibility. The absence of a blindfold, in turn, came to be seen as an omission in need of explanation." Judith Resnik and Dennis Curtis, *Representing Justice: Invention, Controversy, and Rights in City States and Democratic Courtrooms* 74, 96 (2011).

43. *See, e.g.*, Paul H. Thibodeau and Lera Boroditsky, *Metaphors We Think With: The Role of Metaphor in Reasoning*, 6 PLoS ONE 1 (2011); and Paul Thibodeau, James L. McClelland, and Lera Boroditsky, *When a Bad Metaphor May Not Be*

a Victimless Crime: The Role of Metaphor in Social Policy, in PROCEEDINGS OF THE 31ST ANNUAL CONFERENCE OF THE COGNITIVE SCIENCE SOCIETY (N. A. Taatgen & H. van Rijn Eds.) 809 (2009).

44. "The experiment was designed to explore whether simply embedding a common metaphor in an otherwise neutral report about crime can systematically influence people's approach to solving the crime problem. In the task, participants read a report about crime in a fictional city and then answered questions about the city. The report contained mostly crime-relevant statistics, and also two brief instances of either the crime as predator metaphor or the crime as virus metaphor. After reading the report, participants answered questions relating to crime in the city. Critically, in one of these questions, participants were asked to propose a solution to the crime problem. If metaphors in fact have psychological weight, then being exposed to different metaphors for crime may lead people to propose different solutions to the city's crime problem. For example, people exposed to the crime as a predator metaphor might propose toughening law enforcement, while people exposed to the crime as disease metaphor might think about dealing with problems in the community and improving the social environment to prevent future crime. Of course, it is also possible that such metaphors are simply ornamental flourishes of language, and do not influence how people conceive of important social issues like crime." Paul Thibodeau, James L. McClelland, and Lera Boroditsky, *When a Bad Metaphor May Not Be a Victimless Crime: The Role of Metaphor in Social Policy*, in PROCEEDINGS OF THE 31ST ANNUAL CONFERENCE OF THE COGNITIVE SCIENCE SOCIETY (N. A. Taatgen and H. van Rijn, eds.) 809, 810 (2009).

45. Paul Thibodeau, James L. McClelland, and Lera Boroditsky, *When a Bad Metaphor May Not Be a Victimless Crime: The Role of Metaphor in Social Policy*, in PROCEEDINGS OF THE 31ST ANNUAL CONFERENCE OF THE COGNITIVE SCIENCE SOCIETY (N. A. Taatgen and H. van Rijn, eds.) 809, 814 (2009).

46. Paul Thibodeau, James L. McClelland, and Lera Boroditsky, *When a Bad Metaphor May Not Be a Victimless Crime: The Role of Metaphor in Social Policy*, in PROCEEDINGS OF THE 31ST ANNUAL CONFERENCE OF THE COGNITIVE SCIENCE SOCIETY (N. A. Taatgen and H. van Rijn, eds.) 809, 811 (2009).

47. *See, e.g.*, William C. Thompson, *Tarnish on the "Gold Standard": Recent Problems in Forensic DNA Testing*, CHAMPION MAGAZINE (January/February 2006), http://www.nacdl.org/public.nsf/0/6285f6867724e1e685257124006f9177; Osagie K. Obasogie and Troy Duster, *All That Glitters Isn't Gold*, 41 HASTINGS CENTER REPORT 15 (2011); and Michael Lynch, *God's Signature: DNA Profiling, the New Gold Standard in Forensic Science*, 27 ENDEAVOR 93 (2003).

48. Some have questioned why scientists and health professionals continue to use the gold standard metaphor. Tom Love writes: "The 'gold standard' is a pervasive metaphor in health research. Whether it is an argument about establishing a standard for quality of care or a debate about the relative merits of diagnostic investigations, the term is universally used to describe the best care, the best test, or the most certain medical knowledge. . . . [Yet] the gold standard is an outdated, arbitrary form of

defining value that seems to contribute to instability and which has been used only when it suited the country concerned. Is this a good metaphor for the best care, or the most certain medical knowledge?" Tom E. Love, *All That Glisters Is Not Gold*, 321 BMJ 1315 (2003).

49. Dorothy Nelkin and Susan Lindee, *The DNA Mystique: The Gene as a Cultural Icon*, 2 (1995). Nelkin and Lindee argue: "DNA in popular culture functions, in many respects, as a secular equivalent of the Christian soul. Independent of the body, DNA appears to be immortal. Fundamental to identity, DNA seems to explain individual differences, moral order, and human fate. Incapable of deceiving, DNA seems to be the locus of the true self, therefore relevant to the problems of personal authenticity posed by a culture in which the 'fashioned self' is the body manipulated and adorned with the intent to mislead. In many popular narratives, individual characteristics and the social order both seem to be direct transcriptions of a powerful, magical, and even sacred entity, DNA" (2–3).

50. William C. Thompson, *The Potential for Error in Forensic DNA Testing (and How That Complicates the Use of DNA Databases for Criminal Identification)*, conference paper for Forensic DNA Databases and Race: Issues, Abuses, and Actions, June 19–20, 2008, pg. 21, http://www.councilforresponsiblegenetics.org/pageDocuments/H4T5EOYUZI.pdf.

51. J. Jefferson, *Cold Hits Meet Cold Facts: Are DNA Matches Infallible?* 40 TRANSCRIPT MAGAZINE 29 (2008).

52. Linda Geddes, *Unreliable Evidence? Time to Open Up DNA Databases*, NEW SCIENTIST (January 6, 2010), http://www. newscientist.com/article/mg20527424.700-unreliable-evidence-time-to-open-up-dna-databases.html?full=true&print=true.

53. D. E. Kranc et al., *Time for DNA Disclosure*, 326 SCIENCE 1631 (2009).

54. *See, e.g.*, Chris Smith, *DNA's Identity Crisis*, San Francisco Magazine, September 2008, http://www.sanfranmag.com/story/dna%E2%80%99s-identity-crisis (For an example of the injustice that may stem from inaccurate estimates of the likelihood of coincidental matches.)

55. Jason Felch and Maura Dolan, *When a Match Is Far from a Lock*, L.A. TIMES, May 4, 2008, http://articles.latimes.com/print/2008/may/04/local/me-dna4.

56. William C. Thompson, *The Potential for Error in Forensic DNA Testing (And How That Complicates the Use of DNA Databases for Criminal Identification)*, COUNCIL FOR RESPONSIBLE GENETICS 10 (2008), http://www.councilforresponsiblegenetics.org/pageDocuments/H4T5EOYUZI.pdf. The one in 1.1 million figure in the Puckett case used the population figure (i.e. the frequency of the matching profile among Caucasian Americans) as a referent.

57. FBI DNA Advisory Bd., *Statistical and Population Genetics Issues Affecting the Evaluation of the Frequency of Occurrence of DNA Profiles Calculated from Pertinent Population Database(s)*, FORENSIC SCI. COMM., July 2000, http://www2.fbi.gov/hq/lab/fsc/backissu/july2000/dnastat.htm; National Research Council, *The Evaluation of Forensic DNA Evidence: An Update* (1996), http://www.nap.edu/openbook.php?record_id=5141; Jason Felch and Maura Dolan, *When a Match Is Far from a Lock*, LOS ANGELES TIMES, May 4, 2008, http://articles.latimes.com/print/2008/

may/04/local/me-dna4 . *See also* David Kaye, *Taking Liberties with the Numbers*, Sci. & L. Blog, April 18, 2009, http://lawprofessors.typepad.com/science_law/2009/week16/index.html.

58. Jason Felch and Maura Dolan, *When a Match Is Far from a Lock*, Los Angeles Times, May 4, 2008, http://articles.latimes.com/print/2008/may/04/local/me-dna4.

59. *Parents Involved in Community Schools v. Seattle School District No. 1*, 551 U.S. 701, 726 (2007).

60. Chief Justice Roberts notes in the plurality opinion that "working backwards to achieve a particular type of racial balance, rather than working forward from some demonstration of the level of diversity that provides the purported benefits is a fatal flaw under our existing precedent." *Parents Involved in Community Schools v. Seattle School District No. 1*, 551 U.S. 701, 729 (2007).

61. *Ricci v. DeStefano*, 129 S. Ct. 2658, 2673 (2009)

62. *Parents Involved in Community Schools v. Seattle School District No. 1*, 551 U.S. 701, 747-748 (2007).

Chapter 5

1. Angela Onwuachi-Willig, *A Beautiful Lie: Exploring Rhinelander v. Rhinelander as a Formative Lesson on Race, Identity, Marriage, and Family*, 95 Cal. L. Rev. 2393, 2408 (2007).

2. Angela Onwuachi-Willig, *A Beautiful Lie: Exploring Rhinelander v. Rhinelander as a Formative Lesson on Race, Identity, Marriage, and Family*, 95 Cal. L. Rev. 2393, 2409 (2007).

3. Earl Lewis and Heidi Ardizzone, *Love on Trial: An American Scandal in Black and White*, 25 (2001).

4. Angela Onwuachi-Willig notes: "An annulment, as opposed to a divorce, would sever ties completely between the Rhinelanders and Joneses because it would place Leonard and Alice back into their original positions as unmarried persons and, by law, would entirely erase their marital union. Also, in many cases, an annulment importantly left the fraudulent party with no claim to alimony or property and thereby was essential if the Rhinelander family wanted Alice to have no, or at least very little, access to Leonard's or the family's assets. Finally, an annulment was critical because finding that Alice was a colored woman without obtaining an annulment would forever mark Leonard as unmarriageable for a more "suitable" wife, meaning a white woman of the same socioeconomic station and background, and also as unsuitable for the Rhinelander family name." Angela Onwuachi-Willig, *A Beautiful Lie: Exploring Rhinelander v. Rhinelander as a Formative Lesson on Race, Identity, Marriage, and Family*, 95 Cal. L. Rev. 2393, 2411 (2007)

5. Ariela J. Gross, *Litigating Whiteness: Trials of Racial Determination in the Nineteenth-Century South*, 108 Yale L. J. 109 (1998).

6. Ariela J. Gross, *Litigating Whiteness: Trials of Racial Determination in the Nineteenth-Century South*, 108 Yale L. J. 109, 112 (1998).

7. Ariela J. Gross, *Litigating Whiteness: Trials of Racial Determination in the Nineteenth-Century South*, 108 YALE L. J. 109, 156 (1998).

8. *Ozawa v. United States*, 260 U.S. 178, 197 (1922). The Court goes on to say that skin color is a poor measure of race because it "differs greatly among persons of the same race, even among Anglo-Saxons, ranging by imperceptible gradations from the fair blond to the swarthy brunette, the latter being darker than many of the lighter hued persons of the brown or yellow races. Hence to adopt the color test alone would result in a confused overlapping of races and a gradual merging of one into the other, without any practical line of separation"

9. Ian Haney Lopez, *White By Law: The Legal Construction of Race*, 79 (1996).

10. *United States v. Bhagat Singh Thind*, 261 U.S. 204, 215 (1923) The Court continues: "The children of English, French, German, Italian, Scandinavian, and other Europe parentage, quickly merge into the mass of our population and lose the distinctive hallmarks of their European origin. On the other hand, it cannot be doubted that the children born in this country of Hindu parents would retain indefinitely the clear evidence of their ancestry. It is very far from our thought to suggest the slightest question of racial superiority or inferiority. What we suggest is merely racial difference, and it is of such character and extent that the great body of our people instinctively recognize it and reject the thought of assimilation." Thus, racial difference becomes known through the physical attributes of race that are visually observed.

11. Jamie L. Wacks writes: "The Rhinelander case thus put the phenomenon of 'passing' itself on trial for all of America to watch. What mattered most was not who Alice Jones really was but rather how she was defined in the context of the cultural image of black women that were already in social circulation." Jamie L. Wacks, *Reading Race, Rhetoric, and the Female Body in the* Rhinelander *Case, in* INTERRACIALISM: BLACK-WHITE INTERMARRIAGE IN AMERICAN HISTORY, LITERATURE, AND LAW 162, 167 (Werner Sollors, ed., 2000)

12. Milton A. Smith, "America's Most Sensational Mixed Marriages, *Tan Confessions*" 2 (December 1951), quoted in Jamie L. Wacks, *Reading Race, Rhetoric, and the Female Body in the* Rhinelander *Case, in* INTERRACIALISM: BLACK-WHITE INTERMARRIAGE IN AMERICAN HISTORY, LITERATURE, AND LAW 162, 166 (Werner Sollors, ed., 2000)

13. Trial transcript, quoted in Jamie L. Wacks, *Reading Race, Rhetoric, and the Female Body in the* Rhinelander *Case, in* INTERRACIALISM: BLACK-WHITE INTERMARRIAGE IN AMERICAN HISTORY, LITERATURE, AND LAW 162, 168 (Werner Sollors, ed., 2000).

14. Trial transcript, quoted in Angela Onwuachi-Willig, *A Beautiful Lie: Exploring Rhinelander v. Rhinelander as a Formative Lesson on Race, Identity, Marriage, and Family*, 95 CAL. L. REV. 2393, 2416 (2007).

15. Trial transcript, quoted in Angela Onwuachi-Willig, *A Beautiful Lie: Exploring Rhinelander v. Rhinelander as a Formative Lesson on Race, Identity, Marriage, and Family*, 95 CAL. L. REV. 2393, 2429 (2007).

16. Trial transcript, quoted in Angela Onwuachi-Willig, *A Beautiful Lie: Exploring Rhinelander v. Rhinelander as a Formative Lesson on Race, Identity, Marriage, and Family*, 95 CAL. L. REV. 2393, 2429 (2007).

17. In addition to race and ethnicity, the court has extended higher forms of scrutiny beyond rational basis review to classifications based upon national origin, alienage, and children born to unmarried parents.

18. This group of laws, known as the Reconstruction Amendments, includes the Thirteenth Amendment (abolishing slavery) and the Fifteenth Amendment, which extended the right to vote to newly freed slaves.

19. *United States v. Carlene Products*, 304 U.S. 144, 152 (1938).

20. Lewis F. Powell Jr., *Carolene Products Revisited*, 82 COLUM. L. REV. 1087 (1982).

21. Louis Lusky, *Footnote Redux: A Carolene Products Reminiscence*, 82 COLUM. L. REV. 1093, 1105 (1982).

22. *Korematsu v. United States*, 323 U.S. 214, 215 (1944).

23. Justice Black concludes the majority opinion upholding Japanese interment as follows: "It is said that we are dealing here with the case of imprisonment of a citizen in a concentration camp solely because of his ancestry, without evidence or inquiry concerning his loyalty and good disposition towards the United States. Our task would be simple, our duty clear, were this a case involving the imprisonment of a loyal citizen in a concentration camp because of racial prejudice. Regardless of the true nature of the assembly and relocation centers—and we deem it unjustifiable to call them concentration camps with all the ugly connotations that term implies—we are dealing specifically with nothing but an exclusion order. To cast this case into outlines of racial prejudice, without reference to the real military dangers which were presented, merely confuses the issue. Korematsu was not excluded from the Military Area because of hostility to him or his race. He was excluded because we are at war with the Japanese Empire, because the properly constituted military authorities feared an invasion of our West Coast and felt constrained to take proper security measures, because they decided that the military urgency of the situation demanded that all citizens of Japanese ancestry be segregated from the West Coast temporarily, and finally, because Congress, reposing its confidence in this time of war in our military leaders—as inevitably it must—determined that they should have the power to do just this. There was evidence of disloyalty on the part of some, the military authorities considered that the need for action was great, and time was short. We cannot—by availing ourselves of the calm perspective of hindsight—now say that at that time these actions were unjustified." *Korematsu v. United States*, 323 U.S. 214, 224–225 (1944).

24. Kenji Yoshino, *Assimilationist Bias in Equal Protection: The Visibility Presumption and the Case of "Don't Ask, Don't Tell,"* 108 YALE L.J. 485, 489 (1998).

25. *Bowen v. Gilliard*, 483 U.S. 587, 602 (1987) (citing *Lyng v. Castillo*, 477 U.S. 635, 638 (1986).

26. *San Antonio Independent School District v. Rodriguez*, 411 U.S. 1, 28 (1973).

27. *San Antonio Independent School District v. Rodriguez*, 411 U.S. 1, 28 (1973).

28. I emphasize the importance of visibility over immutability since critiques have been exhaustive and the Court has effectively subsumed immutability under visibility. As such, immutability will be discussed only to the extent that it is an implicit part of the visibility prong. *See generally* Donald Bramen, *Of Race and Immutability*, 46 UCLA L. REV 1375 (1998). *See also* Kenji Yoshino, *Assimilationist Bias in Equal Protection: The Visibility Presumption and the Case of "Don't Ask, Don't Tell,"* 108 YALE L.J. 485, 498–499 (1999).

29. *Matthews v. Lucas*, 427 U.S. 495, 506 (1976). *See also* Kenji Yoshino, *Assimilationist Bias in Equal Protection: The Visibility Presumption and the Case of "Don't Ask, Don't Tell,"* 108 YALE L.J. 485, 496–498.

30. *Frontiero v. Richardson*, 411 U.S. 677, 686 (1973). *See also* Kenji Yoshino, *Assimilationist Bias in Equal Protection: The Visibility Presumption and the Case of "Don't Ask, Don't Tell,"* 108 YALE L.J. 485, 496–498.

31. Yoshino attributes the birth of the visibility and immutability factors to "an attempt to isolate the commonalities between the paradigm groups of race and sex in the early 1970s. . . . Rather than operating from *a priori* principles, equal protection jurisprudence has been driven by the groups asking for protection. Generally, the inquiry has not been 'What principles define groups that are worthy of judicial protection?' but rather 'Is group X in or out? . . . Under this group-driven analysis, new groups are admitted by showing that they are like groups that have already established their claim to protection." Kenji Yoshino, *Assimilationist Bias in Equal Protection: The Visibility Presumption and the Case of "Don't Ask, Don't Tell,"* 108 YALE L.J. 559 (1999).

32. Neil Gotanda writes: "Advocates of the color-blind model argue that non-recognition by government is a decision-making technique that is clearly superior to any race-conscious process. Indeed, non-recognition advocates apparently find the political and moral superiority of this technique so self-evident that they think little or no justification is necessary." Neil Gotanda, *A Critique of "Our Constitution Is Color-Blind,"* 44 STAN. L. REV. 1, 16 (1991).

33. *See generally* Andrew Kull, *The Colorblind Constitution* (1992).

34. Ian F. Haney López, *"A Nation of Minorities": Race, Ethnicity, and Reactionary Colorblindness*, 59 STAN. L. REV. 985 (2007).

35. *See generally* Ian F. Haney López, *"A Nation of Minorities": Race, Ethnicity, and Reactionary Colorblindness*, 59 STAN. L. REV. 985, 1012–1021 (2007).

36. Eduardo Bonilla-Silva, *Racism Without Racists: Color-Blind Racism and the Persistence of Racial Inequality in the United States*, 2–3 (2003).

37. *Regents of the University of California v. Bakke*, 438 U.S. 265, 291 (1977).

38. Ian Haney López, *"A Nation of Minorities": Race, Ethnicity, and Reactionary Colorblindness*, 59 STAN. L. REV. 985, 1034 (2007).

39. Powell argues: "Petitioner urges us to adopt for the first time a more restrictive view of the Equal Protection Clause and hold that discrimination against members of the white 'majority' cannot be suspect if its purpose can be characterized as 'benign.' The clock of our liberties, however, cannot be turned back to 1868. It is far too late to argue that the guarantee of equal protection to all persons permits the recognition of

special wards entitled to a degree of protection greater than that accorded others. The Fourteenth Amendment is not directed solely against discrimination due to a 'two-class theory'—that is, based upon differences between 'white' and Negro. Once the artificial line of a two-class theory of the Fourteenth Amendment is put aside, the difficulties entailed in varying the level of judicial review according to a perceived 'preferred' status of a particular racial or ethnic minority are intractable. The concepts of 'majority' and 'minority' necessarily reflect temporary arrangements and political judgments. . . . The white 'majority' itself is composed of various minority groups, most of which can lay claim to a history of prior discrimination at the hands of the State and private individuals. Not all of these groups can receive preferential treatment and corresponding judicial tolerance of distinctions drawn in terms of race and nationality, for then the only 'majority' left would be a new minority of white Anglo-Saxon Protestants. There is no principled basis for deciding which groups would merit 'heightened judicial solicitude' and which would not. . . . The kind of variable sociological and political analysis necessary to produce such rankings simply does not lie within judicial competence—even if they otherwise were politically feasible and socially desirable." *Regents of the University of California v. Bakke*, 438 U.S. 265, 295–296 (1977).

40. Ian Haney López, *"A Nation of Minorities": Race, Ethnicity, and Reactionary Colorblindness*, 59 STAN. L. REV. 985, 1050–1051 (2007).

41. The Court notes: "Federal law requires that a subcontracting clause similar to the one used here must appear in most federal agency contracts, and it also requires the clause to state that 'the contractor shall presume that socially and economically disadvantaged individuals include Black Americans, Hispanic Americans, Native Americans, Asian Pacific Americans, and other minorities, or any other individual found to be disadvantaged by the [Small Business] Administration pursuant to section 8(a) of the Small Business Act.' " 15 U.S.C. §§ 687(d)(2). *Adarand Constructors v. Peña*, 515 US 200, 206 (1995).

42. *Adarand Constructors v. Peña*, 515 US 200, 229 (1995).

43. *Adarand Constructors v. Peña*, 515 US 200, 239 (1995).

44. *Adarand Constructors v. Peña*, 515 US 200, 240 (1995).

45. *Parents Involved in Community Schools v. Seattle School District No. 1*, 551 U.S. 701, 748 (2007).

46. For a persuasive reconsideration of the intent doctrine's genealogy, see Ian Haney López, *Intentional Blindness* 87 N.Y.U. L. Rev. 1779 (2012).

47. *See* Ian Haney López, *Intentional Blindness*, 87 N.Y.U. L. Rev. 1779, 1789–1825 (2012).

48. The Equal Protection Clause applies to the federal government through the due process clause of the Fifth Amendment. The *Davis* court notes: "The central purpose of the Equal Protection Clause of the Fourteenth Amendment is the prevention of official conduct discriminating on the basis of race. It is also true that the Due Process Clause of the Fifth Amendment contains an equal protection component prohibiting the United States from invidiously discriminating between individuals or groups." *Washington v. Davis*, 426 U.S. 229, 239 (1976).

49. *Washington v. Davis*, 426 U.S. 229, 239 (1976).

50. *Washington v. Davis*, 436 U.S. 229, 242 (1976).

51. Ian Haney López, *Intentional Blindness*, 87 N.Y.U. L. REV. 1779, 1807 (2012). Justice White wrote further in *Davis:* "Even agreeing with the District Court that the differential racial effect of Test 21 called for further inquiry, we think the District Court correctly held that the affirmative efforts of the Metropolitan Police Department to recruit black officers, the changing racial composition of the recruit classes and of the force in general, and the relationship of the test to the training program, negated any inference that the Department discriminated on the basis of race or that 'a police officer qualifies on the color of his skin rather than ability.' " *Washington v. Davis*, 426 U.S. 229, 246 (1976).

52. *Pers. Adm'r of Mass. v. Feeney*, 442 U.S. 256, 272 (1979).

53. Reva Siegel offers a brief history of the traditional understanding of this shift toward emphasizing motive in Equal Protection analyses: "The Court embraced the concept of discriminatory purpose as the touchstone for determining the constitutionality of facially neutral state action alleged to discriminate on the basis of race. It was in no sense natural, inevitable, or necessary for the Court to interpret the Equal Protection Clause this way. In the years after *Brown*, prominent legal process scholars such as Alexander Bickel and Herbert Wechsler suggested that it was inappropriate for judges to inquire into the motives of legislators in determining whether statutes comported with constitutional requirements. And the Court itself asserted as much in several of its opinions in the late 1960s and early 1970s. Although in 1960 the Court in *Gomillion v. Lightfoot* stated that 'acts generally lawful may become unlawful when done to accomplish an unlawful end,' by 1968, the Court cast aspersions on the propriety of reviewing legislative motivation in a First Amendment opinion that announced: 'The decisions of this court from the beginning lend no support whatever to the assumption that the judiciary may restrain the exercise of lawful power on the assumption that a wrongful purpose or motive has caused the power to be exerted.' The Court again emphasized this view in *Palmer v. Thompson*, a race discrimination case decided in 1971, which held that a city's decision to close segregated public swimming pools rather than integrate them could not be impugned on the basis of legislative motivation alone. In *Palmer*, the Court announced that 'no case in this Court has held that a legislative act may violate equal protection solely because of the motivations of the men who voted for it,' and proceeded to rehearse again the reasons why it deemed this form of review inappropriate. That same year, in *Griggs v. Duke Power Co.*, the Court held that, under Title VII of the Civil Rights Act of 1964, plaintiffs could prove claims of employment discrimination on a showing of disparate impact evidence alone. A period of uncertainty about constitutional standards ensued. In this period, second-generation legal process scholars, who were critical of the Court's decision in Palmer, began to defend motive review as important in determining the forms of legislative action to which courts should properly defer, while other constitutional commentators began openly to worry about the practical consequences of allowing plaintiffs to challenge facially neutral laws with racially disparate impacts.

A number of federal courts were deciding equal protection challenges to facially neutral state action on the basis of evidence of racial impact alone, and the Court moved sharply to curb this practice. Reversing one such case in 1976, the Court in *Washington v. Davis* announced that there was an important distinction between equal protection and Title VII standards, and drew upon the school segregation cases to assert the general principle that plaintiffs challenging facially neutral state action would have to demonstrate that the state acted with discriminatory purpose in order to make out an equal protection violation. Davis repudiated the Court's prior statements that impugned motive analysis as 'dicta,' and expressly criticized the many appellate court opinions that had found equal protection violations on the basis of impact evidence alone. Thus, in Davis, a case involving a challenge to an employment exam that excluded four times as many African-Americans as whites applying for a position on the District of Columbia police force, and a year later in Village of Arlington Heights v. Metropolitan Housing Development Corp., a case involving a challenge to a zoning ordinance prohibiting the construction of low and moderate income housing, the Court made clear that proving discriminatory purpose was now not only permitted, but required in all cases challenging facially neutral state action having a disparate impact on protected classes. Yet, even as the Court announced its new-found commitment to motive review, it continued to emphasize that plaintiffs might draw upon evidence of racial impact to prove a claim of discriminatory purpose. It was not until its 1979 decision in *Personnel Administrator v. Feeney*, a sex discrimination case in which the Court defined discriminatory purpose under the Equal Protection Clause, that the Court made clear that it had raised quite a formidable barrier to plaintiffs challenging facially neutral state action." Reva Siegel, *Why Equal Protection No Longer Protects: The Evolving Forms of Status Enforcing State Action*, 49 STAN. L. REV. 1111, 1132–1134 (1997). But see Ian Haney López, *Intentional Blindness*, 87 N.Y.U. L. Rev. 1779 (2012) (for a recent critique of Davis and the intent standard).

54. *Pers. Adm'r of Mass. v. Feeney*, 442 U.S. 256, 279 (1979).

55. *Pers. Adm'r of Mass. v. Feeney*, 442 U.S. 256, 272 (1979).

56. Alan Hyde, *Bodies of Law*, 223 (1997).

57. Alan Hyde, *Bodies of Law*, 231 (1997).

58. For a discussion on homosexuals and poor people as putative suspect classes for Equal Protection purposes, see Renee Culverhouse and Christine Lewis, *Homosexuality as a Suspect Class*, 34 S. TEX. L. REV. 205 (1993); and Julie A. Nice, *No Scrutiny Whatsoever: Deconstitutionalization of Poverty Law, Dual Rules of Law, and Dialogic Default*, 35 FORDHAM URB. L. J. 629 (2008).

Chapter 6

1. Individuals have worn hooded garments since at least the twelfth century for various reasons, but the 1930s ushered in what may consider the first commercial distribution and use of hooded sweatshirts. *See, e.g.*, Brian Palmer, *When Did Hoodlums Start Wearing Hoodies?* SLATE, March 22, 2012; and Katherine Boyle,

Trayvon Martin's Death Has Put the Spotlight on Perceptions About Hoodies, WASHING-
TON POST, March 25, 2012. *See also* Dennis Wilson, *A Look Under the Hoodie*, NEW YORK
TIMES, December 23, 2006, http://www.nytimes.com/2006/12/23/opinion/23wilson
.html?_r=1.

2. *Florida Suspect Told 911 Victim Looked Suspicious*, ASSOCIATED PRESS, March 21,
2012, http://www.sfgate.com/crime/article/Florida-suspect-told-911-victim-looked-
suspicious-3425778.php.

3. Isabelle Zehnder, *George Zimmerman's 911 Call Transcribed*, EXAMINER.COM,
March 24, 2012, http://www.examiner.com/article/george-zimmerman-s-911-call-
transcribed.

4. *See generally* Florida Statute 776.013.

5. Kris Hundley, Susan Taylor Martin, and Connie Humburg, *Florida Stand Your
Ground Law Yields Some Shocking Outcomes Depending on How Law Is Applied*, TAMPA
BAY TIMES, June 3, 2012, http://www.tampabay.com/news/publicsafety/crime/article
1233133.ece.

6. Katherine Fung, *Geraldo Rivera: Trayvon Martin's Hoodie Is as Much Responsible
for [His] Death as George Zimmerman*, HUFFINGTON POST, March 25, 2012, http://www
.huffingtonpost.com/2012/03/23/geraldo-rivera-trayvon-martin-hoodie_n_1375080.html.

7. Michael D. Shear, *Obama Speaks Out on Trayvon Martin Killing*, NEW
YORK TIMES, March 23, 2012, http://thecaucus.blogs.nytimes.com/2012/03/23/
obama-makes-first-comments-on-trayvon-martin-shooting/.

8. Dan Klepal and Cindi Andrews, *Stories of 15 Black Men Killed by Police Since 1995*,
CINCINNATI ENQUIRER, April 15, 2001, http://www.enquirer.com/editions/2001/04/15/
loc_stories_of.html.

9. Dan Horn, *Cincinnati: 2001 Year of Unrest*, CINCINNATI ENQUIRER, December 30,
2001, http://www.enquirer.com/unrest2001/.

10. *See generally Trayvon Martin and "the Talk" Black Parents Have with
Their Teenage Sons*, NEW YORK TIMES, March 26, 2012, http://parenting.blogs
.nytimes.com/2012/03/26/trayvon-martin-and-the-talk-black-parents-have-with-
their-teenage-sons/.

11. In a letter to the *Orlando Sentinel*, Robert Zimmerman (George's father) wrote
that his son is "Hispanic and grew up in a multiracial family . . . [and that he] would
be the last to discriminate for any reason whatsoever." Rene Stutzman, *George Zimmerman's Father: My Son Is Not a Racist, Did Not Confront Trayvon Martin*, ORLANDO
SENTINEL, March 15, 2002, http://articles.orlandosentinel.com/2012-03-15/news/os-
trayvon-martin-shooting-zimmerman-letter-20120315_1_robert-zimmerman-letter-
unarmed-black-teenager.

12. *See generally* Jeannine Bell, *Hate Thy Neighbor: Racial Violence and the Persistence of Segregation in American Housing* (2013).

13. The *Tampa Bay Times* analysis of Florida's "stand your ground" law also
"found that people who killed a black person walked free 73 percent of the time, while
those who killed a white person went free 59 percent of the time." Susan Taylor, Artin,
Kris Hundley, and Connie Humburg, *Race Plays Complex Role in Florida's "Stand*

Your Ground" Law, TAMPA BAY TIMES, June 4, 2012, http://www.tampabay.com/news/publicsafety/races-complex-role/1233152.

14. One notable example to the contrary was when President Obama commented on Henry Louis Gates's 2009 arrest when neighbors thought he was breaking in to what turned out to be his own house. President Obama said at the time, "I think we know separate and apart from this incident that there's a long history in this country of African-Americans and Latinos being stopped by law enforcement disproportionately. That's just a fact." Michael D. Shear, *Obama Speaks Out on Trayvon Martin Killing*, NEW YORK TIMES, March 23, 2012, http://thecaucus.blogs.nytimes.com/2012/03/23/obama-makes-first-comments-on-trayvon-martin-shooting/.

15. Randall Kennedy, *The Persistence of the Color Line*, 224 (2011).

16. *Transcript: Illinois Senate Candidate Barack Obama*, WASHINGTON POST, July 27, 2003, http://www.washingtonpost.com/wp-dyn/articles/A19751-2004Jul27.html.

17. Ginger Thompson, *Seeking Unity, Obama Feels Pull of Racial Divide*, NEW YORK TIMES, February 12, 2008, http://www.nytimes.com/2008/02/12/us/politics/12obama.html?pagewanted=all.

18. In this speech, Obama notes that "Reverend Wright's comments were not only wrong but divisive, divisive at a time when we need unity; racially charged at a time when we need to come together to solve a set of monumental problems—two wars, a terrorist threat, a falling economy, a chronic health care crisis and potentially devastating climate change; problems that are neither black or white or Latino or Asian, but rather problems that confront us all." *Obama Race Speech: Read the Full Text*, HUFFINGTON POST, November 17, 2008, http://www.huffingtonpost.com/2008/03/18/obama-race-speech-read-th_n_92077.html.

19. In an interview with the *Rolling Stone*, President Obama said: "Look, race has been one of the fault lines in American culture and American politics from the start. I never bought into the notion that by electing me, somehow we were entering into a post-racial period. On the other hand, I've seen in my own lifetime how racial attitudes have changed and improved, and anybody who suggests that they haven't isn't paying attention or is trying to make a rhetorical point. Because we all see it every day, and me being in this Oval Office is a testimony to changes that have been taking place." Jann S. Wenner, *Ready for the Fight: Rolling Stone Interview with Barack Obama*, ROLLING STONE, April 25, 2012, http://www.rollingstone.com/politics/news/ready-for-the-fight-rolling-stone-interview-with-barack-obama-20120425?print=true.

20. Janell Ross, *Congressional Black Caucus Members Criticize Obama on Unemployment*, HUFFINGTON POST, June 7, 2011, http://www.huffingtonpost.com/2011/07/07/congressional-black-caucus-unemployment_n_892702.html.

21. *See generally* Sumi Cho, *Post-Racialism*, 94 IOWA L. REV. 1589, 1593 (2009).

22. Sumi Cho writes that "based on his 1989 essay, Francis Fukuyama authored the 1992 book, *The End of History and the Last Man*. In it he reinterpreted Hegel's concept of universal history, arguing that the fall of global communism and its revelation represent an 'end of history' insofar as there are no more viable competitors to free-market capitalism and liberal democracy. Post-racialism represents a similar

'end of history' type of ideology in that it represents itself as the evolutionary idea for a society that has transcended the pursuit of racial subordination and remedy by the state." Sumi Cho, *Post-Racialism*, 94 IOWA L. REV. 1589, 1593 (2009).

23. *See generally* Sumi Cho, *Post-Racialism*, 94 IOWA L. REV. 1589, 1603 (2009).

24. *Obama Race Speech: Read the Full Text*, HUFFINGTON POST, November 17, 2008, http://www.huffingtonpost.com/2008/03/18/obama-race-speech-read-th_n_92077 .html.

25. *See* Sumi Cho, *Post-Racialism*, 94 IOWA L. REV. 1589, 1597–1600 (2009).

26. After noting the hardships endured by his Kenyan father and White mother and their ability to build lives for themselves and opportunities for him, Obama embraced the post-racialist rhetoric of universal struggle and transcendence: "I stand here knowing that my story is part of the larger American story, that I owe a debt to all of those who came before me, and that in no other country on Earth is my story even possible. Tonight, we gather to affirm the greatness of our nation not because of the height of our skyscrapers, or the power of our military, or the size of our economy; our pride is based on a very simple premise, summed up in a declaration made over two hundred years ago: 'We hold these truths to be self-evident, that all men are created equal . . . that they are endowed by their Creator with certain inalienable rights, that among these are life, liberty and the pursuit of happiness.' That is the true genius of America." *Transcript: Illinois Senate Candidate Barack Obama*, WASHINGTON POST, July 27, 2003, http://www .washingtonpost.com/wp-dyn/articles/A19751-2004Jul27.html.

27. In the context of post-racialism, Cho defines the redemption of Whiteness as "a sociocultural process by which whiteness is restored to its full pre–civil rights value. In the civil rights era that ushered in egalitarian commitments, whiteness' unjust enrichment from and complicity with white supremacy infringed upon the normative value of whiteness. The post-racial era effectuates the restoration of the full value of white normativity by disaggregating unjust enrichment and complicity from whiteness through the redemptive and symbolic 'big event' of racial transcendence." Sumi Cho, *Post-Racialism*, 94 IOWA L. REV. 1589, 1596 (2009). Cho understands this redemption project primarily through post-racialism. I want to offer an expanded account of this redemption project that accentuates the synergistic effect of the twin rise of colorblindness as a normative claim of how society should be and post-racialism as a descriptive account of how society is that fundamentally stymies any real effort at racial justice.

28. *See generally* Cheryl I. Harris, *Whiteness as Property*, 106 HARV. L. REV. 1707 (1993).

29. *See, e.g.*, W. Parker Frisbie et al., *The Increasing Racial Disparity in Infant Mortality: Respiratory Distress Syndrome and Other Causes*, 41 DEMOGRAPHY 773 (2004); George Farkas, *Racial Disparities and Discrimination in Education: What Do We Know, How Do We Know, and What Do We Need to Know?* 105 TEACHERS COLLEGE RECORD 1119 (2003); Algernon Austin, *Uneven Pain: Unemployment by Metropolitan Area and Race, Economic Policy Institute Issue Brief #278*, June 8, 2010, http://www.epi .org/page/-/ib278/ib278.pdf; Pew Center on the States, *One in 100: Behind Bars in America 2008*, http://www.pewstates.org/uploadedFiles/PCS_Assets/2008/one%20in%20100.

pdf; Vincent Moor et al., *Driven to Tiers: Socioeconomic and Racial Disparities in the Quality of Nursing Home Care*, 82 MILBANK QUARTERLY 227 (2004); Lisa C. Welch et al., *End of Life Care in Black and White: Race Matters for Medical Care of Dying Patients and Their Families*, 53 JOURNAL OF THE AMERICAN GERIATRICS SOCIETY 1145 (2005).

30. For an extended discussion, see Ian Haney López, *Is the "Post" in Post-Racial the "Blind" in Colorblind?* 32 CARDOZO L. REV. 807 (2011).

31. "The typologist stresses that every representative of a race has the typical characteristics of that race and differs from all representatives of all other races by the characteristics 'typical' for the given race. All racist theories are built on this foundation. Essentially, it asserts that every representative of a race conforms to the type and is separated from the representatives of any other race by a distinct gap." Ernst Mayr, *Typological Versus Population Thinking*, in CONCEPTUAL ISSUES IN EVOLUTIONARY BIOLOGY (Elliot Sober, ed.), 159 (1994).

Epilogue

1. *In Time*, 20th Century Fox (2011).

2. *In Time*, 20th Century Fox (2011).

3. *In Time*, 20th Century Fox (2011).

4. For an accessible review of this literature, see generally Nancy Adler et al., *Reaching for a Healthier Life: Facts on Socioeconomic Status and Health in the U.S.*, MacArthur Foundation (2009), http://www.macses.ucsf.edu/downloads/Reaching_for_a_Healthier_Life.pdf.

5. *See generally* Laura Gómez, *A Tale of Two Genres: On the Real and Ideal Links Between Law and Society and Critical Race Theory*, in BLACKWELL COMPANION TO LAW AND SOCIETY (Austin Sarat, ed.). (2004).

Appendix A

1. Developed during the late nineteenth century, classical legal thought in the academy reflected the belief that "properly organized, law was like geometry.... Each doctrinal field revolved around a few fundamental axioms, derived primarily from empirical observation of how courts had in the past responded to particular sorts of problems. From those axioms, one could and should deduce—through uncontroversial, rationally compelling reasoning process—a large number of specific rules or corollaries.... [Legal classicists believed that,] once purified of anomalies and errors, the law would be 'complete' (capable of providing a single right answer to every dispute) and elegant." William W. Fisher et al., *American Legal Realism* (Fisher et al., eds.) xii (1993). *See also* William M. Wiecek, *The Lost World of Classical Legal Thought: Law and Ideology in America, 1886–1937* (1998).

2. Allan Hutchinson and Patrick J. Monahan, *Law, Politics, and the Critical Legal Scholars: The Unfolding Drama of American Legal Thought*, 36 STAN. L. REV. 199, 200–201 (1984).

3. Susan S. Silbey and Austin Sarat, *Critical Traditions in Law and Society Research,* 21 Law & Soc'y Rev. 165, 173 (1987).

4. Mark Tushnet writes: "Critical legal studies is a political location for a group of people on the Left who share the project of supporting and extending the domain of the Left in the legal academy. On this view, the project of critical legal studies does not have any essential intellectual component, which is why I cannot readily identify a great deal that is common in the intellectual production going under the heading of critical legal studies. There should be nothing surprising about this conclusion, of course, in light of the proposition common to most cls authors that law is politics. For if law is politics, presumably one might also believe that legal intellectual positions are politics too." Mark Tushnet, *Critical Legal Studies: A Political History,* 100 Yale L. J. 1515, 1516–1517 (1991).

5. *See generally* William W. Fisher et al., *American Legal Realism* (Fisher et al., eds.) (1993).

6. William W. Fisher et al., *American Legal Realism* (Fisher et al. ed.) xiv–xv (1993).

7. David Trubek, *Where the Action Is: Critical Legal Studies and Empiricism,* 36 Stan. L. Rev. 575, 578 (1984). Regarding legal formalism, Roberto Unger, a key CLS scholar, writes: "What I mean by formalism in this context is a commitment to, and therefore also a belief in the possibility of, a method of legal justification that can be clearly contrasted to open-ended disputes about the basic terms of social life, disputes that people call ideological, philosophical, or visionary. Though such conflicts may not be entirely bereft of criteria, they fall far short of the rationality that the formalist claims for legal analysis. The formalism I have in mind characteristically invokes impersonal purposes, policies, and principles as an indispensable component of legal reasoning. Formalism in the conventional sense—the search for a method of deduction from a gapless system of rules—is merely the anomalous, limiting case of this jurisprudence." Roberto Mangabeira Unger, *The Critical Legal Studies Movement,* 96 Harv. L. Rev. 561, 564 (1983). Unger describes objectivism as "the belief that the authoritative legal materials—the system of statutes, cases, and accepted legal ideas—embody and sustain a defensible scheme of human association. They display, though always imperfectly, an intelligible moral order." Roberto Mangabeira Unger, *The Critical Legal Studies Movement,* 96 Harv. L. Rev. 561, 565 (1983). The basic idea here is that law assumes that its rules impartially reflect rather than produce various social arrangements.

8. J. Paul Oetken, *Form and Substance in Critical Legal Studies,* 100 Yale L. J. 2209, 2211 (1991).

9. *See generally* Duncan Kennedy, *The Structure of Blackstone's Commentaries,* 28 Buffalo L. Rev. 209 (1979); J. Paul Oetken, *Form and Substance in Critical Legal Studies,* 100 Yale L. J. 2209, 2212 (1991).

10. J. Paul Oetken, *Form and Substance in Critical Legal Studies,* 100 Yale L. J. 2209, 2212 (1991).

11. Allan C. Hutchinson and Patrick J. Monahan, *Law, Politics, and the Critical Legal Scholars: The Unfolding Drama of American Legal Thought,* 36 Stan. L. Rev. 199, 209 (1984).

12. Mark Tushnet notes that "in its weakest version the critique of rights argues that there is no necessary connection between winning legal victories and advancing political goals; in a somewhat stronger version it argues that, more frequently than most lawyers think, winning legal victories either does not advance political goals or actually impedes them." Mark Tushnet, *The Critique of Rights*, 47 S. M. U. L. REV. 23 (1993). Tushnet connects the critique of rights to the Critical Legal Studies perspective on law's indeterminacy: "The critique of rights is connected to the indeterminacy thesis. The most straight-forward connection is this: According to the indeterminacy thesis, nothing whatsoever follows from a court's adoption of some legal rule (except insofar as the very fact that a court has adopted the rule has some social impact—the ideological dimension with which the critique of rights is concerned). Progressive legal victories occur, according to the indeterminacy thesis, because of the surrounding social circumstances. If those circumstances support material as well as ideological gains, well and good. And, of course, as long as those circumstances are stable, the legal victory will be so as well. But, if circumstances change, the 'rule' could be eroded or, more interestingly, interpreted to support anti-progressive change. Another connection between the critique of rights and the indeterminacy thesis results from the combination of the individualism of rights in our legal culture with the dialectic of rights and counter-rights. Sometimes progressive lawyers propose changes that, their critics say, infringe on constitutional rights. Recent controversies over regulating hate speech and pornography illustrate the issue (although those proposals have been controversial within progressive ranks as well). Conservatives who in other contexts would not blink at suppressing speech, particularly sexually explicit speech, suddenly become ardent (in the case of hate speech regulation) or ambivalent (in the case of pornography) defenders of the First Amendment" (32–33).

13. Allan Hutchinson and Patrick J. Monahan, *Law, Politics, and the Critical Legal Scholars*, 36 STAN. L. REV. 199, 216–217 (1984).

14. Mari J. Matsuda, *Looking to The Bottom: Critical Legal Studies and Reparations*, 22 HARV. C. R.—C. L. L. REV. 323, 327–328 (1987).

15. Mari J. Matsuda, *Looking to The Bottom: Critical Legal Studies and Reparations*, 22 HARV. C. R.—C. L. L. REV. 323, 327–329 (1987).

16. Mari J. Matsuda, *Looking to The Bottom: Critical Legal Studies and Reparations*, 22 HARV. C. R.—C. L. L. REV. 323, 327-329–330 (1987).

17. Monica Bell, *The Obligation Thesis: Understanding the Persistent "Black Voice" in Modern Legal Scholarship*, 68 U. PITT. L. REV. 643, 681 (2006).

18. Kimberlé Crenshaw et al., Introduction, in *Critical Race Theory: The Key Writings That Formed the Movement* (Kimberlé Crenshaw et al., eds.) xxii–xxiii (1995).

19. Kimberlé Crenshaw et. al., Introduction, in *Critical Race Theory: The Key Writings That Formed the Movement* (Kimberlé Crenshaw et. al., eds.) xxiii (1995).

20. For a description of CLS's attempt to modify its instrumentalist position, see Kimberlé Crenshaw et al., Introduction, in *Critical Race Theory: The Key Writings That Formed the Movement* (Kimberlé Crenshaw et al., eds.) xxiv (1995).

21. Kimberlé Crenshaw et al., Introduction, in *Critical Race Theory: The Key Writings That Formed the Movement* (Kimberlé Crenshaw et al., eds.) xxv (1995).

22. Kimberlé Crenshaw et al., Introduction, in *Critical Race Theory: The Key Writings That Formed the Movement* (Kimberlé Crenshaw et al., eds.) xxv (1995).

23. *See generally* Mark Tushnet, *An Essay on Rights*, 62 TEX. L. REV. 1363 (1983). *See also* Duncan Kennedy, *The Critique of Rights in Critical Legal Studies*, in LEFT LEGALISM/LEFT CRITIQUE (Brown and Halley, eds.) 2002; and Karl Klare, *Labor Law as Ideology: Toward a New Historiography of Collective Bargaining Law*, 4 INDUS. REL. L. J. 450 (1981).

24. Mark Tushnet, *An Essay on Rights*, 62 TEX. L. REV. 1363, 1386 (1983).

25. Patricia Williams writes: "What is too often missing from CLS works is the acknowledgement that our experiences of the same circumstances may be very, very different; the same symbol may mean different things to each of us. At this level, for example, the insistence of Mark Tushnet, Alan Freeman, and others that the 'needs' of the oppressed should be emphasized rather than their 'rights' amounts to no more than a word game. It merely says that the choice has been made to put 'needs' in the mouth of a rights discourse—thus transforming 'needs' into a new form of right. 'Need' then joins 'right' in the pantheon of reified representations of what it is that you, I and we want from ourselves and from society. While rights may not be ends in themselves, it remains that rights rhetoric has been and continues to be an effective form of discourse for blacks. The vocabulary of rights speaks to an establishment that values the guise of stability, and from whom social change for the better must come (whether it is given, taken or smuggled). Change argued for in the sheep's clothing of stability (i.e., 'rights') can be effective, even as it destabilizes certain other establishment values (i.e., segregation). The subtlety of rights' real instability thus does not render unusable their persona of stability." Patricia J. Williams, *Alchemical Notes: Reconstructing Ideals from Deconstructed Rights*, 22 HARV. C. R.—C. L. L. REV. 401, 410 (1987).

26. Richard Delgado, *The Ethereal Scholar: Does Critical Legal Studies Have What Minorities Want?* 22 HARV. C. R.—C. L. L. REV. 301, 304. (1987).

27. Richard Delgado, *The Ethereal Scholar: Does Critical Legal Studies Have What Minorities Want?* 22 HARV. C. R.—C. L. L. REV. 301, 305. (1987).

28. Martin Luther King Jr., *Wall Street Journal*, November 13, 1962, excerpted from http://www.mlkonline.net/quotes.html.

29. Williams notes: "To say that blacks never fully believed in rights is true; yet it is also true that blacks believed in them so much and so hard that we gave them life where there was none before. We held onto them, put the hope of them into our wombs, and mothered them—not just the notion of them. We nurtured rights and gave rights life. And this was not the dry process of reification, from which life is drained and reality fades as the cement of conceptual determinism hardens round— but its opposite. This was the resurrection of life from 400 year old ashes; the parthenogenesis of unfertilized hope. The making of something out of nothing took immense alchemical fire: the fusion of a whole nation and the kindling of several

generations. The illusion became real for only a very few of us; it is still elusive and illusory for most. But if it took this long to breathe life into a form whose shape had already been forged by society and which is therefore idealistically if not ideologically accessible, imagine how long would be the struggle without even that sense of definition, without the power of that familiar vision. What hope would there be if the assignment were to pour hope into a timeless, formless futurism? The desperate psychological and physical oppression suffered by black people in this society makes such a prospect either unrealistic (i.e., experienced as unattainable) or other-worldly (as in the false hopes held out by many religions of the oppressed." Patricia J. Williams, *Alchemical Notes: Reconstructing Ideals from Deconstructed Rights*, 22 HARV. C. R.—C. L. L. REV. 439 (1987).

30. Kimberlé Crenshaw et al., Introduction, in *Critical Race Theory: The Key Writings That Formed the Movement* (Kimberlé Crenshaw et al., eds.) xvii (1995).

31. Bell develops this theory in relation to what he sees as the stagnant effects of *Brown v. Board of Education,* where he "contend[s] that the decision in *Brown* to break with the Court's long-held position on [racial segregation] cannot be understood without some consideration of the decision's value to whites, not simply those concerned about the immorality of racial inequality, but also those whites in policymaking positions able to see the economic and political advances at home and abroad that would follow abandonment of segregation. First, the decision helped to provide immediate credibility to America's struggle with Communist countries to win the hearts and minds of emerging third world peoples. . . . Second, *Brown* offered much needed reassurance to American blacks that the precepts of equality and freedom so heralded during World War II might yet be given meaning at home. . . . Finally, there were whites who realized that the South could make the transition from a rural, plantation society to the sunbelt with all its potential and profit only when it ended its struggle to remain divided by state-sponsored segregation. Thus, segregation was viewed as a barrier to further industrialization in the South." Derrick A. Bell Jr., *Brown v. Board of Education and the Interest–Convergence Dilemma*, 93 HARV. L. REV. 518, 524–525 (1979).

32. Kimberlé Crenshaw et al., Introduction, in *Critical Race Theory: The Key Writings That Formed the Movement* (Kimberlé Crenshaw et al., eds.) xiv (1995). Crenshaw et al. note: "In identifying liberal civil rights tradition and the Critical Legal Studies movement as key factors in the emergence of Critical Race Theory, we do not mean to offer an oversimplified genealogy in which Critical Race Theory appears as a simple hybrid of the two. We view liberal civil rights scholarship and the work of the critical legal theorists not so much as rudimentary components of Critical Race Theory, but as elements in the conditions of its possibility. In short, we intend to evoke a particular atmosphere in which progressive scholars of color struggled to piece together an intellectual identity and a political practice that would take the form both of a left intervention into race discourse and a race intervention into left discourse." Kimberlé Crenshaw et al., Introduction, in *Critical Race Theory: The Key Writings That Formed the Movement* (Kimberlé Crenshaw et al., eds.) xix (1995);

33. In an annotated bibliography from 1993, Richard Delgado and Jean Stefanic identify ten different strands of writing that have come under the Critical Race Theory corpus: (1) critique of liberalism; (2) storytelling/counterstorytelling; (3) revisionist interpretations of American civil rights law and progress; (4) a greater understanding of the underpinnings of race and racism; (5) structural determinism; (6) the intersection of identity characteristics (race, class, sex, etc.); (7) essentialism and anti-essentialism; (8) cultural nationalism and separatism; (9) legal institutions, critical pedagogy, and minorities in the bar; and (10) criticism of Critical Race Theory. The wide-ranging nature of this bibliography belies any attempt to describe this list as definitive of Critical Race Theory, as many of these foci are replicated in other fields, significantly overlap with each other, or have waned in influence within Critical Race Theory since this annotated bibliography was published in 1993. *See generally* Richard Delgado and Jean Stefanic, *Critical Race Theory: An Annotated Bibliography,* 79 VA. L. REV. 461 (1993).

34. *See generally* Michael Omi and Howard Winant, *Racial Formation in the United States: From the 1960s to the 1990s* (1994). The idea that various social experiences are "constructed" dates as far back as 1966. *See generally* Peter L. Berger and Thomas Luckman, *The Social Construction of Reality: A Treatise in the Sociology of Knowledge* (1966).

35. Kimberlé Crenshaw et al., Introduction, in *Critical Race Theory: The Key Writings That Formed the Movement* (Kimberlé Crenshaw et al., eds.) xii (1995).

36. Ian Haney López, *The Social Construction of Race: Some Observations on Illusion, Fabrication, and Choice,* 29 Harv. C. R.—C. L. L. Rev. 3, 4 (1994).

37. "Traditional notions of intent do not reflect the fact that decisions about racial matters are influenced in large part by factors that can be characterized as neither intentional—in the sense that certain outcomes are self-consciously sought—nor unintentional—in the sense that the outcomes are random, fortuitous, and uninfluenced by the decisionmakers' beliefs, desires, and wishes. Americans share a common historical and cultural heritage in which racism has played and still plays a dominant role. Because of this shared experience, we also inevitably share many ideas, attitudes, and beliefs that attach significance to an individual's race and induce negative feelings and opinions about nonwhites. To the extent that this cultural belief system has influenced all of us, we are all racists. At the same time, most of us are unaware of our racism. We do not recognize the ways in which our cultural experience has influenced our beliefs about race or the occasions on which those beliefs affect our actions. In other words, a large part of the behavior that produces racial discrimination is influenced by unconscious racial motivations." Charles Lawrence, *The Id, the Ego, and Equal Protection: Reckoning with Unconscious Racism,* 39 STAN. L. REV. 317, 322 (1986).

38. Ford "employs two lines of analysis in [his] examination of political space. The first demonstrates that racially identified space both creates and perpetuates racial segregation. The second demonstrates that racially identified space results from public policy and legal sanctions—in short, from state action—rather than being the unfortunate but irremediable consequence of purely private or individual choices.

This dual analysis has important legal and moral consequences: if racial segregation is a collective social responsibility rather than exclusively the result of private transgressions, it must either be accepted as official policy or be remedied through collective action." Richard Thompson Ford, *The Boundaries of Race: Political Geography in Legal Analysis*, 107 HARV. L. REV. 1841, 1845 (1993).

39. Barbara Flagg, *Was Blind, But Now I See: White Race Consciousness and the Requirement of Discriminatory Intent*, 91 MICH. L. REV. 953, 957 (1992). *See also* Amanda E. Lewis, *"What Group?" Studying Whites and Whiteness in the Era of Color-Blindness*, 22 SOCIOLOGICAL THEORY 623 (2004).

40. Flagg writes: "In constitutional law, facially race-neutral criteria of decisions that carry a racially disproportionate impact violate the Equal Protection Clause only if adopted with a racially discriminatory intent. This rule provides an excellent vehicle for reconsidering white race consciousness, because it perfectly reflects the prevailing white ideology of colorblindness and the concomitant failure of whites to scrutinize the whiteness of facially neutral norms. In addition, the discriminatory intent rule is the existing doctrinal means of regulating facially neutral government decisionmaking. When government imposes transparently white norms it participates actively in the maintenance of white supremacy, a stance I understand the Fourteenth Amendment to prohibit. We need, therefore, to reevaluate the existing discriminatory intent rule from the perspective of the transparency phenomenon, and to consider a revised approach to disparate impact cases that implement the insights gained from that assessment." Barbara Flagg, *Was Blind, But Now I See: White Race Consciousness and the Requirement of Discriminatory Intent*, 91 MICH. L. REV. 958 (1992).

41. Cheryl Harris, *Whiteness as Property*, 106 HARV. L. REV. 1707, 1714 (1992).

42. Harris notes that in the past, passing as White "meant gaining access to a whole set of public and private privileges that materially and permanently guaranteed basic subsistence needs and, therefore, survival. Becoming white increased the possibility of controlling critical aspects of one's life rather than being the object of others' domination." Cheryl Harris, *Whiteness as Property*, 106 HARV. L. REV. 1713 (1992). Harris contends that while this exact situation no longer exists and that things have improved considerably, the overall dynamic regarding relative property interests in race is still relevant.

43. Cheryl Harris, *Whiteness as Property*, 106 HARV. L. REV. 1715 (1992).

44. "The legal affirmation of whiteness and white privilege allowed expectations that originated in injustice to be naturalized and legitimated. The relative economic, political, and social advantages dispensed to whites under systemic white supremacy in the United States were reinforced through patterns of oppression of Blacks and Native Americans. Materially, these advantages became institutionalized privileges, and ideologically, they became part of the settled expectations of whites—a product of the unalterable original bargain. The law masks what is chosen as natural; it obscures the consequences of social selection as inevitable. The result is that the distortions in social relations are immunized from truly effective intervention, because the existing inequities are obscured and rendered nearly invisible. The existing state of affairs is considered neutral and fair, however unequal and unjust it is

in substance. . . . Through legal doctrine, expectation of continued privilege was rei-fied; whiteness as property was reaffirmed." Cheryl Harris, *Whiteness as Property*, 106 HARV. L. REV. 1707, 1777–1778 (1992).

45. *See generally* Patricia Hill Collins, *Black Feminist Thought: Knowledge, Consciousness, and the Politics of Empowerment* (2000). "Intersectionality refers to particular forms of intersecting oppressions, for example, intersections of race and gender, or of sexuality and nation. Intersectional paradigms remind us that oppression cannot be reduced to one fundamental type, and that oppressions work together in producing injustice". Kimberlé Crenshaw, *Mapping the Margins, Intersectionality, Identity Politics, and Violence Against Women of Color*, 43 STAN. L. REV. 1241, 1245 (1991).

46. Crenshaw draws an interesting analogy when describing intersectionality: "Consider an analogy to traffic in an intersection, coming and going in all four directions. Discrimination, like traffic through an intersection, may flow in one direction, and it may flow in another. If an accident happens in an intersection, it can be caused by cars traveling from any number of directions and, sometimes, from all of them. Similarly, if a Black woman is harmed because she is in the intersection, her injury could result from sex discrimination or race discrimination. Judicial decisions which premise intersectional relief on a showing that Black women are specifically recognized as a class are analogous to a doctor's decision at the scene of an accident to treat a victim only if the injury is recognized by medical insurance. Similarly, providing legal relief only when Black women show that their claims are based on race or on sex is analogous to calling an ambulance for the victim only after the driver responsible for the injuries is identified. But it is not always easy to reconstruct an accident: . . . In these cases the tendency seems to be that no driver is held responsible, no treatment is administered, and the involved parties simply get back in their cars and zoom away." Kimberlé Crenshaw, *Demarginalizing the Intersection of Race and Sex: A Black Feminist Critique of Antidiscrimination Doctrine, Feminist Theory, and Antiracist Politics*, 1989 U. CHI. LEGAL F. 139, 149.

47. Dorothy Roberts, *Punishing Drug Addicts Who Have Babies: Women of Color, Equality, and the Right of Privacy*, 104 HARV. L . REV. 1419, 1421 (1991).

48. Kimberlé Crenshaw, *Demarginalizing the Intersection of Race and Sex: A Black Feminist Critique of Antidiscrimination Doctrine, Feminist Theory, and Antiracist Politics*, 1989 U. CHI. LEGAL F. 139, 150 (1989).

49. *See generally Rogers v. American Airlines*, 527 F. Supp. 229 (S.D.N.Y. 1981).

50. Peter Kwan writes: "Intersectionality risks theoretical collapse as categories multiply. . . . Even if, hypothetically, one can precisely reduce, define and fully describe this complex matrix of identities, and repeat this process on everyone else, we are left with a comprehensive intersectional model of all individuals, but no way of comparing each individual's experiences. . . . [Moreover this prevents] the forging [of] ideological coalitions, political allegiances, or communities of support. Ultimately, intersectionality forces one to decide *a priori* which identities matter, and this is theoretically no different than a pre-intersectionality approach." Peter Kwon, *Jeffrey Dahmer and the Cosynthesis of Categories*, 48 HASTINGS L. J. 1257, 1277 (1997)

51. *See generally* Peter Kwon, *Jeffrey Dahmer and the Cosynthesis of Categories,* 48 HASTINGS L. J. 1257, 1280–1281 (1997)

52. Darren Lenard Hutchinson, *Out Yet Unseen: A Racial Critique of Gay and Lesbian Legal Theory and Political Discourse,* 29 CONN. L. REV. 561, 641 (1997). *See also* Darren Lenard Hutchinson, *Identity Crisis: Intersectionality, Multidimensionality, and the Development of an Adequate Theory of Subordination,* 6 MICH. J. RACE AND L. 285 (2000).

53. Osagie K. Obasogie, *Anything but a Hypocrite: Intersectional Musings on Race, Colorblindness, and the Redemption of Strom Thurmond,* 18 YALE J. L. FEMINISM 451, 488 (2006).

54. Adrienne Katherine Wing, *Essentialism and Anti-Essentialism: Ain't I A Woman?* in CRITICAL RACE FEMINISM: A READER (Adrienne Katherine Wing, ed.) 7 (1997).

55. Adrienne Katherine Wing, *Essentialism and Anti-Essentialism: Ain't I A Woman?* in CRITICAL RACE FEMINISM: A READER (Adrienne Katherine Wing, ed.) 7 (1997).

56. Angela P. Harris, *Race and Essentialism in Feminist Legal Theory,* 42 STAN. L. REV. 581, 585 (1990).

57. Trina Grillo and Stephanie M. Wildman, *Obscuring the Importance of Race: The Implication of Making Comparisons Between Racism and Sexism (Or Other—Isms),* 199 DUKE L. J. 397, 399 (1991).

58. Trina Grillo and Stephanie M. Wildman, *Obscuring the Importance of Race: The Implication of Making Comparisons Between Racism and Sexism (Or Other—Isms),* 199 DUKE L. J. 397, 399 (1991).

59. Derrick A. Bell, *Who's Afraid of Critical Race Theory?* 1995 U. ILL. L. REV. 893 (1995).

60. Neil A. Lewis, *Race Theory Challenges Goal of a Colorblind Society,* AUSTIN AMERICAN STATESMAN, June 8, 1997, J1.

61. Monica Bell, *The Obligation Thesis: Understanding the Persistent "Black Voice" in Modern Legal Scholarship,* 68 U. PITT. L. REV. 643 (2006).

62. Kimberle Crenshaw et al., Introduction, in *Critical Race Theory: The Key Writings That Formed the Movement,* xii (1995).

63. *See generally* Derrick Bell, *Faces at the Bottom of the Well: The Permanence of Racism,* 158–194 (1995).

64. Derrick Bell, *Faces at the Bottom of the Well: The Permanence of Racism,* 194 (1995).

65. Patricia J. Williams, *Alchemical Notes: Reconstructing Ideals from Deconstructed Rights,* 22 HARV. C. R.—C. L. L. REV. 401 (1987).

66. Cheryl Harris, *Whiteness as Property,* 106 HARV. L. REV. 1707, 1711 (1993).

67. Kimberlé Crenshaw et al., Introduction, in *Critical Race Theory: The Key Writings That Formed the Movement,* xii (1995).

68. Russell Robinson, *Perceptual Segregation,* 108 COLUM. L. REV. 1093 (2008).

69. Russell Robinson, *Perceptual Segregation,* 108 COLUM. L. REV. 1093 (2008).

70. Daniel Farber and Suzanna Sherry, *Beyond All Reason: The Radical Assault on Truth in American Law*, 4–5 (1997). *See also* Daniel Farber and Suzanna Sherry, *Is the Radical Critique of Merit Anti-Semitic?* 83 CAL. L. REV. 853 (1995).

71. Kennedy writes that Critical Race Theorists "fail to support persuasively their claims of racial exclusion or their claims that legal academic scholars of color produce a racially distinctive brand of scholarship." Randall Kennedy, *Racial Critiques of Legal Academia*, 102 HARV. L. REV. 1745, 1749 (1988).

72. Randall Kennedy, *Racial Critiques of Legal Academia*, 102 Harv. L. Rev. 1745, 1815–1817 (1988).

73. Daniel Farber and Suzanna Sherry, *Telling Stories out of School: An Essay on Legal Narratives*, 45 STAN. L. REV. 807, 808 (1993).

74. Daniel Farber and Suzanna Sherry, *Telling Stories out of School: An Essay on Legal Narratives*, 45 STAN. L. REV. 807, 809 (1993).

75. Jeffrey Rosen, *O. J. Simpson, Critical Race Theory, the Law, and the Triumph of Color in America*, THE NEW REPUBLIC, December 9, 2006.

76. Ian Haney López, *The Social Construction of Race: Some Observations on Illusion, Fabrication, and Choice*, 29 HARV. C. R.—C. L. L. REV. 1, 6 (1992).

77. Ian Haney López, *The Social Construction of Race: Some Observations on Illusion, Fabrication, and Choice*, 29 HARV. C. R.—C. L. L. REV. 1, 7 (1992).

78. Trina Jones, *Shades of Brown: The Law of Skin Color*, 49 DUKE L. J. 1487, 1493 (1999).

79. Trina Jones, *Shades of Brown: The Law of Skin Color*, 49 DUKE L. J. 1487, 1497 (1999).

80. Jones writes: "The practice of race-mixing in the United States produced a population with skin tones of varying hues. Over time, society attached various meanings to these color differences, including assumptions about a person's race, socioeconomic class, intelligence, and physical attractiveness. In order to understand the development of the color hierarchy in the United States and the meanings attributed to skin color today, a survey of history is necessary." Trina Jones, *Shades of Brown: The Law of Skin Color*, 49 DUKE L. J. 1487, 1499 (1999).

81. Taunya Lovell Banks, *Colorism: A Darker Shade of Pale*, 47 UCLA L. REV. 1705, 1710 (1999).

82. Taunya Lovell Banks, *Colorism: A Darker Shade of Pale*, 47 UCLA L. REV. 1705 (1999). *See generally* Jennifer Hochschild, *When Do People Not Protest Unfairness? The Case of Skin Tone Discrimination*, 73 SOCIAL RESEARCH 473 (2006) (questioning why the discrimination associated with colorism does not elicit political action).

83. Taunya Lovell Banks, *Colorism: A Darker Shade of Pale*, 47 UCLA L. REV. 1705, 1738 (1999).

84. 527 F. Supp. 229 (S.D. N.Y. 1981)

85. 527 F. Supp. 229, 232 (S.D. N.Y. 1981)

86. Paulette M. Caldwell, *A Hair Piece: Perspectives on the Intersection of Race and Gender*, 1991 DUKE L. J. 365, 379 (1991).

87. Paulette M. Caldwell, *A Hair Piece: Perspectives on the Intersection of Race and Gender*, 1991 DUKE L. J. 365, 383 (1991). Caldwell only offers an article from the New York Times to support this argument.

Appendix B

1. *See* David E. Gray, *Doing Research in the Real World* (2004).

2. Hilary Arksey and Peter T. Knight, *Interviewing for the Social Sciences* 32 (1999).

3. *See* Stephen A. Richardon et al., *Interviewing: Its Forms and Functions,* 36 (1965); and David E. Gray, *Doing Research in the Real World,* 215 (2004).

4. Robert S. Weiss, *Learning from Strangers: The Art and Method of Qualitative Interview Studies,* 17 (1994).

5. Robert S. Weiss, *Learning from Strangers: The Art and Method of Qualitative Interview Studies,* 21 (1994).

6. *See generally* Nielsen Net Ratings, *Three out of Four Americans Have Access to the Internet: Online Population Surges Past 200 Million Mark for the First Time,* Press Release, March 18, 2004.

7. Robert S. Weiss, *Learning from Strangers: The Art and Method of Qualitative Interview Studies,* 29 (1994).

8. Robert S. Weiss, *Learning from Strangers: The Art and Method of Qualitative Interview Studies,* 30 (1994).

Index

accent, 59, 64–65

Adarand Constructors v. Peña (1995), 116–17, 153–54, 244n41

affirmative action: *Adarand Constructors v. Peña*, 116–17, 153–54, 244n41; colorblindness for countering, 117, 120, 151, 234n20; and *Plessy v. Ferguson* debate, 233n18; post-racialism rejects, 170, 172; *Regents of the University of California v. Bakke*, 151–52, 153, 156, 234n20, 243n39; *Richmond v. Croson*, 152–53; *Washington v. Davis*, 155–56, 245n51, 246n53

African Americans. *See* Blacks

Allen, Garland, 220n25

Allen, Theodore, 29

ancestry, 1, 55, 56, 68

anti-essentialism, 194, 196–97

Asians: critiques of mainstream assessments of merit may harm, 199; differences between the way blind minorities and blind whites understand race, 69–71; and digital cameras, 40–41, *41*; eyes, 54, 58; *Ozawa v. United States*, 139, 241n8; smell, 66; *United States v. Thind*, 141, 241n10. *See also* Japanese

Banks, Taunya, 202–3

Bell, Derrick, 190, 197, 198, 254n31

Berger, Martin A., 35

Berger, Peter, 25

bias, interviewer, 211–12

Black, Hugo, 13, 21n114, 242n23

Blacks: anti-White bias, 114–15, 117; blind people's understanding of race and its impact on their everyday lives, 98–105; characteristics for identifying, 58; colorblindness theory freezes status quo for, 117, 151; colorism, 201–3; differences between the way blind minorities and blind whites understand race, 69–71; on Oscar Grant killing, 72–74, 75–79; hair, 65, 100–101, 203–4; how blind people come to understand race visually, 81–93; institutional racism, 93–98; intraracial discrimination, 102–3; on LeBron James "Decision," 74–79; Martin-Zimmerman case, 163–68; passing as White, 139, 193,

198, 256n42; racial determination
trials, 139–43; racial disparities
continue, 115; scientific racism
becomes new type of social control
for, 22; skin texture, 65–66; smell,
66, 67, 90, 92; unemployment
among, 169
blind people's understanding of
race, 60–64; blindness as racial
experience, 71; blind since birth
versus becoming blind later in
life, 52–53, 209; capacity to have
visual understanding of race
does not depend upon ability to
see, 71; colorblindness as seen by
the blind, 127–28; colorblindness
concept rests upon, 125; differences
between the way blind minorities
and blind whites understand race,
69–71; formal equality associated
with, 124–27, 128–29; how blind
people come to understand race
visually, 81–98; how sighted people
think they understand race, 58–59;
impact on their everyday lives,
98–105; lack of scholarly attention
to, 1–2; Obama and, 174–75; positive
images of blindness, 237n39; and
presumption that salience of
race comes from what is seen, 51;
research design for, 52–53, 205–14;
secondary characteristics of race
used by, 64–69; as visual, 3–4, 7, 36,
60–64, 68, 80, 127, 158, 181; what it can
contribute to race literature, 33–38
Bonilla-Silva, Eduardo, 151
Boroditsky, Lera, 121, 131–32, 238n44
Brown v. Board of Education (1954), 118,
120, 137, 148, 173, 234n20, 254n31
Burchard, Esteban Gonzalez, 27, 222n38

Caldwell, Paulette, 203–4
Caucasians. *See* Whites

Chinese, *Life* magazine on
distinguishing Japanese from, 12–18,
14, 16, 217n3
civil rights: in Harlan's *Plessy v. Ferguson*
dissent, 119–20; movement, 120, 173,
176, 226n70
class, 23, 30–31, 103, 148, 168, 179, 186, 188
coding, 213–14
colorblindness, 109–37; as backlash,
120, 151; blind people's perspectives
on, 127–28; constitutional, 120,
144, 148, 150–56, 160; in countering
affirmative action, 117, 120, 151,
234n20; defined, 216n4; destabilizing
as a metaphor, 124–29; framing
shared with blindness, 125; fraud
perpetrated by, 137; in Harlan's
Plessy v. Ferguson dissent, 118–20,
124–25; how it became legitimate,
117–21; and how sighted people
think blind people understand race,
58; intent doctrine as product of,
156–57; metaphoric significance of,
117, 121–37; as normative ideology of
racial non-recognition, 115, 171, 172;
and post-racialism, 171–74, 176, 180,
181; reactionary, 152; seen as leading
to equitable outcomes, 7; three
disassociations of, 116, 136; visual
approach to race in, 2; what it is,
115–16
colorism, 201–3
color line, 22, 93, 96, 109, 113
complexion, 31, 225n63
computer vision, 39–44, 228n1
constitutive theory of race, 48–51;
"constitutive" defined, 49;
expanding Critical Race Theory
to, 181, 201, 204; and how blind
people understand race, 62, 104–5;
on producing ability to see race, 18;
raises profound questions about
Equal Protection jurisprudence, 181;